WOMBS
of
EMPIRE

WOMBS *of* EMPIRE

Population Discourses and Biopolitics in Modern Japan

SUJIN LEE

STANFORD UNIVERSITY PRESS
Stanford, California

Stanford University Press
Stanford, California

© 2023 by Sujin Lee. All rights reserved.

No part of this book may be reproduced or transmitted in any form or by any means, electronic or mechanical, including photocopying and recording, or in any information storage or retrieval system, without the prior written permission of Stanford University Press.

Printed in the United States of America on acid-free, archival-quality paper

ISBN 9781503636392 (cloth)
ISBN 9781503637009 (paperback)
ISBN 9781503637016 (electronic)

Library of Congress Control Number: 2022060436

Library of Congress Cataloging-in-Publication Data available upon request.

Cover design: Daniel Benneworth-Gray
Cover art: *National Eugenic Map*, 1941, Edited by Ministry of Health and Welfare, Published by the National Eugenics League, National Diet Library.
Typeset by Elliott Beard in Sabon LT Pro 10/13

To my family and M

CONTENTS

	List of Figures	ix
	Acknowledgments	xi
	A Note on Romanization and Names	xv
	INTRODUCTION Population: A Discursive Site of En-gendering Life	1
ONE	The Population Problem and Utopian Remedies	16
TWO	Voluntary Motherhood: The Feminist Politics of Birth Control	45
THREE	Scientific and Imperialist Solutions to Overpopulation	71
FOUR	Building a Biopolitical State: The Mobilization of Health for Total War	102
FIVE	"Fertile Womb Battalion": The Gender and Racial Politics of Motherhood	133
	EPILOGUE The Continued Politics of the "Population Problem"	158
	Glossary	165
	Notes	167
	Bibliography	205
	Index	225

LIST OF FIGURES

1.1. Cover of *Sanji seigen kenkyū*, 1923 — 37
1.2. Poster of Pro-BC's birth control exhibition, 1931 — 43
2.1. Cover of the *Birth Control Review*, 1921 — 51
4.1. The Eugenic Marriage Consultation Office, 1940 — 127
4.2. Yasui Hiroshi at the Eugenic Marriage Consultation Office, 1940 — 128
4.3. Ten Maxims for Marriage, 1941 — 129
4.4. "Twenty Thousand People's Radio Calisthenics," 1941 — 131
5.1. Family portrait of Shiroto family with sixteen children, 1940 — 140
5.2. Family portrait of Shino family with eleven children, 1940 — 141
5.3. Family portrait of Tsunoda family with twelve children, 1943 — 142
5.4. Handbook for the Expectant Mother, 1942 — 144
5.5. Pregnant woman and newborn health examination form from Handbook for the Expectant Mother, 1942 — 144
5.6. Medical Inspection Report Form appended to ATIS report, 1945 — 155

ACKNOWLEDGMENTS

This book is a product of many inspiring encounters I had with people, ideas, and historical narratives over the past decade. My initial, unprocessed curiosity about vociferous discussions among modern Japanese intellectuals around population issues was nurtured and polished over time through formal and informal conversations with mentors, researchers, colleagues, students, and friends. The growth of this book project was not only temporal but also spatial. Repeated relocations and transitions across borders––more or less normalized in academia––have brought numerous opportunities to engage with different research communities with diverse approaches to historicizing the politics of population. First and foremost, I am deeply indebted to my academic mentors at Cornell University. Naoki Sakai, Katsuya Hirano, J. Victor Koschmann, and Suman Seth introduced me to critical approaches to the study of modernity, state and colonial governance, and knowledge production. Cornell also provided me with a space for intellectually stimulating interactions and discussions with scholars and peers: Chris Ahn, Ai Baba, Brett De Bary, Shiau-Yun Chen, Shoan Yin Cheung, Tyran Grillo, Jihyun Han, TJ Hinrichs, Sookyeong Hong, Junliang Huang, Akiko Ishii, Marcie Middlebrooks, Rachel Prentice, and Kristin Roebuck.

This book would not have been possible without the help of research grants and fellowships. The Japan Foundation Dissertation Fellowship enabled me to conduct nearly one year of research under the mentorship of Ichirō Tomiyama at Doshisha University, Kyoto. The inclusive intellectual community I encountered at Doshisha generously and passionately supported my archival research, commented on my work, and taught me the importance of sharing ideas. I owe thanks to Yujin Jeong, Kazuki Nishikawa, Setsuko Kiriyama, Asato Yoko, and Yea-Yl Yoon who provided encouragement and friendship. I also benefited from the expertise of Tomoko Tanaka and Akinori Odagiri in conducting in-depth research about Senji Yamamoto and the interwar birth control movement in Kansai region. In addition, the UCLA Terasaki Postdoctoral Fellowship in Japanese Studies offered me an invaluable opportunity to teach and communicate my work and to reorient my approach to the study of population discourse to engage with gender and race questions. I give my special thanks to Mariko Tamanoi, Junko Yamazaki, Wakako Suzuki, William Marotti, Kelly Midori McCormick, Sung Eun Kim, and Tomoko Bialock for their support of my postdoctoral research. Also, I cannot miss expressing thanks to the Centre for Asia-Pacific Initiatives at University of Victoria (UVic) for awarding me a visiting fellowship that allowed me to devote a substantial amount of time and energy to completing this book. Besides the above-mentioned fellowship opportunities, I was fortunate to be awarded a range of grants and awards, without which this book would have not come into existence: Japan Studies Travel Grant, Einaudi Center International Research Travel Grant, Dissertation Writing Group Grant, and Timothy Murray Graduate Travel Grant at Cornell University; Taniguchi Medal Award from the Asian Society for the History of Medicine; Graduate Student Best Paper Prize from the Northeast Asia Council of the Association of Asian Studies; and Internal Research and Creative Project Grant at UVic.

Parts of this book were presented in various forms at conferences and workshops, where I received invaluable comments and suggestions, and in journals, from which I enjoyed constructive conversations with numerous scholars. I am deeply grateful to John DiMoia, Alisa Freedman, Tatsushi Fujiwara, Susan Greenhalgh, Aya Homei, Christine Hong, Yu-Ling Huang, John Kim, Sonja M. Kim, Michael Shiyung Liu, Jin-kyung Park, Jennifer Robertson, Stefan Tanaka, and the late Aaron Stephen Moore. Despite the extraordinary challenges the pandemic has posed over the past years, I was able to build virtual support groups with researchers across the Pacific, to whom I am indebted for stimulating discussions and critical comments. Special thanks to Hirotaka Kasai, Sunho Ko, Seok-Won Lee, Margherita Long, Anne McKnight, Chizuko Naito, Young Sun Park, and Setsu Shigematsu. I especially express my gratitude to my colleagues at UVic for their tremendous support and encouragement: Angie Chau, Richard Fox, ann-elise lewallen, Cody Poulton, Victor V. Ramraj, and Lisa A. Surridge.

It goes without saying that I am truly blessed to work with the wonderful editor Dylan Kyung-lim White of Stanford University Press, who showed trust and confidence in my work throughout the whole process of publishing this book. The hard work of Sarah Rodriguez, David Zielonka, Emily Smith, and Jennifer Gordon, as well as Mary Mortensen, made the process extremely smooth for the neophyte author. I sincerely appreciate two anonymous reviewers for their insightful comments and suggestions. Parts of Chapter 1 appeared previously in "Technologies of the Population Problem: The Neo-Malthusian Birth Control Movement in Interwar Japan," *Annual Review of Cultural Studies* 5 (2017): 37–58, https://doi.org/10.32237/arcs.5.0_37; and parts of Chapter 2 were published as "Differing Conceptions of "Voluntary Motherhood": Yamakawa Kikue's Birth Strike and Ishimoto Shizue's Eugenic Feminism," *U.S.–Japan Women's Journal* 52 (2017): 3–22, doi:10.1353/jwj.2017.0009. I thank both the Association of Cultural Typhoon and University of Hawaii Press for the permissions to reproduce them. Fuji shuppan generously gave permission to reproduce an image of the Pro-BC poster from their collected works.

The journey to this book would have not been possible without mentors, friends, and, most of all, family members who have motivated me along the way. I am thankful to my intellectual mentor at Yonsei University, Sung Mo Yim, for introducing me to critical Japanese studies. My parents have never stopped encouraging me to pursue my goals no matter how unconventional they may be. Finally, I dedicate this book to my husband, Samuel Sang-Hyun Ahn, who gave me loving and steadfast support during the ups and downs of the journey.

A NOTE ON ROMANIZATION AND NAMES

I used the revised Hepburn system for Japanese terms and names and the McCune-Reischauer romanization for Korean. Exceptions were made for some regional names (e.g., Tokyo instead of Tōkyō) to reflect conventional use of such terms. As for names, I followed the standard order of Asian names (i.e., the surname followed by the given name) with some exceptions where Asian authors published their work in English.

WOMBS
of
EMPIRE

INTRODUCTION

Population

A DISCURSIVE SITE OF EN-GENDERING LIFE

> I think there is a relation between the thing which is problematized and the process of problematization. The problematization is an "answer" to a concrete situation which is real.
>
> MICHEL FOUCAULT, *Discourse and Truth: The Problematization of Parrhesia* (1983)

Déjà Vu: All-Too-Familiar Problems and Solutions

For decades, Japan has struggled with low fertility rates and rapid population aging issues. Its fertility rate has been hovering around 1.4 births per woman since the mid-1990s, which caused a series of demographic challenges, including the nation's aging and shrinking population and a labor shortage. The Japanese government has drawn up some solutions in response to the multifaceted population problem. Notably, Kōsei rōdō-shō (Ministry of Health, Labor, and Welfare of Japan) has taken the initiative in providing financial and medical support for infertility treatments for married couples since the early 2000s.[1] Their initiative culminated in enforcing the national health insurance coverage program for infertility treatments starting in April 2022. The program aims to relieve the financial burdens of married couples with fertility issues by including certain types of infertility treatments (i.e., artificial insemination, in vitro fertilization, and micro insemination) in the national health insurance package.[2] Working closely with advisory groups such as the Japan Society of Obstetrics and Gynecology and the Central Social Insurance Medical Council, the Ministry of Health, Labor, and Welfare has sought to facilitate medical and technological intervention in reproduction and thereby increase the nation's birth rate. Although the infertility treatment support program is expected to incentivize married couples with fertility problems (who account for 35% of all married couples with wives younger than 50 in Japan)[3] to opt for medical treatments, some drawbacks cannot be overlooked. Conspicuously, the fact that only married couples with wives under age 43 are eligible for the program reveals conservative gender binaries underlying the government's population policies. More specifically, while the Japanese government normalizes heterosexual families as the basic unit for procreation, it reaffirms the norm of women's natural motherhood according to which female infertility is seen as abnormal and pathological. In this view, both heteronormativity and motherhood norms are instrumental in fulfilling the Japanese government's plan to address the demographic challenge.

Government and medical intervention in reproduction and fertility as primary means of population control are by no means new tactics. They are reminiscent of modern population discourse that attempted to address pressing population issues in multiple ways in the interwar and wartime periods. Since the late 1910s, there was a growing call among social scientists and social reformers to solve the "population problem" (*jinkō mondai*), which became a buzzword in prewar Japan. Unlike today, Japan wrestled with high fertility rates and the allegedly resultant economic issues, primarily poverty and unemployment, back in the interwar period between the 1920s and 30s. Despite the difference in demographic patterns between the early twentieth century and today, interwar discussions on tackling the pressing demographic issues among scholars, activists, and government bureaucrats reveal more similarities than differences with the ongoing social discussions of population challenges. Particularly, birth control activists, feminists, eugenicists, and social scientists argued for the regulation of population size and the optimization of its quality on eugenic grounds. The interwar discussions on the control of the population evolved into the pronatalist, comprehensive population policies under the total war regime (1937–1945), which sought to transform its population into readily mobilizable human resources for the war efforts and to instrumentalize women's bodies under the slogan of the "fertile womb battalion" (*kodakara butai*).

Wombs of Empire: Population Discourses and Biopolitics in Modern Japan traces the trajectory of population discourse in interwar and wartime Japan and illuminates population as a critical site where different visions of modernity came into tension and rationalized differences among bodies. I define population discourse as a constellation of interconnected practices, including knowledge production, social movements, and policymaking for problematizing, regulating, and governing the quantity and quality of a population. Historically, population discourse manifested in the forms of birth control movements, the eugenics movement, and various public health policies and programs involving population science. Although national circumstances influence how population discourse emerge and develop, nation-states are not the predetermined condition for population discourse to exist but their forms of expression that necessitate borders and boundaries between nations, in tandem with racial and gender differentiation. The patterns of how population discourse have emerged and diverged are, in fact, transnational as the discourse have produced protean justifications for dominance, that is, ethnonationalism and racism, colonialism and imperialism, and gender segregation.

It is noteworthy that the notion of population (*jinkō*) was already introduced in Japan well before different mechanisms of problematizing the Japanese population emerged in the late 1910s. The Meiji government established Tōkei-kyoku (Statistics Bureau) in Naimu-shō (Ministry of Home Affairs) in 1885 and surveyed population dynamics every five years starting in 1898. The centralized survey of demographic statistics in the late Meiji period enabled the quantification of life for the first time in the modern Japanese state.[4] Discussions of population quality emerged at the same time with the introduction of eugenics into Japan. Pioneering eugenicists including Unno Yukinori (1879–1954) and Nagai Hisomu (1876–1957) played an essential role in initiating intellectual discussion regarding eugenics. These early eugenicists called for the need to improve the quality of the Japanese race on eugenic grounds.[5] The historical narratives around the emergence of the concept of population in modern Japan reveal that population became rendered as a quantifiable form of life on one hand and that the problem of its quality was subsumed under that of the Japanese race on the other. The dyad representation of the population as quantity and quality during the Meiji period set the discursive tone for interwar social discussions and movements around various population issues.

What was distinctive about interwar population discourse compared to the preceding discussions around population was that an inextricable link between quantity and quality problems in the Japanese population began to be established. What was also new about population discourse that emerged in the late 1910s was that the population problem became associated with broader political, economic, biological, and moral problems. How was the intersection between the quantity of population (*jinkō no ryō*) and the quality of population (*jinkō no shitsu*) understood by those who called for the need to address a volatile problem labeled as a "population problem"? If particular patterns of population discourse shaped the idea of population, did the population problem actually exist in social reality or did it remain only as a social imaginary? How did the varying discussions of the population problem constitute a focal point where solutions to the problem were justified? In response to these questions, this book delves into ideas, movements, and policies that co-constructed a discursive site where they discussed and deployed various mechanisms of regulating and governing human life instead of searching for the presumed objective truth underlying demographic facts.

Since the late 1910s, when the so-called Great War ended, Japanese reformers and intellectuals actively referenced European and American discourse on population quantity and quality and reproduced them to address contemporary socioeconomic crises experienced in Japan. The formation and growth of neo-Malthusianism, the leftist birth control movement, the eugenics movement, population science and policy during the interwar period reveals multidimensional social and intellectual responses to the crisis of modernity such as economic inflation and depression, class stratification, and social instability. What these various forms of population discourse collectively did was to formulate the modern crises as the problem of population and reproduction, and accordingly, to seek out solutions that primarily involved population control and management either genetically or socially. Despite varying definitions of the population problem, different actors in the population discourse ultimately reimagined wombs as a controllable, predictable, and optimizable entities for their own causes. Given this, the interwar buzzword "population problem" is not descriptive but symptomatic of increasing social, medical, and government interventions in the size and health of the Japanese population to overcome pressing socioeconomic issues. What Michel Foucault calls "problematization"—by which he denotes the discursive process of rendering certain behaviors, phenomena, or processes as a problem—provides critical insight into this discursive construction of "population problem."[6] This book characterizes the wide range of discussions and practices around the population problem as a technology of life constituting certain truths about social relations instead of presuming the existence of *the* truth about the problem.

Although population discourse arose in response to the predicament of modernity, the historical trajectory of population discourse from the interwar to the wartime period in Japan suggests that both social and governmental sectors attempting to solve the population problem did not necessarily overcome modernity. They rather *consummated* modernity by maximizing various aspects of modern ideas, practices, and institutions. During the interwar years, neo-Malthusianists ascribed poverty to overpopulation and, therefore, advocated birth control to address the imbalance between population and resources. The idea of controlling overreproduction and fertility aimed both to optimize the population size and improve its quality, which would ultimately contribute to national progress from the neo-Malthusianist viewpoint. The interplay between scientific knowledge and nationalism is also found in the role of interwar think tanks that produced population science and developed a blueprint for governing various demographic aspects. As will be discussed in more detail in Chapters 4 and 5, the interwar blueprint for managing the quantity and quality of population comprehensively (e.g., fertility and mortality, nuptiality, the standard of living, public health, sanitation, employment, labor productivity, distribution of resources, food production and consumption, migration, and so forth) eventually came into effect under the wartime regime.

With the notion of a "biopolitical state," I emphasize the integration of interwar population discourse into the wartime state systems and practices that sought to optimize both the quantity and quality of a selected population. The ways in which the total war state orchestrated knowledge and institutions to rationalize demographic management under the quintessential slogan "healthy soldiers and healthy people" (*kenpei kenmin*) indicate that the wartime regime materialized the interwar initiative to institutionalize population control. By looking into how the wartime fascist regime consummated the interwar blueprint for biopolitical rationalities and institutions, I emphasize the maximization of modern systematic and scientific intervention in the population, as opposed to the blind equation of fascism with merely an irrational, regressive form of power. In so doing, I aim to dissociate Japanese fascism from a culturalist and particularist account and, instead, situate it among various inflections of biopolitical modernity that valorized the systematic, scientific management of bodies.

Population: A Protean Site of Problematizing Life

Previous scholarship on population discourse in modern Japan has primarily examined particular patterns of state control over and knowledge formation around the quality of the Japanese population. Most existing work on state intervention into population control delves into the formation of a range of social policies, including public health and family support policies in the interwar period and discusses the growing importance of population quality (*jinkō shishitsu*) to the modern Japanese state that ultimately enforced eugenics policies under the National Eugenic Law during wartime.[7] The development of social movements and scientific knowledge around eugenics is another central subject of the existing literature on Japan's population discourse. A body of work on the history of eugenics in the context of Japan illuminates how, on the one hand, eugenic ideas and practices rationalized government and technological intervention into reproduction in the name of science and progress, and, on the other hand, normalized discriminatory treatment of *others*—whose inferiority was defined on health, genetic, racial, and sexual grounds.[8] Meanwhile, there has been an increasing body of literature on the control of women's sexuality and reproduction in prewar and wartime Japan employing a critical approach to the questions of gender and sexuality.[9] Although the concept of population is only indirectly touched upon in the existing research on state and social control over women's bodies in modern Japan, their critical observation of the history of birth control movements, abortion laws, eugenics laws, and other measures to regulate reproduction has contributed to understanding the politics of sexuality and reproduction—in other words, the social construction of women's bodies as a primary site of state and scientific intervention in the name of national and racial progress.

As mentioned above, both Japanese and English language scholarships have mainly focused on government-level policies and intellectual discussions that sought to improve the quality of the Japanese population either by enhancing their living conditions or by controlling reproduction. While most existing literature has discussed population control without necessarily explicating what population signified in modern Japan, there is a small body of research that traces the trajectory of the development of population policies to highlight the continuity between the prewar, wartime, and postwar government's interest in optimizing both the quantity and quality of the Japanese population.[10] By defining population policy broadly to include a wide range of government measures addressing both the size and health of the population—for example, the interwar public hygiene and demographic research initiated by Hoken eisei chōsakai (Hygiene Investigation Committee) and Jinkō shokuryō mondai chōsakai (Population and Food Problems Investigation Committee), the wartime National Eugenic Law and pronatalist policy, and the postwar family planning campaign and Shin seikatsu undō (the new life movement)—this body of research on Japanese population policies elucidates that consistent efforts were made to increase control over the life of the population as an aggregated body while individual reproduction became instrumental to the state's population control measures.[11]

While this book echoes previous works that highlight the continuity of population policies in transwar Japan, it expands the scope of discussion to include a broad range of intellectual discussions and social movements that problematized the quantity and quality of the population in different ways. The concept of "population discourse" is deliberately adopted to avoid the reductive assumption that population has been merely an object of *policies*; instead, I argue that population has been a site of *politics* that seeks to redefine modernity through the biological reordering of human societies. A critical approach to population as a discursive space has been embraced by some scholars who dissociated themselves from the conception of objectivity underlying so-called demographic facts to unveil the complexity of institutional, ideological, and technological landscapes that have legitimized the problematization of a population.[12] These scholars have contributed to a renewed understanding of population as a discursive form whose elements are not only quantified but also "selectively disaggregated and made the objects of social policy and projects," as Bruce Curtis puts it.[13]

If a population is a discursively composed entity to identify subjects to be governed, a population problem is "discovered" to facilitate institutional, ideological, and technological interventions into individual health and reproduction.[14] Therefore, close scrutiny of population discourse allows us to understand the patterns of how a population is constituted as a demographic truth; of how a population problem is constructed vis-à-vis economic indicators, political ideologies and identities, and social and biological hierarchies; and lastly of how such discovered problems legitimize the interplay of institutional and scientific control of a population to address larger issues than a population itself. As Alison Bashford keenly observes, population has always been more than the politics of sex and reproduction; it has "touched on almost everything: international relations; war and peace; food and agriculture; economy and ecology; race and sex; labor, migration, and standards of living."[15]

Revisiting Japanese Modernity, Biopolitics, and Governmentality

Adding to the growing body of research that critically engages with the politics of population, this book focuses on the genealogy of population discourse in the Japanese historical context to revisit particularized narratives of Japanese modernity on one hand, and to create a non-teleological yet rather constructive dialogue of population discourse in general on the other. First, the former goal of reviewing Japanese modernity through the lens of population primarily concerns a challenge to the characterization of wartime Japan as a deviation or distortion from universal modernity and, not unrelatedly, the disjunctive periodization of the twentieth-century history of Japan—that is, prewar/interwar, wartime, and postwar periods—in history writing. As J. Victor Koschmann explains, since the immediate postwar period, the approach to Japanese wartime history has been dominated by the idea that the wartime social structures (mainly manifested as fascism, militarism, and imperialist expansionism) were pathological consequences of Japan's premodern residues.[16] Maruyama Masao's analysis of the ascendance of ultra-nationalism in wartime Japan echoes this prevailing narrative given his claim that Japan failed to acquire mature forms of modern nationalism—that is, nationalism tied with "bourgeois democracy and popular sovereignty as seen in classic Western nationalism"[17]—due to remaining feudalist social relations. The denunciation of the wartime fascist regime in postwar Japan was ingrained in the postwar social imaginary that sought a "new beginning"[18] to make a complete break from the dark side of incomplete modernity.

Given this, the discursive rupture between the wartime and the postwar eras evolved out of a dual desire: that is, collective memory building in postwar Japan to reconstruct itself into a liberal democratic state on the one hand, and a longstanding endeavor to consummate "modernity," a concept referring to the imagined unity of the West that has dictated *History* or the universal flow of historical development, on the other.[19] The postwar narrative that particularizes Japan as an incomplete yet catching-up-in-the-progress modern state is therefore closely interlinked with the narrative of exceptionalizing wartime Japan. The underlying temporal binary between modern and premodern is both spatially and hierarchically translated to render the West as rational, civilized, and universal as opposed to the non-West as irrational, feudalistic, and particular.

Against this logic of particularizing both Japan and the wartime regime, this book aims to de-colonize the notion of modernity and illuminate a collective inertia to control and govern life by mobilizing government institutions and scientific knowledge throughout the first half of the twentieth century and beyond. The revisiting of modern Japanese history through the lens of population discourse will allow us to understand how consistently yet variably population has been problematized as an object of state control and scientific investigation since the interwar period. Furthermore, it will help us grasp how the wartime fascist regime appropriated and even augmented elements of modern government apparatuses—for example, statistics, population science, eugenics, and public health administrations. My argument, which focuses on the historical continuity of population discourse, does not claim that Japan achieved modernity in a Western-centric historicist sense. Instead, I aim to unsettle such a claim as an inevitable step toward unveiling the heterogenous nature of modernity that Japan, just like anywhere in the world, struggled to consummate and overcome simultaneously.

A second goal of this book is to create a constructive dialogue with broader discussions of Michel Foucault's "biopolitics" and "governmentality" without subsuming the historical narrative surrounding Japan's population discourse under the alleged universality of Foucauldian theories of power. It is no exaggeration that Foucault has had a considerable impact on academic discussions regarding tactics and technologies of power. The notions of biopolitics and governmentality have been significantly influential among scholars whose work shed light on legislative and administrative regulation and management, and on scientific knowledge and technological intervention that center on various aspects of population phenomena, such as sexuality, reproduction, health, welfare, and so forth. While this book, too, draws upon Foucault's analytical concepts that he primarily developed vis-à-vis European historical contexts, it does so by acknowledging an inherent tension between theoretical frameworks and historical experiences and by critically engaging with a conversation with historical complexity and specificity.[20]

In his lectures at the Collège de France between 1975 and 1976, Foucault sketched out the emergence of biopolitics. For Foucault, biopolitics is a crucial framework for explaining a new technology of power that emerged in the second half of the eighteenth century and took precedence over, if not replacing completely, existing sovereign power. This new technology of power, according to Foucault, "deals with the population, with the population as a political problem, as a problem that is once scientific and political, as a biopolitical problem and as power's problem."[21] The essence of biopolitics is that it regulates a population as an aggregated form of life to make subjects live and let them die. This principle is radically different from the sovereign power that wields rights to take subjects' lives and let them live. Biopolitics also differs from disciplinary power, another modern technology of power that emerged in the first half of the eighteenth century, in the sense that whereas disciplinary power is exercised over "man-as-body," biopolitical power is directed at "man-as-species," that is, a massified, quantified, and regulated form of life called "population."[22] Foucault suggests that with the emergence of biopolitics, new regulatory mechanisms of power relations are introduced: biopolitical mechanisms of regulating a population involve "forecasts, statistical estimates, and overall measures" to achieve an equilibrium of demographic indicators, unlike disciplinary power that seeks to correct or modify conducts at an individual level.[23]

In the succeeding years, while the notion of biopolitics was largely put aside, Foucault's interest turned to "governmentality": that is, an art of government and governmental rationality whereby he delved into the underlying problem of the state and population.[24] According to Foucault, governmentality, which he called an "ugly word" presumably due to its substantial obscurity,[25] is broadly defined as follows:

> The ensemble formed by institutions, procedures, analyses and reflections, the calculations and tactics that allow the exercise of this very specific albeit complex form of power, which has its target population, as its principal form of knowledge political economy, and as its essential technical means apparatuses of security.[26]

As Mitchell Dean points out, the relationship between biopolitics and governmentality remains unclear in Foucault's accounts due to his, whether intended or not, failure to articulate how the two themes are distinguished from each other.[27] If population is both a biopolitical problem and a governmental problem, and both the target of biopolitical power and of governmentality, why did Foucault not use a single framework in the first place? I argue, though, that the ambiguity of the connection of biopolitics and governmentality does not necessarily unveil the weaknesses of Foucault's accounts of power but rather urges us to look into how the notion of governmentality reorients the question of power relations. Considering the abovementioned definition of governmentality, it is worth noting that the problem of government is much larger than that of institutions or functions of political technologies. By focusing on governmental rationality and its practices underlying power relations, multiple domains where different technologies and mechanisms of power intersect to optimize their target population come into view. For Foucault, it is both the external and internal structure of the state that becomes a focal point through the analytic lens of governmentality. The modern state, according to him, is not a uniformed entity possessing power, but it is merely constitutive of totalizing governmental rationalities, as he puts it, the " 'governmentalization' of the state."[28]

This book draws on the notion of governmentality to underline the complex dynamics of power relations that led to the construction of population as an object of scientific inquiry, regulatory management, and disciplinary control in modern Japan. In so doing, this book opposes interpreting population policies from merely a top-down perspective and instead situates policy-level discussions within the broader genealogy of population discourse. Taking such an approach as a premise, I use the term "biopolitical state" to conceptualize the Japanese wartime state's incorporation of population governance into its system, which in turn led to the transformation of the state into a constitutive of governmental rationalities aiming to optimize population quantity and quality. A close investigation into the continued patterns of population discourse in interwar and wartime Japan will help us identify the location of the Japanese biopolitical state in the broader map of modern governmentality.

It is noteworthy that the use of Foucault's frameworks in analyzing particular historical experiences of modern Japan requires an elaborate approach to the tensions between theory and history and that between the general and the particular. These tensions by no means stem from the presumed incommensurability between the West and the Rest but from common misconceptions of theory as teleological texts and of history as self-enclosed narratives.[29] To avoid such misconceptions, this book will utilize the account of biopolitics and governmentality as a window through which to examine why and how population became rendered as a multifaceted political problem during interwar and wartime Japan. By doing so, I seek to create a constructive dialogue between the biopolitical frameworks of modernity and modernity as lived experiences in the Japanese colonial empire.

Particularly, this book will delve into two crucial questions that have been neglected in the account of biopolitics and governmentality. These questions include, first, how Japanese colonialism and imperialism informed population discourse in Japan proper (*naichi*) and vice versa, and second, how bodies were not only massified in the form of population but also differentiated and excluded along the lines of gender and race. As for the question of colonialism and imperialism, the missing link between metropole and colony in Foucault's account will be articulated to dissect colonial desire inseparable from political discussions and governmental measures to control the Japanese population.[30] The close attention to the historical conditions of Japan's colonial empire will allow us to grasp the discursive proximity between biopolitical rationality and colonial political economy.

In the meantime, the second question regarding the differential ordering of bodies will be examined mainly through the discursive construction of motherhood (*bosei*) in modern Japan. The problem of reproduction was foregrounded in various forms of population discourse due to its instrumentality in national productivity, race betterment, and masculine imperialism. The interwar birth control and eugenics movements, as well as wartime population policies, made wombs a pivotal focal point on which to optimize the quantity and quality of a selected population. Therefore, motherhood became a political means by which different population discourse reified the gender binary and valorized scientific and administrative interventions into reproductive bodies. By de-essentializing the norms of motherhood, I will illuminate how the biopolitical regime in the Japanese imperial context reordered life through the gender lines to instrumentalize wombs as a source of the health and welfare of the Japanese race and, thereby, how reproductive functionality embodied in the subjectivity of motherhood intersected with and reinforced racial and ethnic differences in the Japanese colonial empire. In sum, the history of population discourse in modern Japan will reveal to us both inclusive and exclusive dimensions of modern power relations that primarily manifested in knowledge, practices, and policies concerning the quantity and quality of a selected population.

Chapter Outline

The body of this book is arranged in both chronological and thematic order. The first three chapters examine interwar population discourse that variously constituted and responded to the "population problem" and discuss how the cacophony of population discourse in the 1920s and 1930s essentially indicates multifaceted versions of restructuring modernity through population governance. The last two chapters turn to the wartime population policies and inquire into how the total war state incorporated preceding population discourse into its mobilization strategies and practices, and how the state's effort to consummate modernity through population governance imperatively necessitated exclusion and differentiation along gender and racial lines.

Chapter 1 examines how Japanese neo-Malthusianists and leftists articulated the population problem differently in the interwar period. In response to salient symptoms of the crisis of modernity, Japanese social reformers and labor activists waged a heated debate around the issue. The term "population problem" remained undefined because there was no consensus on what ought to be problematized, let alone agreement on how to tackle it. Notwithstanding their disagreement, both sides advocated birth control as a biological tool to achieve their respective political goals. By tracing the history of the population debate in interwar Japan, this chapter illuminates different utopian visions channeled through population control and their reconfiguration of modernity as biological progress.

In Chapter 2, I trace the historical trajectory of prewar feminist discussions on voluntary motherhood. Since the early 1920s, the rise of the birth control movement and the introduction of contraceptives allowed feminist thinkers to envision alternatives for natural conception that they thought to be constraints on women's empowerment. The idea of artificial birth control created a new basis for thinking beyond the naturalness of women's maternity far before the emergence of the women's liberation movement in the postwar era. This chapter elucidates the historical link between feminists' rearticulation of motherhood and contraceptive technologies by focusing on the transpacific circulation of the "voluntary motherhood" slogan. A close investigation into this birth control activism allows us to understand heterogeneous feminist approaches to the fashioning of ideal motherhood and the underlying gender schemas applied to positioning women within the nexus of ethnic nation (*minzoku*), race, and class.

Chapter 3 turns to the roles of scholars in legitimizing the "scientific" governance of the Japanese population. Against the backdrop of worldwide economic depression and the rise in agrarian and industrial disputes across the nation, leading scholars in economics, statistics, public policy, and sociology took the initiative in developing population science and joined think tanks, including Jinkō shokuryō mondai chōsakai (Population and Food Problems Investigation Committee, established in 1927 and dissolved in 1930) and Jinkō mondai kenkyūkai (Population Problem

Research Society, established in 1933). The principles laid out by these scholars range from social scientific reconfigurations of the Japanese population to the necessity of a permanent national institution to regulate and manage the population. Through a close reading of a range of population investigations, this chapter casts light on the inflection of population science against the backdrop of the foundation of Manchukuo in 1932 and discusses the historical entanglement between population governance and colonial domination in the context of the expanding empire.

Chapter 4 explores the process by which the Japanese wartime population policies were established under the banner of total mobilization. The historical trajectory from the creation of Kōsei-shō (Ministry of Health and Welfare) to the establishment of Kenmin-kyoku (Healthy People Bureau) under Kōsei-sho in November 1943 allows us to raise crucial questions about why the wartime fascist regime functioned as the primary agency of population discourse, and what roles a set of Japanese wartime population policies played in the transformation of a population to human resources (*jintekii shigen*). In arguing that the wartime population policies materialized the interwar blueprints for the biopolitical state, this chapter offers a critical look at the conventional association of Japanese fascism with a deviation from universal modernity. It also illuminates how the fascist regime reified biopolitical rationalities to transform the population into mobilizable human resources for the war efforts. Ironically, the perpetual wartime mode of life under fascism created a murky zone where the lines between life and death, biopolitics and necropolitics, and welfare and warfare became indistinguishable.

Chapter 5 shifts the analytic focus to the government's increasing attention on the maternal body during wartime. The chapter situates the wartime pronatalist policy under the slogan "give birth and multiply" (*umeyo fuyaseyo*) within the broader context of population discourse and discusses the gendered nature of the biopolitical state that normalized the roles of female Japanese citizens in producing as many superior and healthy citizens as possible. A set of wartime population policies such as the government's "fertile womb battalion" (*kodakara butai*) commendations and "Ninsanpu techō" (Handbook for the Expectant Mother) of July 1942 offer a revealing look at the instrumentality of motherhood and family in the governmentalization of the state. In addition to the gendered division of citizenship, this chapter further examines the differential effects of biopolitical rationalities along racial and class lines. So-called comfort women, or military sexual slaves mobilized across the Japanese colonial empire, were transformed into women unfit for motherhood.

Their fertility was denied by the imperial total war regime that mobilized "comfort women" only as disposable sexual resources.

In the Epilogue, I provide a brief insight into the impacts of interwar and wartime discourse of population on postwar Japanese society. After the defeat of Japan in World War II in 1945, Japan underwent a drastic change in its political, economic, and social structures: the deconstruction of the Japanese empire and the reconstruction of the nation-state. However, this post-imperial postwar process of rebuilding Japan continued to involve the remaking of population discourse, particularly population control through the family planning campaign and eugenic policies to accelerate economic recovery. The continued politics to control the population and reorganize gender relations makes clear the necessity to reconsider the historical legacy of population discourse in Japan and beyond.

ONE

The Population Problem and Utopian Remedies

> The Roman proletariat lived at the expense of society, while modern society lives at the expense of the proletariat.
>
> KARL MARX, *The Eighteenth Brumaire of Louis Bonaparte* (1852)

> Although workers are humans with freedom and independence, they must sell the labor power they possess to make a living.... Furthermore, as far as labor is a commodity [urimono], it will inevitably obey the so-called principle of supply and demand in economics. As the number of workers grows, the labor power will increase accordingly. [Then,] the value of the labor power, that is, wages will necessarily fall. Therefore, if the population of workers was not limited, it would not be conceivable to expect a wage increase. As matters stand today, the workers always outnumber what the capitalists demand.
>
> ABE ISOO, *Seikatsu mondai kara mita sanji chōsetsu* [Birth control from the perspective of living problems] (1931); translation is mine

The Problematization of Population in Interwar Japan

In July 1922, Japanese birth control advocate Baron Ishimoto Keikichi presented a paper titled "The Population Problem in Japan" at the Fifth International Neo-Malthusian and Birth Control Conference in London.[1] Since the first International Neo-Malthusian Conference held in Paris in August 1900, it had developed into a major event for birth control advocates and eugenicists exclusively from Western countries, including the United States, Britain, France, Germany, Netherlands, and Austria.[2] Two

Asian nations were included as official participating countries at the fifth conference: Japan and India. Baron Ishimoto attended the conference as a Japanese delegate, along with a few Japanese birth control proponents such as Abe Isoo and Kaji Tokijirō, to discuss manifold social issues presumably caused by overpopulation based on the Malthusian theory of population. In his presentation, Baron Ishimoto noted that "the only way for Japan to meet the problem presented by a growing population and a static food supply" was birth control.[3] This claim encapsulates his ideas of the population problem facing Japan and the essence of neo-Malthusianism in general. Attendees from other countries shared the idea that birth control would eliminate many issues resulting from overpopulation and even improve the quality of the race.

The global rise of neo-Malthusianism is symptomatic of what Alison Bashford called a "revival of Malthusian ideas" that made the "struggle for room and food" global in the aftermath of the First World War.[4] While the movement traces its history back to 1877, when the Malthusian League, the world's first birth control advocacy group, was founded in Britain,[5] the substance of neo-Malthusian arguments underwent marked changes after the First World War. Bashford elucidates this transition of the population discourse in the postwar global context, which she sums up as the integration of biopolitics into geopolitics.[6] The first global war between 1914 and 1918 proved that a failure to address the spatial and material limit of human expansion would only invite violence. Whereas a war was an inevitable option for Thomas Robert Malthus (1766–1834) to curb population growth, his successors in the twentieth century prioritized international collaboration to maintain the optimal size of the population and thereby to ensure global peace. Charles Vickery Drysdale, British neo-Malthusianist and president of the 1922 conference, made opening remarks verifying the increasing consensus on the need for population control for global security: "No event in the whole history of the movement is of such good augury for the future peace of the world, and for the progress of the cause; as the greatest obstacle to its acceptance is the fear of the superior fertility of the high birth-rate nations."[7]

While neo-Malthusianists around the world were striving to address overpopulation for food and military security, their contemporary socialists and communists tackled population issues from a markedly different perspective. Radical leftists harshly criticized the neo-Malthusian arguments by adopting Karl Marx's criticism of Malthus's population theory. Marx denounced Malthus's biological reckoning of population by reorienting the issue of poverty from overpopulation to capitalism.[8]

Whereas Malthus attributed the cause of surplus population to the law of human reproductive nature, Marx argued that surplus population was independent of the absolute population size. For Marx, "relative surplus population" was produced due to the mechanism of capitalist production that continuously set free exploitable populations only to accumulate capital.[9]

The critique of Malthus's population theory was carried on by German socialist August Bebel (1840–1913) and Bolshevik leader Vladimir Lenin (1870–1924).[10] Both Bebel and Lenin rebutted Malthusian myths about the correlation between poverty and fecundity. Bebel concluded that the root cause of poverty is "not due to a lack of food" but "an unequal distribution of same" under the capitalist mode of production.[11] Likewise, Lenin condemned bourgeois ideology shared among contemporary neo-Malthusianists, which illuminates leftists' dominant responses to the birth control movement:

> The working class is not perishing, it is growing, becoming stronger, gaining courage, consolidating itself, educating itself and becoming steeled in battle. We are pessimists as far as serfdom, capitalism and petty, production are concerned, but we are ardent optimists in what concerns the working-class movement and its aims. We are already laying the foundation of a new edifice and our children will complete its construction. That is the reason—the only reason—why we are unconditionally the enemies of Neo-Malthusianism, suited only to unfeeling and egotistic petty-bourgeois couples, who whisper in scared voices: "God grant we manage somehow by ourselves. So much the better if we have no children."[12]

The opposition between Malthus's population theory and Marx's critique of the capitalist mode of production had evolved into the debate on population issues between neo-Malthusianism and socialism in the early twentieth century. The fundamental disagreement between the two sides concerned the source of poverty. Whereas neo-Malthusianists blamed unchecked population growth for poverty and its attendant problems, leftists considered structural inequality under capitalism to be the root cause of poverty. Their different views on the origin of poverty informed different solutions to the population issue: the approach of the neo-Malthusianists was to resolve the global issue of overpopulation using contraceptives; leftists, on the other hand, advocated a proletarian revolution based on an optimistic assumption that once capitalism was overthrown, the suffering of the working classes would be addressed.

The debate between neo-Malthusianism and socialism was symptomatic of growing tensions of modernity in the early twentieth century. The tensions of modernity hardly concern the side effects of modern progress, but there are intrinsic tensions to modernity. Takeuchi Yoshimi's definition of modernity is helpful to grasp the complex nature of modernity. In Takeuchi's view, modernity as the "self-recognition of Europe," and Europe—namely the spirit of modernity and self-proclaimed universality—"barely maintains itself through the tensions of its incessant self-renewals."[13] The movement of European self-realization in various forms— including capitalism, colonialism, rationalization, progress, scientific knowledge, and technological advances—is in constant flux to strive to close the gap between ideology and practice. The inherent tensions between European universality and historical particularity evoke different political responses. When it comes to the population debate, different political strategies emerged in response to the growing tensions between the ideology of human progress and social stratification under capitalism. Whereas neo-Malthusianism proposed a biological solution to amend capitalism, socialists and communists denounced capitalism altogether to pursue the ultimate form of human progress.

Japan was not immune to the unfolding tension of modernity. Notably, World War I brought about political, economic, and ideological changes in Japan just as it did in Europe. Between 1914 and 1918, Japan underwent a temporary boom due to a growing demand for Japanese products in the absence of European goods. Although the brief increase in demand caused an increase in Japanese workers' incomes, the surge in workers' wages did not necessarily elevate their standard of living. The general level of prices for goods, especially food prices, grew more than enough to offset any wage increases.[14] Furthermore, wartime inflation was followed by nationwide postwar economic hardship, symbolized by the Rice Riots of 1918. The Rice Riots were a series of nationwide riots against the high price of rice. With the wartime inflation that caused the price of rice to almost double in many areas, the urban and the rural poor revolted against the rice merchants and jostled with the police. The Rice Riots exemplify growing social and political contradictions in post–World War I Japan, and more importantly, the emergence of class conflicts in the form of food crises.[15]

In response to salient symptoms of the crisis of modernity, Japanese social reformers and labor activists had a heated debate around the "population problem." That interwar buzzword remained undefined as there was no consensus on what ought to be problematized between neo-

Malthusian reformers and leftist activists, let alone consensus on how to tackle it. What was distinctive about the population debate in interwar Japan was that both sides advocated birth control as a biological tool to achieve their respective political goals. For neo-Malthusianists, as seen above, birth control was a panacea for overpopulation and its resultant social issues. For leftists, on the other hand, birth control was a stopgap measure to mitigate the hardship confronting the working classes, whereas the proletarian revolution was the only way to liberate the masses from the evils of capitalism thoroughly.

This chapter examines how Japanese neo-Malthusianists and leftists articulated the population problem differently in the interwar period. I will argue that the population problem or *jinkō mondai* was discursively formulated to problematize various symptoms of modernity primarily in a biological way. I am mainly interested in how the population discourse deployed by neo-Malthusianists and leftists each articulated the relationship between human reproduction, capitalism, and the idea of progress in their own way. As discussed below, the history of the population debate in interwar Japan presents us with multiple utopian programs entailed by different political movements. Despite conflicting views on the population problem, their utopian programs agreed at least on one thing: population lies at the root of the modern crisis.

The Schema of the Population Problem: Census, Eugenics, and Utopia

The historical condition for the emergence of population debates was the introduction of the concept of population (*jinkō*). In Japan, it was not until the late Meiji period that population, a quantified and massified form of life governed by a modern state, became incorporated into government's policies and practices. The Meiji government adopted the household registration system (*koseki*) in 1871 to compile nationwide household registers. Under *koseki*, the government documented the information of households instead of individuals. Although the *koseki* system is often credited with being the first modern demographic statistics, it had not yet produced comprehensive demographic data, particularly data on individuals in the population.[16] Pioneering statistician Sugi Kōji (1827–1917) who worked for Daijō-kan (Grand Council of State) to establish the general statistical system in the 1870s, took the initiative to transform household-level surveys into individual-level demographic statistics.[17] His effort to improve the accuracy of population statistics following the German census model culminated in the demographic survey in Kai province (present-day Yamanashi Prefecture) in 1879, which became the prototype for the national census in Japan.[18] With the establishment of Tōkei-kyoku (Statistics Bureau) under Naimu-shō (Ministry of Home Affairs) in 1885, existing household surveys that local governments had carried out were replaced by the centralized dynamic statistics of population in 1898.[19] The survey of population dynamics that aimed to collect data on birth and death rates, population growth rates, and sex ratios remained the central pillar of the population statistics system until a national census system was introduced in 1920 in Japan proper.

Given the transition from household surveys to individual-level population statistics at the turn of the twentieth century, one may wonder why it took two more decades to undertake the national census in Japan. In fact, with the passing of Kokusei chōsa ni kansuru hōritsu (National Census Bill) in 1902 in the Imperial Diet, the Meiji government originally planned to conduct the first census in 1905. Naitō Morizō, a lower house member who led the committee on the Census Bill, strongly advocated for undertaking a census survey in Japan to build a foundation for administering general affairs of the state by ensuring the collection of demographic data.[20] Naitō's emphasis on the importance of census in the state's governing strategy echoes what Foucault calls the "science of the state," or *statistics* in modern government.[21] Foucault identifies statistics as a modern technology of government that made it "possible to quantify specific phenomena of population."[22] In the same vein, the Census Bill aimed to keep track of and manage general phenomena of the population at a national level modeling on Western countries including the United States, Britain, France, and Germany.[23] This modernization effort was eventually disrupted due to the Russo-Japanese War (1904–1905) and the resultant shortage of budget.

Interestingly, the first national census in the Japanese empire was conducted in Taiwan instead of Japan proper. In 1905, the Japanese colonial government in Taiwan conducted a census to take control of the colonized population and their land.[24] This illuminates that colonies were integral in experimenting with different visions and practices of modernity in the Japanese colonial empire. Ann Laura Stoler points out in her observation of biopower in Dutch colonial contexts that "the hallmarks of European cultural production have been sighted in earlier ventures of empire and sometimes in the colonies first."[25] There is a clear parallel between European empires and the Japanese empire: similar to the Dutch empire, colonies were instrumental for the Japanese empire's development of a modern technology to trace the biological and socioeconomic traits of population. This modern technology was eventually brought back to Japan proper in 1920 when a national census (*kokusei chōsa*) was executed. The first national census presented comprehensive demographic data in the metropole and its colonies—that is, Taiwan, Korea, Karafuto Prefecture or the present-day South Sakhalin, and Kwantung Leased Territory—that translated population into a quantifiable resource and reified a demographic phenomenon into a set of problems including population density, sex ratio, ethnicity, and productivity.[26]

The birth of the census system marked a watershed in the genealogy of population discourse. Its importance does not lie in the fact that the census identified problems in Japan's demographic phenomenon with scientific data; more essentially, the census problematized a population by putting certain demographic phenomena into question and reorganizing them into measurable factors. The population growth rate and the density in the census data reified the Malthusian theory of population into the pressing issue of overpopulation allegedly facing Japan. For example, Baron Ishimoto, a pioneering birth control activist, raised a concern about a fast-growing population in Japan proper based on the census data of 1920. He argued that

> although the Japanese staple food is rice, the current rice production is not enough to meet the population's demand. . . . According to the census reported last year, the Japanese population increases every year by six to seven hundred thousand. The gist of the problem is how to deal with our suffering from overpopulation as the population continues to overflow.[27]

As the quote suggests, Baron Ishimoto drew on a set of quantitative data such as birth rates and population density to substantiate the neo-Malthusian view of overpopulation; however, the essential role of the census data was to represent the population as being quantifiable, hence visible, rather than to verify the truth of the population problem.

While the introduction of the census system facilitated the neo-Malthusian analysis of the quantity of the population, eugenics added a qualitative layer into the schema of the population problem. The term "eugenics" was originally coined by English mathematician and geneticist Francis Galton (1822–1911) who defined it as "the science of improving stock" by taking cognizance of "all influences that tend in however remote a degree to give to the more suitable races or strains of blood a better chance of prevailing speedily over the less suitable than they otherwise would have had."[28]

Galton's idea of eugenics was first introduced by Unno Yukinori (1879–1954) who published *Nihon jinshu kaizōron* (On reforming the Japanese race) in 1910 to stress the urgent need to improve the Japanese race from an evolutionary perspective and to discuss both positive and negative eugenics—the former foregrounds measures to encourage reproduction among those with desirable traits while the latter seeks ways to decrease undesirable traits through reproductive control—as feasible measures to race betterment in Japan.[29] Since the late 1910s, eugenics had taken root in scientific and media discussions on Japan's status amid intensifying international conflicts as exemplified by World War I. Against the backdrop of geopolitical tensions, leading scientists such as zoologist Oka Asajirō, plant cytologist Yamanouchi Shigeo, and physiologist Nagai Hisomu investigated both genetic and social factors that allegedly contributed to the quality of the Japanese race and popularized eugenic theories. Especially, in 1917 Yamanouchi founded Dai nihon yūsei kai (Greater Japan Eugenics Society) in collaboration with early eugenics supporters, including educator Ichikawa Genzō and agricultural geneticist Abe Ayao, which gave rise to the eugenics movement in the interwar period.[30] In the 1920s, specialized magazines including *Yūseigaku* (Eugenics), published between 1924–1943, and *Yūsei undō* (The eugenics movement), published between 1926–1930, played an integral role in spreading eugenic ideas among the Japanese public. In 1930, Nagai Hisomu founded Nihon minzoku eisei gakkai (Japanese Academy of Race Hygiene), renamed Nihon minzoku eisei kyōkai in 1935, to promote German-inspired eugenic theories, which eventually became instrumental in the wartime implementation of the National Eugenic Law.[31]

The incorporation of quantitative frameworks into population discourse is indicative of the growing influence of eugenics in interwar Japan. In addition to scientists who took the initiative in popularizing eugenics, bureaucrats and social scientists also paid attention to eugenic theories from different perspectives. For example, bureaucrats in the Department of Home Affairs such as Ujihara Sukezō and Saitō Itsuki envisioned eugenics as a radical, biological approach to public health. In 1914, Ujihara Sukezō published "Minzoku eisei gaku" (The study of racial hygiene), where he stressed the need to apply effective eugenics measures to the Japanese race to compete against the threatening "white race."[32] For Ujihara, eugenics measures ought to incorporate both positive and negative eugenics practices to encourage people with desirable traits to procreate and nurture their children in an ideal environment on one hand and to prevent those with undesirable traits from procreating by banning marriage on the other. In his view, bodies with undesirable traits referred to those who have mental diseases, hereditary diseases, and criminal traits.[33]

Whereas Ujihara focused on addressing the problem of race by appropriating American and German eugenics measures, bureaucrat Saitō Itsuki reframed eugenics as a biological solution to the issues of Westernized modernity. Immediately after the end of World War I, Saitō published an article "Yūshu-ron" (The study of eugenics) serialized in *Shakai to kyūsai* (Society and relief) to revisit the dominant ideologies of Western-modeled modernity, including materialism, laissez-faire individualism, and social Darwinism, which would threaten civilization in his observation.[34] While denouncing destructive modern values, Saitō supported eugenics to improve individual quality of life and ultimately achieve human progress. In Saitō's view, the ideal condition for rebuilding civilization was to build an "organism in complete harmony" (*yūkiteki kon'itsutai*)[35] comprised of individuals, nations, and humankind. Despite its semblance to holism, Saitō's vision of eugenics required the exclusion of those with undesirable qualities to fulfil humanity's ideal goal. The irony of eugenics—specifically, biological exclusion as a precondition to imagine an inclusive community—is exemplified in his articulation on the population problem. Saitō contended that

> the focus of the population problem, now, turns to the quality of the population. Whereas those who are considered desirable to reproduce are a superior type, those whom their neighbors do not welcome are subjected to annihilation for the benefits of social progress and nation-building.[36]

Despite differing views on the Westernization of Japanese society, Saitō's emphasis on the quality of the population echoes Ujihara's claim for race betterment. For both bureaucrats, eugenics was not only a biological measure to ensure the quality of the Japanese population but also a biopolitical tool to legitimize inclusion and exclusion.

The quality (*shitsu*) of population was by no means bureaucratic jargon but widely used by intellectuals and activists who formed the backbone of the population discourse. Regardless of the different views on the root cause of the population problem, academic and activist circles expressed interest in the quality of the Japanese population on eugenic grounds. For example, Takano Iwasaburō (1871–1949), a social statistician of the Tokyo Imperial University and a founding member of Ōhara shakai mondai kenkyūsho (Ōhara Institute for Social Research), echoed the need for eugenic policies. While his advocacy for further population growth was at odds with contemporary neo-Malthusianism, Takano reformulated the population question into a dual question of quantity and quality and highlighted a virtuous circle between economic progress and population growth. In his lecture at Shakai seisaku gakkai (the Social Policy Conference), Takano articulates the dual meaning of population growth which, he believed, needed to be incorporated into the realm of social policies.

> It should be noted that population growth refers to quality improvement and an increase in quantity. We must find ways to improve the population's health, knowledge, and morality. The right path to do so is the fair distribution of wealth and the improvement of living standards. In much the same way, the economic progress conditions population increase. Population growth is both quality-wise and quantity-wise conditioned by economic progress.[37]

Takano's attention to the qualitative improvement of the population indicates the incorporation of the language of eugenics into the population discourse. Echoing Saitō's emphasis on the population's quality, Takano criticized the heretofore "lack of attention to the qualitative dimension of the population" while demanding aggressive social policies for the "improvement of livelihood and nutrition, and moral advancement."[38] The ways in which population was rendered into a quantity question complicated the definition of human quality rather than clarifying it. Given this, eugenics was a prescriptive technology that translated human differences into the problem of quality to prevent undesirable traits. Whether desirable traits ought to be defined by socioeconomic status or biological characteristics was less of a concern than the idealized goal of eugenics. Its supreme goal was, as Galton puts it, "to bring as many influences as can be reasonably employed, to cause the useful classes in the community to contribute *more* than their proportion to the next generation" (italics in Galton).[39]

The two pillars of the population discourse—census and eugenics—contributed to forming the population problem in post–World War I Japan. Academics and bureaucrats problematized the quantity and quality of the Japanese population to identify negative social phenomena and determine the fundamental cause of social ills. In this process, those who actively participated in discussing the population problem, whether it be liberal neo-Malthusianists or pro–birth control leftists, discovered a utopian remedy by their own definition. For both sides, it was legitimate for different political apparatuses to govern the size and health of the population to fulfill their respective utopian desire—namely, national development for neo-Malthusianists and the proletarian revolution for leftists.

The logic behind their *oversimplified* solutions for overdetermined modern problems indicates the historical embeddedness of utopia. Frederic Jameson stresses the creation of utopian space as an effect and a continuation of existing social relations contrary to the conventional understanding of utopia as a radical rupture with reality. Jameson illuminates the historical precondition for utopia to be formulated by arguing that "the view that opens out onto history from a particular social situation must encourage such oversimplifications; the miseries and injustices thus visible must seem to shape and organize themselves around one specific ill or wrong."[40] This account suggests that utopias cannot be separated from reality. In other words, utopias are the product of the recognition of social reality from which a group of people desires to break away using an overly simplistic remedy. In view of this, a growing interest in birth control among social reformers, labor activists, and intellectuals in interwar Japan points to multiple utopian enclaves being formulated against the backdrop of socioeconomic crises. Although different remedies were desired, both neo-Malthusianists and leftists were utopian dreamers evolved out of modernity.

Birth Control for a Nation: A Neo-Malthusian Panacea for Overpopulation

In March and April 1922, Margaret Sanger (1879–1966), American birth control activist and the founder of the American Birth Control League (ABCL), visited Japan to promote the idea of birth control. Sanger's visit was arranged by Kaizō-sha, a major publishing house based in Tokyo. In an effort to introduce contemporary Western ideas to the Japanese audience, Kaizō-sha launched a lecture series featuring prominent figures of the time, including British philosopher Bertrand Russell (1872–1970), German-born physicist Albert Einstein (1879–1955), and Irish writer and social reformer George Bernard Shaw (1856–1950).[41] Of the guest speakers invited by Kaizō-sha, Sanger was the most controversial, given the debate about birth control in Japanese society. The Japanese government banned her from holding any public lectures on contraceptives.[42] While bypassing the controversial subject, Sanger turned to the less scandalous yet fundamental idea underlying birth control: neo-Malthusianism. In her first lecture, held at the Tokyo Young Men's Christian Association (YMCA) on March 14, Sanger addressed an audience of over 500 people on the subject of war and population.[43] Sanger attributed colonization and militarism to an overflowing population, as debatably illustrated by the situation of Germany before the outbreak of World War I, and she urged Japanese audiences to address similar issues facing Japan. Sanger's accounts of overpopulation were anchored in the neo-Malthusian argument that birth control is integral to ensuring the balance between population size and resource supply. She concluded that Japan's rising population would lead to domestic problems as well as international conflicts.

Sanger's lectures addressing the question of overpopulation had social ramifications. Despite the Japanese government's effort to control the information on birth control, Sanger's presence stirred up public interest in contraceptive methods and intellectual debates over social problems presumably tied to overpopulation. During her visit, sexologist Yamamoto Senji, who served as Sanger's interpreter, likened her visit to the Black Ships of the Taishō era.[44] Yamamoto's analogy indicates Sanger's wide-ranging implications for the Japanese audience in rearticulating the relationship between human reproduction and socioeconomic development. It was particularly social reformers and activists who were drawn to Sanger's neo-Malthusian account of overpopulation due to their shared concerns about a wide range of social issues (*shakai mondai*)—including poverty, unemployment, physical and moral degeneration, poor living standards both in rural and urban areas, and so forth—that they considered the burdens of modernity.

Against this backdrop, the first birth control movement group in Japan, Nihon sanji chōsetsu kenkyūkai (Japanese Society for the Study of Birth Control), hereinafter Chōsetsukai, was founded in Tokyo in May 1922. Chōsetsukai appeared at the intersection between the domestic discourse of the population problem in the aftermath of World War I and the growing birth control movements worldwide. Its founding members included baroness and feminist Ishimoto Shizue, Baron Ishimoto Keikichi, socialist feminist Yamakawa Kikue, physician Kaji Tokijirō, Christian socialist and Waseda University professor Abe Isoo, and labor activist Suzuki Bunji. Despite different political views among its founding members, Chōsetsukai formally adopted a neo-Malthusian rationale for advocating birth control.[45] In an effort to raise awareness of birth control among the Japanese public, the members of Chōsetsukai published the magazine *Shōkazoku* (Small family) and a series of booklets.[46] The following prospectus of Chōsetsukai suggests that various social problems be attributed to the rapid population growth in Japan proper.

> The fact that the population in Japan has increased by approximately 700,000 every year both causes fierce competition for survival domestically and complicates foreign relations. Moreover, even at an individual level, the excess of births results in the world's highest mortality rate and various women's illnesses. Ultimately, high birth rates pose significant mental and financial burdens and prevent the betterment of children and women. . . . It is also necessary to prevent men and women with hereditary defects from having children.[47]

As seen in the prospectus, Chōsetsukai argued that the population growth negatively affected the standard of living, the health of mothers and children, and Japan's international relations. Their argument implies that the quantity and quality of the population are not mutually exclusive, but the former (that is, population size) is determinant of the population's quality. By combining the neo-Malthusian logic of overpopulation with eugenics discourse, Chōsetsukai essentially ascribed overpopulation to uncontrolled fertile bodies. Insofar as the population problem was inseparably linked with individual sexual reproduction, it was logical to advocate population control as *the* ultimate solution. Chōsetsukai promoted contraceptive use as a panacea for the social ills that they claimed to be caused by overpopulation while they opposed traditional solutions—such as late marriages, infanticide, and abortion—on the grounds that those had caused "inhumane outcomes."[48]

In this regard, the founding members of Chōsetsukai articulated a meaning of birth control that went far beyond simply a means of reproductive control. For the members, birth control was essentially the technique of government whereby individuals were held accountable for the well-being of the population and, at the same time, subjected to disciplinary institutions for the sake of the betterment of the population. The neo-Malthusian theory of the population problem thus was based on this discursive link between individual reproductive bodies and the population as a totality. This link was repeatedly emphasized in Chōsetsukai's discussions on birth control to justify individuals' self-discipline as well as the public intervention in reproductive control.

Most representatively, Abe Isoo (1865–1949), one of the founding members of Chōsetsukai and a committed birth control activist, emphasized the new morality of parents, arguing that "leaving procreation to nature is a big sin. Parents have a huge responsibility for controlling reproduction artificially and having a child only when they want one."[49] While Abe's argument dovetails into the neo-Malthusian view of individuals' reproductive responsibility, he framed the desirable roles of parents in practicing selective reproduction in moral terms. In his schema, scientific knowledge and morality worked to redefine each other. Birth control and eugenics were incorporated into the realm of moral responsibility as the moral principles in the age of eugenics shifted away from natural reproduction towards the selective production of desirable descendants. In the same vein, Abe stressed the need for teaching hygienic sexual desire (*seiyoku eisei*) to help biological males moderate their sexual desires and prevent syphilis among the youth.[50] Notably, hygiene refers to the reproductive health of parents or potential parents who were supposedly responsible for producing and fostering healthy children.

The discursive framing of scientific reproduction as parental morality indicates the disciplinary mechanism of modern knowledge, which Foucault calls "technologies of the self." Dissecting the axes of power, knowledge, and subjectivity, Foucault highlights "technologies of the self," which

> permit individuals to effect by their own means or with the help of others a certain number of operations on their own bodies and souls, thoughts, conduct, and ways of being, so as to transform themselves and attain a certain state of happiness, purity, wisdom, perfection, or immortality.[51]

Abe's moralization of birth control exemplifies a disciplinary technology necessary to construct modern parents who problematize their bodies, identify themselves with the wider population, and control sexuality and reproduction with responsibility.

Abe's emphasis on disciplinary technologies is also reflected in his view of class issues. Concurring with his fellow neo-Malthusianists, Abe attributed poverty to population growth exceeding resource production. However, Abe's view of population issues was distinctive in the sense that he rearticulated the population problem by situating population at the heart of labor issues such as unemployment, low wages, and exploitative labor conditions. Drawing the law of supply and demand in economics, Abe argued that labor as a commodity (*urimono*) was governed by the principle of supply and demand, and thereby, the value of the labor power inevitably decreased as the number of workers increased.[52] Although Abe was sympathetic to the working class under capitalism, his account of the capitalist system conformed to a dogmatic framework that rendered the commodification of human relations into an objective law of capitalism. In this fictional narrative of a laissez-faire economy, capitalist social relations that quantified and determined the value of labor power remained unquestioned. As illustrated in Abe's argument that "the system of the reserve army naturally arises out of overpopulation,"[53] what was questioned instead was the excessive reproduction of the working class. If the root cause of the surplus labor lay in the working-class sexuality and low wages were necessary by-products of a surplus labor supply, birth control would solve the social and economic difficulties of the working class. It is noted that Abe's advocacy for birth control to address poverty and exploitation facing the working class was not intended to stand *against* the capitalist system. On the contrary, he promoted birth control as a self-help technique to cope with life *under* capitalism. Considering this, Abe reconfigured class stratification and inequality as the issue of the working-class body and sexuality. His birth control solution essentially legitimized the unevenness between workers and capitalists while transforming workers' bodies into a site of discipline.[54]

In addition to disciplinary technologies, the neo-Malthusian advocates of Chōsetsukai emphasized the need for state intervention to address the population problem. The group argued that poverty relief efforts were inadequate because the fundamental cause of overpopulation and its concomitant social problems was unchecked human reproduction.[55] Chōsetsukai, instead, emphasized the importance of the state to address the population-based issues more thoroughly and systematically. For example, the group published a booklet titled "Birth Control from a Biological Perspective" authored by entomologist Matsumura Shōnen who argued that the non-selective approach of charity work only aggravated counter-selection tendencies and increased the burden placed on the state and society. In his view, it was *inhumane* to aid degenerates with inferior genetic traits or criminal tendencies, while birth control was a eugenically desirable and thus *humane* way of reducing unwanted offspring.[56] To that end, the state's role was indispensable for promoting birth control among the Japanese public. Matsumura argued that

> birth control cannot be governed by individuals alone as it is crucial to national security . . . for the benefit of the nation and on eugenic grounds, the government should spare no efforts in looking into ways of prohibiting the reproduction of people who have genetic diseases or disabilities, and those who are morons [*hakuchi*].[57]

Matsumura's call for the state's active role in controlling childbirth on eugenic grounds was echoed by both neo-Malthusianists and contemporary feminists in support of the protection of motherhood. Among neo-Malthusian advocates, Abe demanded the state's role in keeping the "unfit" population in check by promoting birth control. He had a firm faith in the fundamental logic of eugenics, demarcating fit from unfit. In his view, the category of the unfit included the poor; criminals; people with disabilities, low intelligence, and potentially hereditary diseases such as tuberculosis and leprosy—all of whom ought to be discouraged from having children using birth control.[58] Apparently, there is ambiguity in determining the unfit because he lumped physical, mental, and social traits together as genetic diseases and pathologized the so-called unfit bodies. For Abe, this ambiguity was not problematic, which indicates that eugenics was a versatile concept for valorizing biological hierarchies. In other words, eugenics did not prove whether genetic or social factors played a key role in determining the reproductive fitness of individuals but only problematized individual human bodies and prescribed birth control as preventive medicine. Therefore, the unfit was not provable but only preventable. In Abe's view, the state's role was essential in stamping out the conflated genetic and social issues facing the poor.

On top of promoting birth control for the control of the population quality, Abe envisaged that eugenic sterilization would contribute to the relief of the poor, the improvement of public health, and ultimately the strengthening of the nation; to that end, he demanded the enforcement of eugenic sterilization policies.[59] With a particular interest in compulsory sterilization in the United States, Abe translated *Sterilization for Human Betterment* (published in 1929, co-authored by Ezra Seymour Gosney and Paul B. Popenoe) and introduced compulsory sterilization laws to the Japanese public.[60] He believed that eugenic sterilization would address the pressing issues—such as, alcoholism, criminality, tuberculosis, and leprosy—facing the "genetically burdened" working class.[61] As the second Sino-Japanese war broke out in 1937, Abe even retreated from his long-held position on birth control and advocated compulsory sterilization and pronatalist policies. Abe's shifted position cannot be interpreted, though, as an abrupt retraction from his neo-Malthusian creed, but rather an adjustment of his population control tactics to amplify the importance of the population quality.[62] The utopian vision for compulsory sterilization eventually came into existence with the enactment of Kokumin yūsei hō (National Eugenic Law) in 1940, examined in detail in Chapter 4.

In the meantime, maternal feminists whose advocacy for gender equality was centered around women's *re-gendered* maternal instinct also demanded that the state take responsibility for protecting mothers and children.[63] Hiratsuka Raichō (1886–1971), pioneering feminist and founder of the women's literary magazine *Seitō* (Bluestocking), and anarchist feminist Takamure Itsue (1894–1964) upheld a maternalism that glorified motherly love and rendered women's reproductive roles into a public duty toward the Japanese nation. As we discuss in Chapter 2, Hiratsuka had promoted the state protection of mothers since the late 1910s. While her maternal feminism inspired by Swedish feminist Ellen Key is well known, the fact that her advocacy for motherhood protection was couched in the language of the population discourse is little discussed in scholarship on Japanese maternal feminism. Echoing the contemporary neo-Malthusianists, Hiratsuka incorporated eugenics into her feminism and argued that "the new task of motherhood is a matter not simply of bearing and raising children, but of bearing sound children and raising them well."[64] Also, her belief in eugenic principles evolved to the point where she demanded the state force eugenic marriage and sterilization policies.[65] Meanwhile, Takamure's maternalist vision foregrounded women's atavistic motherly love and instinct, according to which she challenged the patriarchal view of families while reinforcing both gender binary and anti-modern nationalism.[66] Maternalist feminism that was blended with nationalism anticipated the wartime co-optation of feminist activists by the state, as fully examined in Chapter 5. Hiratsuka's and Takamure's cooperation with the wartime regime to mobilize the home front hardly symptomized their drastic political conversion but their long-term goal of empowering women by virtue of women's reproductive capacity.[67]

The role of neo-Malthusian advocates, as well as maternal feminists, in popularizing eugenics for their own political agendas allows us to revisit the historical association of eugenics with authoritarian fascist regimes.[68] As seen above, neo-Malthusian advocates took the initiative to raise public awareness of overpopulation and required the state to take responsibility for the control of both the quantity and quality of the population. Compared to these birth control advocates who were active since the early 1920s, the Japanese government was a latecomer to the discourse of the population problem. It was not until the late 1920s that the government paid attention to the population problem and its resultant social issues and put institutional efforts to initiate research into demographic challenges and possible solutions. This time gap suggests that governmentality, a modern form of power that aims to optimize its target population, is not necessarily initiated by the state institution but is envisioned and validated by various social forces whose desires to increase their control over human reproduction converged into the governmentalization of the state.[69] However, the utopian desire shared among the neo-Malthusian advocates to rationalize the quantity and quality of the Japanese population was harshly attacked by contemporary leftists who built their own utopian enclave to break away from the wretched realities under capitalism. In what follows, I will turn to the leftist birth control movement to delve into another utopian remedy imagined in response to the crisis of modernity.

Birth Control for the Proletarian Revolution

When a group of birth control advocates organized Chōsetsukai in Tokyo, Yamamoto Senji (1889–1929), budding biologist and sexologist based in Kyoto, published a booklet titled "Sanga joshi Kazoku seigen hō hihan" (The critique of Ms. Sanger's "Family Limitation," hereinafter referred to as "Kazoku seigen hō hihan") in May 1922. The booklet was a Japanese translation of "Family Limitation" authored by Margaret Sanger in 1914. Despite his intention to advocate rather than criticize Sanger's birth control movement, Yamamoto deliberately included the term "critique" in the title to avoid censorship. The arbitrary nature of Japanese censorship laws during the Taishō period (1912–1926) simultaneously restricted the freedom of the press and left the door open for circumventing the censorship measures under the pretext of academic purpose.[70] Yamamoto understood the arbitrariness of the censorship laws. Although the publication and distribution of sex-related materials were deemed a violation of manners and morals (*fūzoku*) under the Publication Law of 1893, the Home Ministry administration showed exceptional leniency toward academic work. Using this loophole, Yamamoto published the first edition of "Kazoku seigen hō hihan" and distributed 2,000 copies to medical professionals and academics.

Yamamoto's booklet marked a watershed event for his manifold ventures as a scientist-cum-political activist over the next decade. Influenced by Charles Darwin's evolution theory and the liberal Unitarian Church, which inspired him to reconcile his religious beliefs with his pursuit of scientific truth, Yamamoto studied zoology at Tokyo Imperial University between 1917 and 1920. After graduation, he began his academic career as a lecturer in biology and sexology at both Kyoto Imperial University and Dōshisha University in 1920. In his lectures, Yamamoto emphasized sex as a central element of human biology while refuting the conventional approach of pathologizing sex, what he called "sexual obscurantism" (*seiteki inpeishugi*).⁷¹ In protest of the prevailing obscurantism that had hindered the Japanese public from obtaining scientific knowledge on sexual activities, Yamamoto advocated sex education for the public. The goals of sex education, he proclaimed, were to provide individuals with sufficient scientific knowledge to prevent unpredictable risks, to help them cultivate self-awareness, self-respect, and self-discipline by demonstrating how to overcome blind instinct with reasoned self-control, and ultimately, to inspire them to enjoy daily lives to the fullest and foster an ability to contribute to the fellow country people (*dōhō*).⁷² In his view, sex education had a broader social value than how it was conventionally understood. Yamamoto emphasized that sex education could play an instrumental role in practicing both euthenics (*gense kaizengaku*)⁷³ and eugenics by advancing both living environments and human qualities.

Yamamoto's efforts to enlighten the public about sexual and reproductive biology culminated in his participation in birth control activism. When Sanger visited Japan upon the invitation of Kaizō-sha, Yamamoto interviewed Sanger in person and translated the lecture she gave at the Kyoto Municipal Medical Association.⁷⁴ His firsthand conversations with Sanger inspired Yamamoto to translate Sanger's "Family Limitation" to raise public awareness of the pressing need for birth control and to spread scientific knowledge about contraception. "Kazoku seigen hō hihan" is largely divided into two parts. The first is Yamamoto's translation of the original text of "Family Limitation" where Sanger presented technical information about available contraceptives, including coitus interruptus, douches, condoms, pessaries, sponges, and vaginal suppositories. The second part contains Yamamoto's comments on the legitimacy of contraception on eugenic grounds. Underlining natural selection as the essential mechanism of human evolution, Yamamoto argued that human beings had always used birth control to prevent those with inferior traits from reproducing, although specific birth control methods had varied over time.⁷⁵ Then, he contextualized the importance of birth control in Japanese society while couching his advocacy of birth control mainly in the language of eugenics:

> The so-called educated class chant "give birth, multiply, and fill the earth!" but they fail to understand the social reality of how the unfit produces more offspring than the fit does just as Gresham's Law says bad money drives good money out of circulation. The educated class are

merely obsessed with the obsolete laissez-faire ideology—namely, "after me, the deluge." It is extremely suspicious that they have no consideration of eugenics facilities aiming to encourage the superior to produce offspring and sterilize the inferior and the imbecile, nor they bother to look into birth control with a sense of social solidarity.[76]

As this quote indicates, Yamamoto expected both sexual enlightenment and birth control to fulfill the purpose of eugenics by enabling scientific interventions in natural selection, or as he put it, "selecting good sperm."[77] From a eugenics perspective, birth control would serve as a means to improve hereditary factors and environmental conditions. Given this, Yamamoto's reasoning for birth control contrasts with contemporary neo-Malthusian reformers whose primary goal for the birth control campaign was to address overpopulation. While Yamamoto refuted the neo-Malthusian account of birth control as a way of curbing population growth, he instead stressed its potential contribution to the eugenics ideals. Moreover, unlike neo-Malthusianists who blamed the public's unrestrained fertility for the population problem, Yamamoto criticized the inaccessibility of scientific knowledge for the general public due to the knowledge monopoly held by the educated class. By bringing the issue of class disparities in knowledge distribution to the fore, Yamamoto reoriented the discussion of birth control toward the sexual enlightenment of the underprivileged.

His rearticulation of birth control in light of eugenics and class struggle soon gained traction among labor activists. In Osaka, Mitamura Shirō (1896–1964), Bolshevist and one of the leading members of Nihon rōdō kumiai sōdōmei (Japan Federation of Labor), abbreviated as Sōdōmei, acquired Yamamoto's "Kazoku seigen hō hihan" through a printworker who printed the booklet at his workshop.[78] Inspired by the booklet, Mitamura suggested to Yamamoto that they collaborate to promote birth control among the working class. The collaboration between Mitamura (labor union leader) and Yamamoto (sexologist and biologist) resulted in the publication of a popular edition of "Kazoku seigen hō hihan" in December 1922.[79] Approximately 2,000 copies of this edition with a confidential stamp were circulated among Kansai-based workers (the western region of mainland Japan). With the extensive circulation of the booklet, both Mitamura and Yamamoto sought to facilitate a consensus about the pressing need for birth control among the working-class people in the region.

In January 1923, this growing consensus bore fruit: the first leftist birth control organization in Japan, Sanji seigen kenkyūkai, hereinafter

Seigenkai, was founded in Osaka. Seigenkai consisted of labor activists as well as medical and scientific experts. In addition to Yamamoto and Mitamura, the members of the Osaka affiliate of Sōdōmei—including Noda Ritsuta, Noda Kimiko (Noda's wife), Ōya Shōzo, Kutsumi Fusako, and physician Yasuda Tokutarō (Yamamoto's cousin)—participated in organizing Seigenkai. Within a month, several branches of Seigenkai were established in Nagoya, Kyoto, Kobe, Okayama, and other cities in the Kansai region.[80]

Seigenkai's primary strategy for promoting birth control among the working class was holding public lectures. Unlike printed materials that could potentially violate censorship laws, a public lecture was a legitimate and relatively efficient way to educate the audience about birth control methods. No sooner was Seigenkai founded than the group held its first public lecture at the YMCA Hall in Kobe and its second one at the Osaka Grand Municipal Hall.[81] These two public lectures (which attracted audiences of 400 and 1,000, respectively) drew considerable media attention. The *Osaka Asahi Shinbun* carried a series of articles that cast a positive light on the labor union's involvement in the birth control movement and its well-attended lectures.[82] Meanwhile, another major newspaper in the region, *Osaka Mainichi Shinbun*, responded to Seigenkai's campaigns with a critical editorial on contraception.[83] These two contrasting responses reflected a broader debate among contemporary intellectuals over how to tackle the domestic population problem. Whereas the articles in the *Asahi Shinbun* represented a leftist stance that favored birth control to alleviate the sufferings of lower-class families, the *Mainichi Shinbun* spoke for a pronatalist group that appealed to parental morality for the sake of strengthening the nation. The controversy in the media, though, had a promotional effect in favor of Seigenkai's birth control movement.[84] Regardless of whether news reports were favorable to birth control or not, they ended up serving as an efficient outlet to propagate the leftist birth control ideas.

The collaboration between labor activists and scientists led to the rearticulation of birth control as a critique of class disparities in the capitalist mode of production. In May 1923, Noda Kimiko, one of the founders of Seigenkai, published *Sanji seigen kenkyū* (The study of birth control) (Figure 1.1).[85] The tract gives a glimpse into how Seigenkai incorporated birth control into the proletarian movement based on the Marxist critique of capitalism. First and foremost, Seigenkai distinguished its approach to birth control from neo-Malthusianism. Seigenkai denounced the theoretical basis of neo-Malthusianism—namely, Malthus's principle of population—for its failure to grasp the underlying cause of poverty. Contrary to the accounts that attributed the root cause of poverty to excess population, Noda claimed that poverty stemmed from the capitalist system, noting that "the capitalist system based on the private ownership of the means of production conditions unfair ways of production and distribution."[86] According to this view, insofar as the bourgeois class—including the landed gentry—continued to monopolize the means of production and produce profitable commodities by exploiting the proletarian labor force, simply putting a brake on population growth would not eradicate poverty.

From the perspective of Seigenkai members, the neo-Malthusian advocates unequivocally connived with the capitalists by presenting overpopulation as a *fait accompli*. While the neo-Malthusian logic replaced the

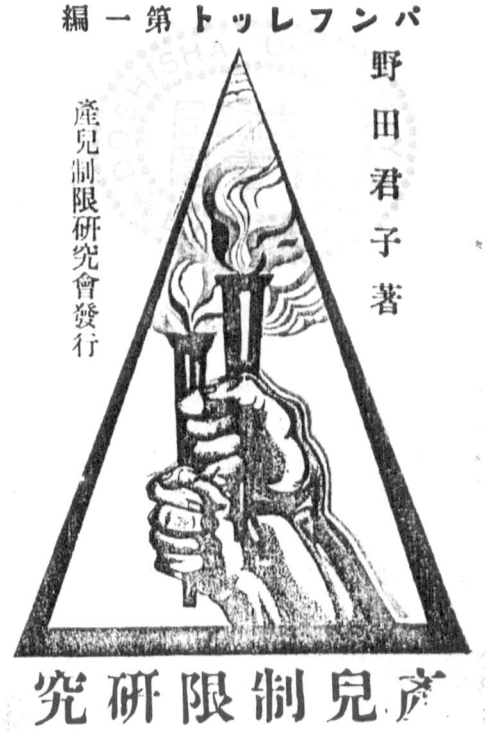

Figure 1.1 The cover of *Sanji seigen kenkyū* [The study of birth control].
Source: Noda, *Sanji seigen kenkyū* (1923).

socioeconomic cause of poverty with the sheer number of the population, capitalists would continue to generate the exploitable labor force, or what Marx calls "industrial reserve army."[87] In *Capital*, Marx underlines that the relative surplus population forms a disposable industrial army under the capitalist mode of production. This suggests that whereas surplus laboring population is independent of the absolute surplus population, the population is subordinate to capital, which continuously sets free exploitable population as it expands. Furthermore, the "industrial reserve army" is a volatile category because the despotic work of capitalism constantly shifts the boundaries of employment, half-employment, and unemployment for the sake of the self-expansion of capital. In view of this, Seigenkai anticipated that the inherently exploitative system under capitalism would perpetuate the poverty of the proletarian class.

Notwithstanding, the members of Seigenkai encouraged the proletarian class to practice birth control, or, as they phrased it, "scientific artificial birth control" (*kagakuteki jinkō sanji seigen*).[88] Thus, birth control became a defensive solution for various problems, such as poverty, illness, and the high infant mortality rate of the proletarian class. In *The Study of Birth Control*, Noda argues that:

> It is most necessary and appropriate to curb excessive reproduction to help bring the proletarians [*musansha*] out of poverty or at least relieve it because poverty is an urgent and imminent problem for them. Even though poverty is a result of capitalism, there is no need to put up with its faulty system. . . . Under no circumstances is it acceptable to encourage workers [*rōdōsha*] to produce more wage slaves when they barely manage to survive on a paltry income.[89]

In contrast to the neo-Malthusianists who legitimized birth control as the ultimate solution to poverty, Seigenkai members viewed birth control as a necessary, if incomplete, defense against capitalism. Insofar as the capitalist system prevailed, birth control could function as an individual defense against poverty. Moreover, birth control could help defend the proletarian class in general by preventing those burdened with many children from dropping out of the class war.[90] Seigenkai's attention to the imminent livelihood issues faced by the proletariat served to counter the concerns of ideologically driven leftists who argued that contraception would weaken proletarian class consciousness. The orthodox Marxists objected to the use of contraception among the proletarian class on the grounds that birth control would primarily serve bourgeois interests.[91] While rebutting the ideological presumption that associate contraception with the bourgeoisie, Seigenkai reformulated a class identity of birth control. In other words, birth control acquired a new meaning as the means of self-defense for the proletariat.

In February 1925, Seigenkai published the first issue of the *Birth Control Review* (*Sanji chōsetsu hyōron*, hereinafter *Hyōron*), a monthly magazine for birth control research and propaganda.[92] Since its founding, Seigenkai had organized public lectures to encourage working-class people to use contraception. The membership of the group expanded to include Japan's internal and external colonies, including Hokkaido, Manchuria, Korea, and Taiwan, and by the beginning of 1925, Seigenkai had recruited more than 5,000 members throughout the Japanese colonial empire.[93] *Hyōron* aimed to provide the members with comprehensive information ranging from scholarly discussions on the legitimacy of birth control to practical knowledge on contraceptive methods. As the magazine's title suggests, *Hyōron* was largely influenced by the *Birth Control Review* Sanger had published since 1917. Yamamoto, a committed subscriber of the *Birth Control Review*, attempted to emulate its extensive coverage of topical and scholarly issues surrounding birth control while adding original content that is geared toward the Japanese proletarian class.

In their efforts to legitimize birth control, the contributors of *Hyōron* foregrounded the rearticulation of science as a new tactic of the class struggle. Notably, leftist birth control advocates deemed eugenics to be the guiding principle of birth control to ensure the scientific reproduction of the proletarian class. What underlies the coupling of socialism and eugenics was the idea of human progress, which likewise facilitated the embracing of eugenics by neo-Malthusianists despite occupying different positions in the political spectrum. As to the malleable nature of eugenics deployed in political discourse and practices in modern times, Diane Paul argues that eugenics has always been a "protean concept" as it has conjoined with a myriad of politico-economic interests ranging from reactionary nationalism to revolutionary socialism.[94] Japanese leftists' birth control advocates on eugenic grounds were situated precisely within the growing wave of the transnational eugenics movement. While sharing the vision of positive eugenics that aimed to encourage the breeding of those with good hereditary qualities, Japanese leftists underlined that birth control would serve the supreme purpose of eugenics: as socialist politician Koike Shirō puts it, the "renovation of the human race" (*jinrui kaizō*).[95]

Hyōron provided a platform for intellectual discussions on the eugenic value of birth control. Particularly, Yamamoto actively introduced Western birth control advocates who foregrounded eugenic purposes. A British birth control activist and the founder of the Society for Constructive Birth Control and Racial Progress (CBC), Marie Stopes was an emblematic figure who broke away from neo-Malthusianism in support of the eugenic value of contraception. As its name implies, the CBC upheld birth control for wise parenthood to protect the child's and mother's health, and ultimately, for racial progress while denouncing the neo-Malthusian claim that contraception mainly aimed at controlling the population size.[96] Echoing Stopes's view of constructive birth control, Yamamoto questioned the actual effectiveness of birth control in controlling the population quantity while reorienting the discussion on the values of birth control toward improving living standards and public health and, essentially, the betterment of population qualities.[97]

A British eugenicist and sexologist, Havelock Ellis, was another influential source for *Hyōron*'s reframing of birth control based on positive eugenics. In support of birth control, Ellis argued that contraception became one of the most excellent channels "through which the impulse toward the control of procreation for the elevation of the race [entered] into practical life."[98] Ellis's advocacy for birth control was couched in the languages of nationalism and humanitarianism. From his eugenics-informed perspective, both nationalism and humanitarianism necessitated the predictability and manipulability of reproduction for the enrichment of the quality of life. This biological representation of human progress—or conversely, the nationalist-cum-humanitarian representation of eugenics—was echoed by leftist birth control advocates in Japan. Through *Hyōron*, Japanese advocates explicitly articulated how essential birth control was for improving the human race and how indispensable artificial selection was in creating ideal biological, medical, and sanitary conditions needed to improve maternal and child health.[99]

Hyōron was eventually discontinued in May 1926 due to financial difficulties, internal conflicts in the proletarian movement, and growing government oppression. In the mid-1920s, the proletariat movement underwent repeated instances of consolidation and dissolution because of internal factionalism and the government's suppression of radicalism. A major split in the proletariat movement occurred in 1925 between its socialist and communist subgroups when Sōdōmei expelled the communists, and a breakaway communist faction founded Nihon rōdō kumiai hyōgikai (Japan Labor Unions Council). The following year, there was the second split between right-wing socialism and centrist socialism when the latter group separately formed Nihon rōdō kumiai dōmei (Japan Labor

Union League). Each labor federation developed into different proletarian parties with different ideological lines.[100] The majority of the leading members of Seigenkai, including Yamamoto, was involved with the labor union movement and then later the political party activities ahead of Japan's first universal male suffrage election in 1928.[101] As a result, the group gradually disbanded, and accordingly, the magazine *Hyōron*— retitled *Sei to shakai* (Sex and society) in October 1925—was terminated.

After the disbandment of Seigenkai, Yamamoto, once a devoted biologist and sexologist, became more deeply involved in the labor movement and political activities. He joined the Labor-Farmer Party shortly after the decision to discontinue the publication of *Sei to shakei* in 1926 and then was elected as a member of the House of Representatives in the first universal male suffrage election of 1928.[102] However, his promising career as a left-wing politician ended with his sudden death. Yamamoto was stabbed to death by a right-wing activist on the same day he made a speech against the retrogressive revision of the Peace Preservation Law in March 1929.[103] The purpose of the revision was to ratify the emergency ordinance stipulating the introduction of the death penalty and widen the definition of political dissidents, which would further tighten the police control over political radicals.[104] Although Japan completed the façade of democracy with the execution of the first universal male suffrage election in 1928, the government at the same time strengthened its crackdown on socialists, communists, and other radical groups. The heightened policing of radical movements culminated in the March 15 Incident of 1928: that is, the mass arrest of the Communist Party members and sympathizers.[105] The murder of Yamamoto by a right-wing activist gives a snapshot of the volatile nature of democracy in interwar Japan. Behind the so-called Taishō Democracy, leftist activists who were deemed serious threats to national polity (*kokutai*) by the government authorities were gradually losing their footing.

Although the leftist movements had faced many political challenges since the late 1920s, leftist advocates' efforts to promote birth control entered a new phase in the early 1930s. Whereas Seigenkai's movement centered on the theoretical justification of birth control, the new leftist birth control organization Musansha sanji seigen dōmei (Proletariat Birth Control League, hereinafter Pro-BC) strove to develop concrete praxis to serve the interests of the working class and renew a strategy of the class struggle by incorporating scientific reproduction. In June 1931, several proletarian organizations—including the Labor Union, the Farmers' Union, the Consumers Union, and a group of physicians and midwives in support of the working class—joined forces to establish Pro-BC in Tokyo. In protest against the increasing commercialization of birth control since the late 1920s, Pro-BC issued the following manifesto: "We adamantly reject the existing reactionary, profit-seeking, and deceptive business of birth control. We advocate birth control to support a liberation front [*kaihō sensen*]. We hope for sexual reform based on scientific birth control."[106] In October, Pro-BC joined Nihon puroretaria bunka renmei (Japan Proletarian Cultural League), or KOP, a newly founded proletarian alliance for cultural and scientific movements. Pro-BC's participation in a broader class-based movement indicates that birth control was a scientific medium through which the birth control activists concretized the proletarian revolution, far beyond merely addressing poverty.

Pro-BC developed three main strategies to encourage the working-class people (primarily, urban manufacturing workers and the poor) to use birth control methods: the propagation of contraceptive methods, the operation of birth control consultation centers, and the organization of local units called "circles" (*ban*) to channel birth control propaganda into working-class families. The information on contraceptives and their ideological rationales was distributed through the alliance's newsletter *Pro-BC News* and birth control exhibitions (Figure 1.2). Birth control consultation centers, another critical campaign strategy of Pro-BC, offered counseling and medical support to those seeking help with reproductive issues. In the meantime, the alliance organized *ban* modeled on the proletariat cultural movement of the Soviet Union, or *Proletkult,* to shift economic or physical burdens of procreation from individual working-class families into the social realm.[107] Over three years, until its dissolution in 1934, Pro-BC pursued the abovementioned strategies to integrate sexual and reproductive issues into the issue of the proletarian class and, accordingly, to reframe birth control as a concrete means of fulfilling the working-class benefits.

However, like its predecessor Seigenkai, Pro-BC did not last long. Despite its constant efforts to expand the birth control campaign, Pro-BC faced challenges due to the increasing state repression of leftist radicals in the early 1930s. After the Manchurian Incident in September 1931,[108] the Japanese government increased its control and suppression of communists, which peaked in 1933 when a central figure in the proletarian movement, Kobayashi Takiji, was tortured to death by Special Higher Police. Widespread suppression caused a split within the proletarian movement, which ultimately led to the dissolution of the KOP and its affiliated organizations in April 1934.[109] With the dissolution of Pro-BC in 1934, the Japanese proletarian birth control movement was also ended.[110] Activists'

Figure 1.2 The poster of Pro-BC's birth control exhibition. The caption reads, "Join the Birth Control Exhibition!"
Source: *Pro-BC News*, no. 6, in *SSJ*, vol. 14 (1931), 8. Originally published October 1, 1931. Reprinted with permission.

utopian vision for the proletarian revolution, by virtue of having control over fertility, did not materialize as they expected, and their enclave was dissolved, if not completely destroyed, into the government's own blueprint in response to modern crises.

Unfinished Utopian Dreams: In Anticipation of Population Remedies

The history of neo-Malthusianists' and leftists' birth control movements in interwar Japan reveals the complex nature of the population debate of the time. *Jinkō mondai* did not merely refer to excess population and poverty as its resultant problem. It was symptomatic of growing interests in the quantity and quality of the Japanese population among reformers and revolutionaries who sought an all-embracing biological solution to a variety of socioeconomic challenges. Despite their conflicting views on the definition of the population problem, both Japanese neo-Malthusianists and leftist birth control advocates played a crucial role in reconfiguring reproduction as a fundamental solution for the modern crises facing the nation.

Different remedies for population problems suggested by neo-Malthusian reformers and leftists remained unfinished business primarily due to the association of birth control with moral and political radicalism. As examined in detail in Chapter 3, the government as well as its advisory group of scholars not only questioned the validity of the use of contraceptives as a solution to overpopulation but also suppressed the birth control movements by issuing Yūgai hininyō kigu torishimari kisoku (Harmful Contraceptive Devices Control Regulation) in 1930. Notwithstanding this oppressive response to birth control measures, the unfinished utopian dreams that had flourished across the political spectrum since the early 1920s should not be regarded as failures. Although the state oppressed birth control advocates, their essential ideas regarding the rational management of the quantity and the quality of the population were eventually carried into practice during the wartime years. As discussed in later chapters in this book, interwar movements to address the population problem preceded the era of population control initiated under the wartime government that co-opted the ideas of managing population size and improving its health for the war effort.

In the meantime, the Japanese' reformers and leftists' utopian dreams were also shared by leading feminists who agreed to bring fertility to the forefront in response to socioeconomic challenges; and these feminists took it even further by allowing women to take control over their fertility, which they called "voluntary motherhood." In the next chapter, I will examine how the interwar population debates valorized the idea of motherhood (*bosei*) as women's political agency and, ironically, how voluntary motherhood became a tool to naturalize the gender binary and reinforce gender and family ideologies. The reconfiguration of motherhood in the interwar population debates will allow us to grasp the process through which reproduction acquired a new discursive value: that is, a site where control and autonomy are imbricated with each other.

TWO

Voluntary Motherhood

THE FEMINIST POLITICS OF BIRTH CONTROL

> Woman's acceptance of her inferior status was the more real because it was unconscious. She had chained herself to her place in society and the family through the maternal functions of her nature, and only chains thus strong could have bound her to her lot as a brood animal for the masculine civilizations of the world. In accepting her role as the "weaker and gentler half," she accepted that function. In turn, the acceptance of that function fixed the more firmly her rank as an inferior.
>
> MARGARET SANGER, *Woman and the New Race* (1920)

> Women's mothering is central to the sexual division of labor. Women's maternal role has profound effects on women's lives, on ideology about women, on the reproduction of masculinity and sexual inequality, and on the reproduction of particular forms of labor power. Women as mothers are pivotal actors in the sphere of social reproduction.
>
> NANCY CHODOROW, *The Reproduction of Mothering* (1978)

Gender Question in Interwar Feminism

The idea of gender differences, once naturalized in the state ideology in Meiji Japan, was constantly redefined during the interwar period. Initially, the Meiji state upheld the value of women's reproductive roles—including procreation, childrearing, and household chores—in the domestic sphere to ensure the management of the family system. Family evolved into an integral site where the modern state materialized and even reinforced gender ideology by shaping it as an exclusively feminine sphere.[1] With the emergence of feminism in Japan, the "good wife, wise mother" (*ryōsai kenbo*) slogan was gradually put into question by early feminist thinkers. The new women's movement that emerged in the 1910s reexamined women's domesticity by adopting the language of liberal politics. Whereas reproductive roles in the family were women's *duties* in the Meiji state ideology, early feminists associated domestic responsibilities for mothering with women's political *rights*. As Barbara Molony notes, gender equality was no longer contested by the late Meiji period.[2] Nevertheless, there was hardly a consensus on how gender differences should be dealt with to elevate women's status even among feminist thinkers, let alone between the state and feminists.

In this context, motherhood became the focus of feminist discourse as early as the 1910s. Whether motherhood was the basis for women's rights or an obstacle to gender equality was a vexing question among leading first-wave feminists. The "motherhood protection debate" (*bosei hogo ronsō*) between 1918 and 1919 is a quintessential example of the feminist reexamination of motherhood. Poet Yosano Akiko (1878–1942) published her criticism of women's dependency on men and the state in the magazine *Fujin kōron* (Women's review), and she inspired three other pioneering feminist critics—socialist Yamakawa Kikue (1890–1980), cofounder of *Seitō* (Bluestocking) Hiratsuka Raichō (1886–1971), and social reformer Yamada Waka (1879–1957)—each elaborated on the nature of motherhood.

Particularly, Yosano and Hiratsuka led the heated debate on motherhood protection, representing different standpoints regarding gender differences. Yosano advocated women's economic independence by means of increasing their participation in the workforce. Yosano equated women's domestic labor with "parasitism" (*iraishugi*) because women's unpaid work at home only inhibited their access to political rights.[3] Whereas Yosano's support for women's economic independence was inspired by South African socialist feminist Olive Schreiner (1855–1920) and her accounts of women's economic empowerment, Hiratsuka endorsed the rights of mothers by drawing on the maternal feminism of Swedish feminist Ellen Key (1849–1926).[4] The gist of Hiratsuka's claim was that the state should provide social assistance to protect women's natural quality as mothers.[5] For her, motherhood was integral to women's political rights considering women's contribution to the state by producing future citizens.

The different views on motherhood between Yosano and Hiratsuka fundamentally lay in their different understanding of gender differences.

Yosano considered differences between the two sexes an obstacle to overcome in order to achieve gender equality. In contrast, Hiratsuka's advocacy for motherhood protection was deeply entrenched in her belief in the sexual division of labor as nature's mandate. Hiratsuka's feminist goal concerned altering the social system to aid mothers' natural vocation instead of dismantling rigid gendered binaries. Similarly, Yamada Waka conveyed a matricentric feminist view by putting motherhood at the center of woman's political rights.[6] Yamada's faith in mothering as women's exclusive vocation was criticized by Yamakawa Kikue, who sarcastically likened Yamada's matricentric feminism to the reactionary ideology of " 'neo' good wife, wise mother" (*shin ryōsai kenbo*).[7] Furthermore, not only did Yamakawa criticize liberal feminism for reducing women to mothers only to sustain the patriarchal family, but she also refuted Yosano's indifference to deeper issues of capitalism. As discussed later in this chapter, women's subjugation under patriarchy was intertwined with class issues under capitalism from Yamakawa's socialist feminist perspective.

The motherhood protection debate was only a prelude to the long-lasting debate on motherhood within the Japanese feminist circle. The feminist thinkers collectively raised their voices to urge rethinking of motherhood vis-à-vis women's political rights, but they nevertheless created a cacophony of differing opinions about whether or not women's reproductive roles were conducive to women's empowerment. Apparently, motherhood as a woman's innate nature remained unproblematic for most feminist activists, as exemplified by Hiratsuka and Yamada. Maternal feminism concerned women's political integration into the state by gendering women, which enabled them to dovetail readily with the gender ideology of the wartime state, as examined in Chapters 4 and 5.[8] Notwithstanding the prominence of motherhood in feminist tenets, a few voices were raised to problematize the unquestioned equation of mothers and women. Most representatively, Yosano put individualism first in envisioning women's political rights while Yamakawa uncovered a complex web of oppression faced by women. Both Yosano's liberal individualism and Yamakawa's socialist feminism suggest alternative womanhood that hardly fits into the mold of motherhood. Such alternative visions for women's rights would reappear in postwar feminist activism, as represented by the women's liberation movement under the slogan of sexual and reproductive self-determination.[9]

Although the contentious debate about motherhood among feminists has drawn interest from historians, there have been few attempts to fill the gap between the understanding of gender differences in feminist discourse and the history of the birth control movement during the interwar period.[10] As examined in this chapter, the interwar birth control activism serves as a bridge between the initial feminist debate on motherhood and the postwar feminist advocacy for women's reproductive rights. Since the early 1920s, the rise of the birth control movement and the introduction of contraceptives allowed some pioneering feminist thinkers to envision alternatives for natural conception, which they thought to be constraints on women's empowerment. The idea of artificial birth control created a new basis for thinking beyond the naturalness of women's maternity far before the emergence of the women's liberation movement in the postwar era. How did feminism and the birth control movement inform each other in articulating women's gender roles? What impacts did birth control, both as concept and practice, have on the reconstitution of motherhood vis-à-vis women's political rights? What does the convergence of feminism and the birth control movement imply about the reconstruction of modernity in the interwar period? These questions will serve as a point of departure for exploring the complex web of politics whereby ideal motherhood was questioned, articulated, and reproduced.

Transpacific Translations of Voluntary Motherhood

As discussed in the previous chapter, with the growing concern over the population problem during the interwar years, motherhood became a site of social and medical debate as well as a primary object of social reform. The role of birth control activists in raising awareness about Japan's population issues became conspicuous as early as the 1920s. The Ōhara Institute for Social Research added a section titled "Population Problem" to the list of social problems in *Nihon rōdō nenkan* (the 1922 labor yearbook of Japan).[11] The new population section summarized demographic data from Japan's first national census executed in 1920 and the key points of a recent debate on birth control in mainland Japan.[12] According to the Ōhara Institute's report, during the previous year, social reformers and elites had become increasingly interested in artificial (*jiniteki*) birth control as a method of tackling a wide array of pressing social issues, including poverty, employment, migration, eugenics, and maternal health.[13] Among various benefits, the report spelled out the benefits of birth control for women (*fujin*) in particular by introducing the opinions of Japan's two leading birth control activists: Ishimoto Shizue (1897–2001, also known as Katō Shizue; her last name changed after marrying labor activist Katō Kanjū in 1944) and Yamakawa Kikue. As pioneering feminist advocates for birth control, both Ishimoto and Yamakawa emphasized the need to use birth control to liberate women from reproductive labor, including childrearing and household chores, and to grant women the right to choose motherhood.[14] For them, women's empowerment was as important as the protection of the lower classes as far as the rationales for the popularization of birth control methods was concerned. In that regard, Ishimoto and Yamakawa were not only on the forefront of the birth control movement, but also occupied a distinctive place in the wide spectrum of the population discourse.

The feminist birth control activism in interwar Japan emerged from the intersection of socioeconomic realities in the domestic context and the growing campaign for birth control led by feminist advocates in North America and Europe. Ishimoto and Yamakawa were trailblazing Japanese feminists who swiftly adopted "voluntary motherhood," an Anglo-American birth control slogan, and translated its agenda into Japanese social contexts to inspire Japanese women to control heretofore uncontrollable conception.

It should be noted that the feminist slogan of voluntary motherhood was continuously being recontextualized over time; it was far from being a finished product imported from the West. The American feminists in the late nineteenth century initially employed the term to promote the idea of sexual morality and protect motherhood in the domestic sphere. As Linda Gordon points out, the free love advocates, one of the radical strains of early American feminism, endorsed voluntary motherhood to give married women more control of their fertility rather than challenging the family system or promoting women's sexual freedom.[15] In the early twentieth century, the feminist understanding of voluntary motherhood shifted as Anglo-American feminists embraced the ideas of birth control and eugenics.[16] Whereas their predecessors vehemently opposed artificial birth control due to their concerns over women's sexual promiscuity as a likely consequence of birth control, emerging feminists supported birth control. For these feminist successors, voluntary motherhood, or women's right to reproductive autonomy, was directly associated with the nation's health.[17]

Margaret Sanger was the most influential figure in Anglo-American feminist birth control activism. As a pioneering activist and an ideologue who coined the term "birth control" in 1914, Sanger contributed to popularizing the catchphrase "voluntary motherhood" by which she promoted women's control over fertility in hopes of ultimately addressing the poverty of the working class.[18] In February 1917, Sanger launched a new monthly magazine titled *Birth Control Review*, which would function as a primary means for the birth control campaign for more than two decades (Figure 2.1). The phrase "the principle of intelligent and voluntary motherhood" on the cover of the *Review* indicates the underlying tenet of birth control activism. The term "voluntary motherhood" remained a slogan until the magazine changed its motto into "agitation, education, organization, legislation" in 1922 to underscore the importance of the concrete action plan.[19] Unlike the feminist predecessors whose overriding concern was a commitment to sexual morality through self-control, Sanger rearticulated voluntary motherhood and associated it with women's conscious efforts to empower themselves and ultimately to improve the quality of a race. In her book *Woman and New Race* published in 1920, Sanger set forth the dual goal of encouraging women to embody "a new morality," that is, "vigorous, constructive, liberated morality" of voluntary motherhood.[20] According to her, voluntary motherhood would "prevent the submergence of womanhood into motherhood" and allow women to move away from "mechanical maternity" toward "the creation of a new race."[21] This attempt to redefine motherhood through incorporating eugenic ideas epitomizes the interplay between the population discourse and feminism during the interwar period.

Sanger's reconfigured slogan, voluntary motherhood, inspired contemporary feminists in Japan. Yamakawa introduced Japanese audiences to the idea of voluntary motherhood in her 1920 article "Tasan shugi no noroi" (The curse of pronatalism) in the magazine *Taikan* (General views). Quoting the following from Sanger's *Woman and the New Race*, Yamakawa advocated *nin'iteki bosei* (literally, motherhood at one's discretion), her translation of voluntary motherhood, to highlight individual mothers' self-conscious choice to give birth:

> Millions of women are asserting their right to voluntary motherhood. They are determined to decide for themselves whether they shall become mothers, under what conditions and when. This is the fundamental revolt referred to. It is for woman the key to the temple of liberty.[22]

Meanwhile, Ishimoto's advocacy of birth control built on Sanger's voluntary motherhood as well, which Ishimoto translated as *jishuteki bosei*, or autonomous motherhood in a literal sense. In her 1921 pamphlet "Shinmarusasu shugi" (Neo-Malthusianism), Ishimoto explained two different terms referring to "voluntarily having a child," that is, birth control (*sanji seigen*) and voluntary motherhood (*jishuteki bosei*).[23] In regard to different terminology, Ishimoto added that "voluntarily having a child inevita-

Figure 2.1 The cover of the *Birth Control Review* 5, no. 2 (1921).
Source: Nineteenth Century Collections Online, http://tinyurl.gale.com/tinyurl/CHJBV9, accessed November 19, 2019.

bly corresponds to the goal of *sanji seigen*" in the "era of capitalism."[24] Similarly to Sanger who considered women's fertility control as a solution to poverty, Ishimoto resorted to individual reproductive autonomy to address poverty under capitalism.

The transpacific movement of the feminist slogan "voluntary motherhood" in the early 1920s exemplifies what Deleuze and Guattari describe as "translation." Here, translation does not mean simply the *re-presentation* of the original language, but "beyond that as the ability of language, with its own givens on its own stratum, to represent all the other strata" and thus to synthesize all of the "flows, particles, codes, and territorialities of the other strata into a sufficiently deterritorialized system of signs."[25] Put another way, translation is the process of creation with which linguistic, nonlinguistic, and extralinguistic factors are variably involved, far from being a mere tool for interlingual communication. Deleuze's and Guattari's understanding of translation questions the unilateral influence of Sanger on Yamakawa and Ishimoto, or that of American feminism on Japanese feminism in general. The polysemic and polyvocal nature of voluntary motherhood neither derives from the supremacy of English language nor the universality of Anglo-American feminism. As examined through its changing meanings over time, the slogan was constantly displaced and rearticulated due to the very transformative nature of language that involves all types of variables including linguistic components, sociopolitical factors, and individual enunciators. This nonlinear process of transpacific translation reconstituted the concept of motherhood in multiple fashions.

The dynamics of translation also created a condition for multiple variations of what voluntary motherhood ought to look like in Japan. Despite reaching an agreement on the need for birth control for women's sake, Ishimoto and Yamakawa's views on the identification of women did not necessarily align. In other words, the category of "woman" was variably identified with different positions, including ethnic nation (*minzoku*), race, and class. The different ways in which Ishimoto and Yamakawa defined women vis-à-vis identity categories informed their political goals underlying the slogan "voluntary motherhood." Whereas the target audience for the birth control campaign was explicitly urban middle-class Japanese women for Ishimoto, Yamakawa focused on the working-class women whose experiences were primarily determined by the interplay of capitalism and patriarchy rather than merely national belonging. The conceptual gaps between Ishimoto's and Yamakawa's views on women's positionality ultimately reflect heterogeneous feminist approaches to the fashioning of ideal motherhood in the interwar period. The irony was that the initial attempts by these leading feminists to articulate motherhood as a political subject were motivated to support women's voluntary choice to *not* become mothers.

In what follows, I will examine Japanese feminist approaches to the birth control campaign and their underlying gender politics, focusing on Ishimoto's and Yamakawa's discussions of motherhood. As the pro–birth control activists as well as women's right activists, their paths crossed frequently in the period between the early and mid-1920s. The 1922 amendment of Article 5 of Chian keisatsu hō (Public Peace Police Law) that recognized women's rights to attend political meetings unleashed a new force in politics. Diverse feminist voices cutting across ideological lines emerged to support Russian famine relief, disaster relief after the Great Kantō Earthquake of 1923, and most importantly, women's suffrage.[26] Ishimoto and Yamakawa worked hand in hand to fulfill these varied agendas despite political division— namely, Ishimoto being at the nationalist end while Yamakawa was at the socialist end. How did their political positions inform their views of motherhood differently? What does it imply about heterogeneous feminist approaches to gendering women? The political division here will not be considered an absolute demarcation between the two feminist figures. Instead, the following will illuminate the different ways in which motherhood is translated into political subjectivity and the underlying gender schemas applied to positioning women in the nexus of ethnic nation, race, class, and even abstract nature.

Ishimoto on Eugenic Motherhood

Ishimoto Shizue was a prominent feminist who initiated the birth control movement in Japan as early as the beginning of the 1920s. Her career as a birth control activist can roughly be divided into two phases. During the early 1920s, Ishimoto strove to popularize the benefits of birth control on socioeconomic and eugenic grounds. Her activism focusing on creating public awareness gradually shifted to include a clinic-based strategy for providing consultations about birth control methods and selling contraceptives to clients in the 1930s. While her approach to the birth control campaign changed over time, the underlying idea of her vocal support for women's reproductive control remained consistent. As discussed below, eugenics and nationalism were deeply entrenched in her advocacy of birth control, embodying the quintessential characteristics of eugenic feminism. According to Asha Nadkarni, "eugenic feminism" is a version of maternal feminism that invests in "biological reproduction as the means of progress and improvement, as the platform for women's rights within the state."[27] I argue that Ishimoto's support for birth control is motivated by her pursuit of maternal feminism, whereby she idealized eugenic motherhood, or mothers who were informed of eugenics and controlled their fertility according to eugenic principles, as the means of women's empowerment and race betterment.

Ishimoto Shizue—originally born to aristocratic, liberal-minded parents—had the privilege of accessing educational opportunities, including a high school curriculum and learning from her uncle, Tsurumi Yūsuke (1885–1973) with his extensive knowledge of Western political thought and literature. In 1914, Ishimoto married Baron Ishimoto Keikichi who studied engineering at the Tokyo Imperial University and believed in Christian humanism. The life of the young aristocratic couple took a new turn when they moved to the island of Kyushu where the Baron Ishimoto worked as a supervisor at the Mitsui Mining Company. During their stay in Kyushu between 1915 and 1917, they observed the impoverished and filthy living conditions of coal miners and their families, which inspired both the baron and Ishimoto (Shizue) to realize the pressing need for social reform to address poverty and class issues. Later, in her autobiography, Ishimoto recollected with sympathy that the miserable lives of the working class inspired her ponder the question, "why must the mother breed and nurse while she works for wages?"[28] This question would arise again in her life as she began to commit to the birth control movement in the early 1920s.

A pivotal point came for Ishimoto when she became acquainted with American birth control activists. In 1919, Ishimoto sailed for the United States following the baron who had moved to New York to study labor issues under capitalism. In New York, the baron became infatuated with socialism, which he deemed to be the ultimate solution for humanity; his utopian vision for social reform outpaced his dreams of being an engineer. Soon after Ishimoto joined her husband in New York, the baron made a trip to Washington, DC, to serve as an interpreter at the International Labor Organization conference for the Japanese delegation. In her husband's absence, Ishimoto attended a secretarial course in the Ballard School of the Young Women's Christian Association. In the meantime, she was befriended by American socialist and birth control activist Agnes Smedley (1892–1950). Through Smedley, Ishimoto became acquainted with American activists in Greenwich Village, a place known for embracing bohemian and radical thoughts at the time.[29] On January 17, 1920, Smedley invited Ishimoto to a tea hosted by Margaret Sanger, with whom Smedley worked at the *Birth Control Review*.[30] It was that day when the long-lasting camaraderie between Ishimoto and Sanger began to develop, which eventually evolved into what Aiko Takeuchi-Demirici called the "transnational birth control movement."[31]

Upon returning to Japan in September 1920, Ishimoto independently worked to promote the idea of birth control to the Japanese masses. She began to gain a reputation as the Margaret Sanger of Japan after writing a few articles for newspapers.[32] In August 1921, Ishimoto published a pamphlet entitled "Shin-marusasu shugi" with the help of a labor activist Ōshima Yoshiharu to attract public attention to the benefits of birth control.[33] This pamphlet contains the salient points of Neo-Malthusian rationales, resembling Sanger's views on population issues. In the pamphlet, Ishimoto raised a concern about Japan's population crisis due to the imbalance between the population's size and food supply.[34] While acknowledging that the population crisis had become a global challenge as seen in the First World War as its most evident consequence, Ishimoto noted that Japan was particularly in urgent need of addressing the high population density caused by its mountainous territory and a lack of metals and fossil fuels.[35] In this light, Ishimoto presented Japan's overpopulation as a *fait accompli* just as many neo-Malthusian ideologues regarded an excess of population as the essence of the population crisis. Insofar as the uncontrolled fertility of Japanese people was the root cause of the population crisis, birth control was a ready-made solution.

Although Ishimoto's understanding of the population problem appears to primarily concern the quantity of population due to its alignment with Malthusianism, she proceeded to push the overpopulation issue beyond the quantity question. In particular, Ishimoto's approach to the population problem is distinctive in that she placed "women's issues" (*fujin no mondai*) at the center of Japan's demographic issues.[36] From a feminist viewpoint, Ishimoto spelled out the negative impacts of multiple pregnancies on women's lives, both financially and in terms of quality of life, which she thought ultimately resulted in women's servitude due to lack of opportunity for self-development. Accordingly, for Ishimoto, women were more vulnerable than men to the consequences of overpopulation because women were deprived of opportunities to develop and enjoy "cultural living" (*bunkateki seikatsu*), a post–WWI neologism meaning a modern life involving consumption, mass media, popular culture, and education.[37]

It is worth noting that Ishimoto did not intend to render women as passive victims whose lives were excluded from the benefits of the urban, middle-class, modern life. Instead, she reoriented the nature of human reproduction away from the quantity question and toward the quality issue. Adopting the tenets of eugenics, Ishimoto's neo-Malthusian vision for fertility control foregrounded the quality of the Japanese population. In the pamphlet, Ishimoto pointed out that uncontrolled fertility caused women's mental and physical exhaustion and had detrimental effects on the health of Japanese children.[38] In this regard, Ishimoto interwove the population problem with women's problems in calling for the use of birth control methods among Japanese women. The intertwined relationship between population and women's issues is clearly indicated in her positive outlook on women's potential to address Japan's population problem.

In concluding remarks, Ishimoto added that "the only solution for the population problem in Japan is birth control . . . [it is] primarily a women's issue. It is not strange at all that women can resolve the population problem that has troubled great male politicians so far."[39] With this, she implied the integral role of motherhood in producing mentally and physically healthy offspring, let alone curbing the population growth.

The pamphlet gives us a glimpse into how Ishimoto shaped new ideals for motherhood to reframe, rather than reconstituting women's gendered subjectivity. Although she pursued women's liberation by encouraging women to use contraceptives, the goal of women's liberation was not synonymous with women's freedom in terms of fundamental civil rights but rather the rearrangement of gender norms through an altered meaning of reproduction. In other words, producing children itself was no longer a desirable expression of womanhood: producing *healthy* children on eugenic grounds was women's new norm. Ishimoto's ideal for motherhood, hence, was a gendered subjectivity embodying eugenics and maternal agency.

Ishimoto's vision of ideal motherhood laid a foundation for her birth control movement. In May 1922, Ishimoto founded Japan's first pro–birth control organization, Nihon sanji chōsetsu kenkyūkai, and launched the campaign to promote birth control measures towards the Japanese masses in earnest.[40] Chōsetsukai functioned as Ishimoto's official channel for justifying birth control for women's sake, although in an ambiguous tone. In her article titled "Fujin kaihō to sanji chōsetsu" (Women's liberation and birth control) published in Chōsetsukai's magazine *Shōkazoku* (Small family), Ishimoto put women's liberation at the forefront of the birth control movement by declaring:

> The birth control movement is a prerequisite for the issue of women's liberation. We women have been ruled by slavish morality and have resigned ourselves to the forced duty of motherhood. However, times have changed. Motherhood in the true sense becomes possible only when a married woman who is physically, mentally, and financially qualified to be a mother gives birth to a beloved baby at her own will. In light of this, birth control can be interpreted as voluntary motherhood.[41]

For Ishimoto, voluntary motherhood was not a goal in itself but a necessary qualification for ideal mothers. What determines "ideal" was the principles of eugenics that reaffirmed gender norms and trapped women back into their maternal bodies while extending the meaning of human reproduction to include its national implications. In a booklet published by Chōsetsukai, Ishimoto explicitly put forward birth control for eugenic purposes in her assertion that "birth control [*sanji seigen*] is to take conscious control of the population, far from endorsing race suicide or sinful abortions. What birth control aims is to awaken people to the goal of breeding better humans on earth."[42] Her claim that women should assert their maternal agency in the ultimate interest of race betterment reflects the quintessential account of eugenic feminism. Ishimoto's eugenic feminism did not simply reiterate the preceding feminist ideas ingrained in maternal feminism but translated them into the intersection of maternal agency and biopolitical discourse. Unlike the mother's natural rights that Hiratsuka pursued, Ishimoto reoriented women's allegedly predetermined maternal responsibility of their ethnic nation. Neo-Malthusianism and eugenics were the two main pillars of her biopolitical logic whereby she justified the role of ideal mothers in addressing overpopulation and its resultant quality issue.

We cannot overlook the paradox of eugenic feminism: the reduction of women into maternity, whether it be actual or potential. Women's liberation from their duty of *involuntary* reproduction still depended on women's reproductive function, namely, female physicality that was allegedly central to femininity. Ishimoto's advocacy for birth control fell short of challenging such an essentialist view of mothers as a predetermined path for biological women. If there was anything new about Ishimoto's vision of motherhood, she attempted to grant partial, if not full-fledged, citizenship to women who could take part in the public sphere only through the medium of their maternal physicality.

Moreover, eugenics was conducive to reinforcing this gendered vision of femininity couched in her language of voluntary motherhood. Ishimoto brought overpopulation into question by arguing that "the sharp increase in the size of the unhealthy population" would "burden the superior and healthy humankind and diminish national strength."[43] The assumption of biological disparities between the superior and the inferior epitomizes what Foucault refers to as "a biological-type relationship."[44] According to Foucault, a biological-type relationship indicates the fundamental mechanism of biopower, namely, a modern form of power ceaselessly addressing the biological continuum of life while creating the caesuras within it. Simply put, Ishimoto, like other adherents of neo-Malthusianism, concluded that the elimination of the unfit ensures the proliferation of the fit. According to this view, individual bodies were never equal in terms of their qualities but differentiated between superior and inferior. Therefore, when it comes to voluntary motherhood, women were subjected not simply to the autonomous choice of giving birth or not giving birth but, more fundamentally, to the biopolitical norms of *being entitled to give birth* and *ought to be banned from giving birth*.

After Chōsetsukai was disbanded, Ishimoto joined forces with male birth control activists in opening Nihon ninshin chōsetsu sōdansho (Japan Birth Control Clinic) in Tokyo in August 1924. Under the leadership of birth control activist Ogawa Ryūshiro and physician Kaji Tokijirō, the clinic provided contraceptive consultation and lectures, published booklets, and sold various contraceptives, including pessaries, cervical caps, condoms, sponges, and emmenagogues.[45] By the mid-1920s, Ishimoto's activism appeared to have evolved into a clinic-based, practical approach, yet her personal life disrupted her birth control campaign. Her husband's desire to seek a seat in the House of Peers forced Ishimoto to compromise her own political goals due to an antipathy shared among political conservatives towards radical activism. Although the baron never succeeded in being elected, their marital relationship began to break down, which further impeded Ishimoto from pursuing birth control activism.[46]

After a few years' hiatus during the mid- to late-1920s, in 1931 Ishimoto resumed her birth control activism.[47] With a growing interest in birth control as a solution to the population crisis, activists from various political backgrounds organized Nihon sanji chōsetsu renmei (Japan Birth Control League) in January 1931. Ishimoto was named president while her long-time fellow activists, Abe Isoo and Majima Kan, were appointed as honorary president and chairman, respectively.[48] The group also gained support from feminist activists and intellectuals including Hiratsuka Raichō, Kawasaki Natsu, Kaneko Shigeri, Niizuma Ito(ko), Akamatsu Akiko, Shibahara Urako, and Muraoka Hanako. These feminist members participated as the board members of the Birth Control League and raised their collective voices in support of the "protection of motherhood" and "voluntary motherhood."[49] These two catchphrases that integrated maternal and eugenic feminism are indicative of leading Japanese feminists' favorable adoption of eugenics as a key principle of validating maternal agency.

Although the league was short-lived, in May 1932 Ishimoto and a number of fellow feminists formed Nihon sanji chōsetsu fujin dōmei (Women's Birth Control League of Japan), hereinafter referred to as Fujin Dōmei, the first women's birth control advocacy group in Japan. In addition to Hiratsuka Raichō, Kawasaki Natsu, and Niizuma Ito(ko) (who had joined forces with Ishimoto a year earlier to form the Birth Control League), socialist Akamatsu Tsuneko (Akamatsu Akiko's sister-in-law), Christian Yamamuro Tamiko (daughter of Yamamuro Gunpei, the founder of the Salvation Army), and physician Yamamoto Sugiko participated in the unprecedented woman-centered birth control group.[50] The primary aim of Fujin Dōmei was to improve maternal and child health by educating the public on accurate and practical methods of contraception.[51] With the creation of this group, Ishimoto realigned her approach to the birth control campaign and implemented a practical, clinic-based strategy for the movement. In 1934, she set up a birth control clinic in the Shinagawa district of Tokyo to provide medical consultations and to manufacture and sell contraceptives such as pessaries and spermicidal jellies.[52]

However, this shift in the strategies of Ishimoto's birth control movement did not necessarily mean the absence of ideological justifications. Her rationale for birth control was still couched in the language of eugenic feminism while it incorporated relatively moderate feminist slogans for motherhood protection. For example, one of the pamphlets published by Fujin Dōmei, "Sechigarai yononaka ni" (In a world full of difficulties) illustrates how motherhood was rendered instrumental for the health of children and the protection of the family.[53] While Ishimoto emphasized the role of birth control in protecting maternal and child health, her previous slogan in support of women's liberation was replaced with a family-centered emphasis on the maternal body (*botai*). What determined the importance of a mother's physicality was her reproductive role: that is, giving birth only to the number of children one could afford and producing and raising healthy children. Moreover, the maternal body was represented as a basic biological unit on which the nation's health depended. The family and the nation-state constituted the two poles of birth control practice in the sense that the former was the main unit of reproduction whereas the latter demarcated the boundary within which a biological relationship was considered valid. The pamphlet reiterated the convergence of nationalism with eugenic feminism, which paradoxically reduced women to breeding machines:

> A child is a family treasure as well as a social treasure. Giving birth to a child is a woman [*josei*]'s vocation. We, Japanese women, should give birth to strong children for the society and to good children for the family.[54]

This declaration reveals the complex structure of ideal motherhood premised on women's gendered subjectivity, eugenics, and nationalist ideology. Ideal motherhood was a product of the politico-scientific discourse of imagining the eugenic chain of life that moved from healthy mothers to healthy offspring and further onto the healthy nation. While Ishimoto previously maintained the ambiguity of universal bodily categories in her eugenic feminism, the representation of organic bodies became enclosed within national borders. In place of the ambiguous terrain between womanhood and motherhood, Ishimoto reconfigured women as mothers—or at least potential mothers—whose vocation and moral obligation was deemed to have healthy children. Thus, Ishimoto's eugenic feminism remained consistent in the birth control movements as she continued to draw both national borders and a biological chain around mothers' bodies.

Birth Strike: Yamakawa Kikue's Critique of Gender and Class

Yamakawa Kikue is one of the most influential figures in the history of the Japanese feminist movement. Yamakawa's role in the feminist movement evolved from a socialist feminist in support of proletarian women's rights in the prewar period to an egalitarian feminist advocating gender equality in postwar Japan.[55] It is well acknowledged that Yamakawa's commitment to addressing women's issues, particularly working-class women's rights, lay in her criticism of the capitalist system that had nurtured inequality along the lines of gender, class, and race. Whereas her socialist feminist thought has drawn attention from scholars, little has been known about Yamakawa's involvement with the birth control movement. The lack of attention to Yamakawa's support of birth control is partly because, unlike Ishimoto, Yamakawa was a theorist rather than an activist in the public debate on birth control during the interwar period. Moreover, her support of birth control was primarily expressed in a series of articles she published in the early 1920s.[56] Her seemingly short-lived participation in the birth control campaign, however, does not verify the triviality of the birth control issue in Yamakawa's socialist feminist agenda. Rather, I argue that Yamakawa's intensive effort to theorize the benefits of birth control attests to her consistent approach to women's issues. As shown in the motherhood protection debate, Yamakawa put emphasis on the liberation of women both from capitalist oppression and patriarchy. Accordingly, to Yamakawa, birth control was a political means for emancipating women from the shackles of the patriarchal family system and alleviating the reproductive burdens of the proletariat. The term "birth strike" (*shussan sutoraiki*) encapsulates Yamakawa's protest against this double burden and her attempt to reorient the goal of birth control toward the critique of gender and class stratification.[57]

Yamakawa was born in Tokyo in a former samurai family. Her mother, Aoyama Chise, was a progressive-minded woman who valued the education of her children.⁵⁸ Owing to her mother's influence, in 1908, Yamakawa enrolled in Joshi eigaku juku (Women's English-Language Academy), the forerunner of Tsuda College founded by educator Tsuda Umeko. During this period, Yamakawa was exposed to various social issues, especially the severe working conditions for female workers. Although the Factory Act was enacted in 1911 to protect female and young workers in factories, it was not until 1916 that the act went into effect. Even when it did, there was a lack of adequate enforcement to limit the work hours for female and child laborers.⁵⁹ Against the backdrop of increasing labor issues, Yamakawa gradually leaned toward socialism and met with leftists from Heiminsha (Commoners' Society), one of the earliest socialist groups. Through the socialist reading group, Yamakawa met Yamakawa Hitoshi, a leading Japanese socialist who later founded the Japanese Communist Party in 1922. Yamakawa (Kikue) married him in 1916 and continued her involvement with the socialist movement for the rest of her life.

Yamakawa quickly gained a reputation for her sharp, sophisticated criticisms of capitalism, published in numerous articles. For nearly a decade beginning in the late 1910s when mass-circulation magazines came to play a significant part in Taishō culture and politics, Yamakawa actively published articles on the intersecting issues of class and patriarchy for magazines such as *Seitō* (Bluestocking), *Fujin kōron* (Women's review), *Kaizō* (Reconstruction), and *Onna no sekai* (Women's world).⁶⁰ In particular, she became famous for the above-mentioned motherhood protection debate. With critical comments on bourgeois, matricentric feminism that failed to reckon with the structural problems of capitalism, Yamakawa was able to increase her presence as a socialist feminist in intellectual circles.⁶¹

In addition to being a prolific writer, Yamakawa was an activist who participated in Sekirankai (Red Wave Society), a women's socialist group founded in 1921 to protest against structural inequalities under capitalism.⁶² Although the group was disbanded within only eight months, Yamakawa continued to engage in leftist activism through the Communist Party and later the Japan Labor Unions Council. Her role in the male-dominated proletarian movement was noteworthy. Yamakawa questioned the absence of women's division inside the Labor Unions Council and the widespread negligence of working women among male activists despite the gravity of women's issues under capitalism. Against the androcentric culture prevalent in the proletarian movement, Yamakawa drafted "Fujinbu te-ze" (Thesis on women's division) to call for creating a women's division within the council and raise awareness about working women's struggles.[63]

In this interwar trajectory of Yamakawa's political activism, her advocacy of birth control appears less visible than other issues of working-class women she strove to tackle. However, it cannot be overlooked that Yamakawa was one of the earliest pioneers who raised awareness of the benefits of birth control. This begs the question of why Yamakawa supported birth control and what connection her advocacy of birth control had with her socialist feminist agenda. As discussed below, Yamakawa's keen interest in birth control attests to her consistent approach to the complex nature of gender inequalities rather than obscuring her feminist theoretical grounds. Moreover, her persistent criticism of the structural conditions for gender inequalities marks her distinctive position in either feminist or socialist circles.

In 1920, Yamakawa introduced Japanese audiences to Sanger's concept of "voluntary motherhood," which she translated into *nin'iteki bosei* to emphasize an individual mother's conscious choice to give birth. Although Ishimoto, too, embraced the same concept in support of Sanger's underlying belief in women's reproductive agency as a way of revolt, there were gaps in Ishimoto's and Yamakawa's understanding of the sociohistorical conditions whereby they justified the need for voluntary motherhood. As discussed earlier, Ishimoto incorporated eugenics into the birth control movement to justify the ethnonational benefits of women's autonomous choice over their bodies. In a similar vein, to Sanger, whose ideological basis on Neo-Malthusianism and eugenics became conspicuous by the beginning of the 1920s, voluntary motherhood would transform women into empowered builders of a healthy race.[64] The concept of voluntary motherhood implied a causal link between a mother's freedom and her potential to improve racial quality. It was thus gendered and racialized freedom that both Sanger and Ishimoto pursued through their birth control movement.

Meanwhile, Yamakawa reconfigured voluntary motherhood as a means of revolt against enforced sexual morality, inhumane exploitation, and oppression under capitalism. She defied feudal patriarchy and capitalism on the ground that both constituted existing social structures "which treat women merely as breeding machines, that is, the machines for supplying workers for capitalists and soldiers for the state."[65] In the fight for women's liberation from the dual shackles of patriarchy and capitalism, Yamakawa championed "women's freedom to love and their rights to choose motherhood."[66] From her viewpoint, birth control was a means to rise against involuntary motherhood, which she considered slave morality and, essentially, a vital strategy for transforming women into political subjects. Therefore, it was crucial for her to resist the reduction of women's sexuality and reproduction into an expression of womanhood or merely to an instrument for race betterment. Yamakawa reoriented reproductive autonomy as women's political agency against power using the notion of voluntary motherhood.

Yamakawa's theorization of birth control as the means of revolt is closely aligned with her sharp criticism of two major responses to the population problem: namely, neo-Malthusianism and socialism. As examined in the previous chapter, despite their different accounts of what caused the population problem, neo-Malthusianism and socialism shared an economic determinism concerning the relationship between population and resources. Whereas neo-Malthusianists conjectured that the balance between population and food resources could be acquired by reducing population growth, socialists advocated a fair distribution of resources to close the gap between the capitalists and the proletariat.[67] Discussion of reproduction as the corporeal experience of women as well as an object of patriarchal exploitation was absent in both branches of mathematical reasoning. Yamakawa positioned herself as a critic of neo-Malthusianism and socialism to remind both groups that birth control had to be a perennial goal even after the issue of overpopulation and poverty was resolved by the proletarian revolution.[68] In her view, voluntary motherhood must not be rendered into economic determinism but instead retained its own merit as an expression of women's basic liberty.

Yamakawa's distinctive position in the interwar population discourse, though, is not without reference to the ongoing debate over the cause of poverty. Yamakawa essentially agreed with Marx's critique of Malthus's theory that population growth would outpace food production. Against this Malthusian dogma shared among her contemporary neo-Malthusianists, Yamakawa argued that "nowadays, it is the unfair distribution of products rather than low productivity relative to population growth that prevents the reduction of poverty in some societies."[69] Her criticism of neo-Malthusianism echoed Marx's language in light of the emphasis on socioeconomic aspects of population dynamics.[70] Yamakawa drew upon the critiques of the population problem developed by Marx, and other leftist theorists including Peter Kropotkin and August Bebel, who presented bright pictures of human progress based on technological development.[71] German socialist Bebel was particularly influential in her thought on production and reproduction under capitalism. Building on

Bebel's work *Woman and Socialism*, originally published in 1879, she argued against the theory that a surplus population could outstrip food resources, labeling it an illusion:

> The relative excess of population that today is continually produced by the capitalistic system to the detriment of the working class and of society, will prove a blessing on a higher level of civilization. A numerous population is not a hindrance to progress. It is, on the contrary, a means to advance progress, just like the present overproduction of commodities and food, the disruption of marriage by the employment of women, children in industry and the expropriation of the middle class by the large capitalists, are the preliminary conditions of a higher stage of civilization.[72]

Bebel considered population growth to be a necessary step toward a higher stage of civilization, that is, a socialist society. While drawing upon Bebel's critique of the bourgeois myth of surplus population, Yamakawa pushed the critique further to dissect the capitalist system that inevitably produced a surplus population. Yamakawa stressed that "relative surplus population, as one of the characteristics of a capitalist society, is produced or increased by capitalism, and at the same time, serves as a necessary condition for capitalism."[73] The concept of "relative surplus population" refers to the excess of laboring population for exploitation, unlike the Malthusian principle of absolute surplus population outgrowing food supply. Her critique of the surplus laboring population, both as the product and the condition for capitalist accumulation, is closely linked to what Marx called the "despotism of capitals" in his analysis of the capitalist mode of production and its creation of the industrial reserve army.[74] Insofar as the capitalist mode of production necessitated the surplus laboring population for the expansion of capital, the exploitation of laborers would continue independently of the size of population.

The notion of relative surplus population refuted both the Malthusian theory of overpopulation and the neo-Malthusian solution for social ills. In Yamakawa's view, the overpopulation problem posed by neo-Malthusianists was merely a displacement of the nature of capitalist exploitation into a purely biological issue. In this light, Yamakawa's view of capitalism was at odd with Sanger's underlying logic behind women's reproductive autonomy. As discussed above, Sanger claimed that the misery of the proletariat stemmed from uncontrolled fertility, and, furthermore, that fertility served capitalism as its accomplice.[75] Whereas Sanger attributed the hardship of the working class to their own fertility,

Yamakawa unpacked the ideological tactics behind the overpopulation discussion, which inverted the causation of poverty. Accordingly, Yamakawa concluded that the fundamental solution to social issues lies in the fair distribution of resources instead of curbing population growth.[76]

Despite her rebuttal of the overpopulation theory, Yamakawa's criticism of the neo-Malthusian accounts begs the question: Why did Yamakawa still support birth control? Her critique of the capitalist system underpinned her advocacy for "birth strike," namely women's use of birth control as a means of protest against capitalism. In her article "Birth Control and Socialism" (1921), Yamakawa lamented that "women, as a tool for procreation, have been treated as machines for supplying workers to capitalists on one hand, and soldiers to the state on the other. Their excruciating efforts to raise their children go down the drain as their children are eventually exploited by capitalism and militarism."[77] Against the structural exploitation under capitalism, Yamakawa demanded proletarian women's birth strike until "the society would guarantee a decent and civilized life for future generations."[78] In light of this, birth strike was intended to redefine birth control as a weapon for the proletarian movement and particularly for the working-class women in their fight against the capitalist instrumentalization of procreation.

Notwithstanding the underlying aim of birth strike, Yamakawa's advocacy of birth control remained controversial among many Japanese socialists of the time. Except for a handful of leftist activists—including Yamamoto Senji and Sakai Toshihiko (1872–1933), who were sympathetic to women's issues—there was widespread indifference to the birth control movement among male socialists who failed or refused to identify a connection between reproduction and class struggle.[79] Yamakawa's conflict with her fellow Japanese socialists centered on recognizing women as both individual subjects and members of the proletariat. To Yamakawa, women's bodies and reproduction lay simultaneously inside and outside the domain of the class struggle because women were not only workers who pursued social equality and liberty but also individuals with freedom of choice. Reproduction could not be an exception and thus had to be respected as included in the realm of individual rights.[80] Although the proletarian movement eventually incorporated birth control into its strategy to fight the class struggle, most socialists not only denied women's individual subjectivity but also downplayed the importance of reproductive issues in the proletarian movement. Yamakawa must have been aware of the prevailing disavowal of women's freedom being outweighed by the goal of proletarian revolution, given her sharp question "what will happen if society can provide welfare for people in the future so that birth control is no longer needed for economic reasons?"[81] This question unveils an inconvenient truth: women's autonomy remained problematic for the male-dominated socialist movement.

Evidence of the conflicting definitions of women and reproduction is found in the debate between Yamakawa and Ishikawa Sanshirō, a Christian socialist turned anarchist.[82] In 1921, Ishikawa published an article, "Shakai shugi sha kara mita fujin kyūsai: ippuippu seido wa shizen de jiyū de junketsu de aru" (A socialist view on the relief of women: monogamy as nature, freedom, and purity), in *Onna no sekai*. Sparked by Ishikawa's essay, Yamakawa and Ishikawa began a debate over the legitimate reasons for birth control. The debate reveals their opposing views largely on the following two issues: first, whether birth control served the interests of bourgeois ideology or women, particularly proletarian women. Second, whether birth control would no longer be needed once the proletarian revolution solved poverty.

With respect to the first question, Ishikawa deemed contraception as merely "the pleasure [*dōraku*] of bourgeois intellectuals" or a "tricky philosophy born out of modern decadence."[83] His objection to birth control reflects his antipathy towards social and relief works whose humanitarianism invariably buttressed capitalist and commercialist interests. In response, Yamakawa denounced Ishikawa's ironically bourgeois mentality in equating contraception merely with "pleasure" while overlooking the manifold challenges faced by women. In her view, "women, particularly proletarian women who are working mothers," bore the burdens of childbirth, parenting, and education that were oftentimes ridiculed by an androcentric nonchalance about women's reproductive labor.[84]

Yamakawa's critique of women's domestic labor suggests that women's exploitation was defined primarily by their *natural* motherhood—that is, the gendered representation of motherhood as biologically predetermined. The widespread assumption on natural motherhood contrasts with class identification as the latter is constructed based on the male homosocial desire that normalized the masculinity of the working class.[85] Whereas homosocial bonds among male subjects mark the working-class identity, Yamakawa exposed non-homosocial experiences shared by proletarian women. Yamakawa was keenly aware of how the gendered categories of sex and class primarily informed women's experiences and, thus, how substantially difficult proletarian women's experiences were due to the dual shackles of feudal patriarchy and capitalism. Her understanding of the intersection of gender and class contrasts with Ishikawa, who overlooked the question of motherhood insofar as class issues are concerned. In Yamakawa's view, Ishikawa was complicit in the subjugation of women because of the androcentrism common to both bourgeois intellectuals and socialist activists who excluded women's reproductive labor—that is, both biological and social reproductive labor—from socioeconomic domains. In other words, the bourgeois and socialist circles were no different from each other in segregating motherhood and reproduction from social practices.

The problem with normalized gender segregation brings us to the second issue: Yamakawa's and Ishikawa's opposing views on the place of women between nature and society, that is, between biological motherhood and social relations under capitalism. While Ishikawa envisioned a socialist state where the economic burden of childbirth and childrearing would thoroughly disappear, Yamakawa argued that women's freedom of voluntary motherhood must be protected even in a post-revolutionary socialist state. In her article "Ishikawa Sanshirō to hininron" (Ishikawa Sanshirō and a discussion of contraception) (1921), Yamakawa asserts:

> In short, [in an ideal society], people should be able to choose whether to give birth or not at their free will, just like they do when deciding marriage.... I have no doubt that the difficulties in getting married for economic reasons will be solved in the future. Nevertheless, we must not jump to the conclusion that women will no longer need reproductive choices. In the same token, we must not confuse contraception for economic reasons and birth control as women's choice about motherhood. [86]

As the quote indicates, Yamakawa emphasized voluntary motherhood by representing women's reproduction within the domain of individual rights. Her equation of reproductive choice as a political right suggests that Yamakawa's understanding of motherhood was couched in the politicized language of rights and freedoms. On the contrary, Ishikawa and many contemporary socialists regarded reproduction as part of the realm of *nature*—that is, the depoliticized, segregated, and gendered rendering of female subjectivity. From their homosocial perspective, a socialist state founded on economic equality and technological advance would address women's financial burden from reproductive labor without necessarily eliminating gender segregation. The question of the proper place of motherhood either in the realm of depoliticized nature or as a site of political subjectification was the underlayer in the socialist debate on the rights and wrongs of birth control. While most socialists depoliticized motherhood by segregating reproduction from social issues, Yamakawa identified reproduction as an overdetermined site of patriarchal and capitalist powers and, therefore, *re-politicized* motherhood in support of women's political membership in the class movement.

It was this new political terrain of reproduction where Yamakawa and Ishimoto formed a common ground. For Ishimoto, overpopulation had to be addressed while women's reproductive choice was a solution to the problematized population and, more significantly, a new political niche for women. Meanwhile, Yamakawa tackled intersectionality between gender and class in both capitalism and the proletarian movement. To Yamakawa, women's reproductive choice was the means of protest against the depoliticized—hence, gendered—realm of reproduction in the androcentric imaginary. Ironically, the different definitions of voluntary motherhood were analogous to each other in terms of the politicization of motherhood. Both feminists adopted the birth control strategy to challenge the androcentric representation of motherhood. By the same reasoning, they reconstructed women's subjectivity to claim women's membership in the nation-state and in the class movement, respectively.

Gender Questions: Between Womanhood and Motherhood

This chapter has delved into the multifaceted meanings and objectives of birth control deployed by Japanese feminists during the interwar period to show how motherhood became a primary site where the population discourse and feminism intertwined to reconstitute existing gender orders. Feminists Ishimoto Shizue and Yamakawa Kikue adopted Sanger's voluntary motherhood to link women's empowerment with women's free choice in reproduction and, more broadly, to associate motherhood with political subjectivity. Ironically, their solidarity in advocating birth control was built on the heterogenous nature of feminism. Their rationales for supporting women's reproductive autonomy differed from each other, essentially due to their differing views of gender differences.

Ishimoto's eugenic feminism illustrates the discursive convergence of maternal feminism, eugenics, and nationalism. Ishimoto put motherhood at the center of womanhood to normalize women's maternal role. While her belief echoed maternal feminist accounts of motherhood as a marker of natural differences between males and females, she reconfigured gender differences as a means to empower women instead of a predetermined obstacle. In her perspective, birth control was a political tool to improve women's agency—not because it would give women free choices to avoid having children, but because it would enable women to produce healthy children for the sake of the Japanese race. In this respect, Ishimoto envisioned women's political agency by re-gendering and racializing women. Yamakawa was fundamentally different from Ishimoto in that Yamakawa foregrounded socioeconomic aspects of gender difference. Her advocacy for birth control was a magnifying lens that reflected the double shackles on women under the patriarchal capitalist system, but it was also a weapon to be used for a "birth strike" against the oppressive system. Yamakawa's account of voluntary motherhood unsettled, if not invalidated, the gendered and classed rendering of motherhood and reclaimed women's subjectivity from "naturalized" femininity.

I began this chapter with a set of questions about the intersection of the population discourse, feminism, and the birth control movement in interwar Japan. The discussion of feminist birth control advocates presented us with heterogeneous feminist approaches to the issue of Japan's growing population. However, close scrutiny of this discussion reveals that both feminists rearticulated motherhood by placing reproduction in the broader context of modernity. In particular, both emphasized the importance of women's reproductive autonomy in ultimately addressing Japan's imperialistic expansion and militarism, capitalist exploitation, and patriarchal oppression, all of which are the symptoms of gendered modernity. In this light, these feminists' advocacy of voluntary motherhood was simultaneously their response to the masculine nature of modernity and the respective criticism of it to seek to reclaim women's subjectivity in the name of reproductive autonomy. Whereas the majority of contemporary birth control advocates, whether neo-Malthusianists or leftists, instrumentalized birth control to tackle what they deemed to be issues relating to imbalance caused by the (lack of) modern development, Ishimoto and Yamakawa created a unique discursive space to unveil hegemonic masculinity embodied by modern institutions—that is, nation, class, and family—and essentially reoriented the value of birth control toward women's autonomy. In this way, regardless of their different ideological visions, both Ishimoto and Yamakawa pushed the naturalized boundaries of gender norms to place motherhood at the center of the population discourse.

However, their pioneering role in advocating birth control and in promoting women's reproductive autonomy was in sharp conflict with the state's population policies. As seen in the next chapter, the government suppressed the birth control movement by issuing a new regulation to ban the sales and distribution of intracervical and intrauterine devices in 1930, which resulted in the arrest of prominent birth control activists such as midwife Shibahara Urako.[87] The wartime pronatalist policy even further limited the space for the birth control promotion. Under such suppressive circumstances, Ishimoto was eventually arrested in December 1937 for her political and birth control activities[88] while Yamakawa turned to less controversial subjects in her writing during the wartime period.[89] Their failure to expand the birth control movement due to the government's clampdown, however, does not necessarily mean a complete failure to fulfill their vision of voluntary motherhood. As will be discussed in Chapter 5, the wartime regime incorporated the feminist perspective of empowered motherhood into its population policies and mobilized the agency of mothers essentially to produce healthy human resources. The ironic resemblance between the interwar feminist approach to motherhood and the wartime state's policies around motherhood protection illuminates the growing importance of reproductive bodies to population governance.

THREE

Scientific and Imperialistic Solutions to Overpopulation

Solutions to the problem of knowledge are solutions to the problem of social order.

STEVEN SHAPIN and SIMON SCHAFFER,
Leviathan and the Air-Pump: Hobbes, Boyle, and the Experimental Life (1985)

The fundamental solution for Japan's population problem lies in recognizing all living beings in the nation as well as the society, achieving nationally and socially unified, transcendent goals, and fostering cooperation among citizens while holding control over them in order to complete the processes of democratization and socialization [shakaika]. The goals and duties of social policies center around ensuring democratic cooperation and social control to fulfill such social purposes and consummate the process of evolution. This is what I call a social-policy approach to the population problem. Explicitly put, it refers to a solution to the population problem based on the social-scientific [shakai kagaku-teki] laws of population as well as the sociological [shakaigaku-teki] or socio-psychological [shakai shinri-teki] laws of population. Put simply, it is a solution to the population problem based on the historical, social, and psychological laws of population. Such a solution differs from one based on the natural law of population or the socialist [shakaishugi-teki] laws of population.

NAGAI TŌRU, *Nihon jinkōron* [The study of the Japanese population] (1929); translation is mine

The Dawning of Governmentality in Japan

The previous chapters focused on Japanese birth control advocates who addressed the population problem from different angles. Neo-Malthusian reformers attributed the fundamental cause of social ills—namely, unemployment, poverty, and physical, mental, and moral deterioration—to overpopulation. Pro–birth control leftists and labor activists dismissed the idea of overpopulation as catering to the interests of the bourgeois class. They reframed birth control as a means of self-defense for the proletariat. Meanwhile, feminists who engaged in the birth control movement invariably prioritized the goals of women's empowerment and reproductive self-determination, regardless of their different ideological positions. These different patterns of the birth control movement during the interwar years, however, had much in common with views on eugenics and, essentially, favorable opinions of social and technological interventions into individual reproductive practices in order to materialize their own utopian alternatives to modernity.

This chapter turns to the roles of intellectuals in the development of population policies during the interwar period. Compared to birth control advocacy groups who had raised population issues since the late 1910s, the Japanese government belatedly took part in discussions regarding population issues in Japan proper. It was not until the late 1920s that the Japanese government began to adopt an all-encompassing approach to population problems and integrate population science into policymaking to address various social issues.

Against the backdrop of worldwide economic depression and the rise in agrarian and industrial disputes across the nation, leading scholars in economics, statistics, public policy, and sociology took the initiative in developing scientific research on a demographic phenomenon to which they linked socioeconomic conflicts occurring both domestically and internationally. Among those scholars in the different branches of social science, some pioneering researchers in "population science"—which I use here to highlight the scientific, extensive dimensions of knowledge produced by investigating various demographic phenomena—worked closely with the government since the 1920s.[1] These scholars formed a think tank for a government initiative to facilitate wide-ranging research on populations and to develop population policies, aiming for rational population governance.

It is worth noting that although both birth control advocates and think tank scholars acknowledged the need to control population growth and to enhance the quality of life on eugenic grounds, they differed significantly in the essential objectives of problematizing the Japanese population. As examined in the previous two chapters, birth control advocates unequivocally concurred about spreading adequate knowledge and methods of birth control among the masses to address various issues of modernity. For those advocates, birth control was a biological means of solving socioeconomic issues that were reductively referred to as the "population problem." In the meantime, the think tank social scientists were not only skeptical of the effectiveness of birth control in curbing population growth, but they also remained critical of the narrow definition of the population problem. The think tank scholars who mapped out the government's population policies foregrounded social scientific approaches to population phenomena in domestic and international contexts and developed scientific knowledge as guiding principles for population management instead of reducing their roles merely into problem solvers.

During the interwar war years, scholars in various fields of population science played an integral role in creating a blueprint for extensive population policies. Their blueprint based on population science aimed at regulating and managing multifaceted dimensions of population: population quantity and quality, density, fertility, mortality, nuptiality, the standard of living, public health, sanitation, employment, labor productivity, distribution of resources, food production and consumption, migration, and so forth. For the think tank scholars, a population was neither the origin of poverty nor the panacea for the evils of modernity. Rather, the population itself was an ultimate goal of governance; hence, it had to be problematized in multiple ways so as to ensure the rational governance of every dimension of the population.

Such an epistemological turn in the governance of population provides a revealing look at Foucault's theory of governmentality. With the notion of "governmentality," Foucault highlights a complex form of power that encompasses institutions, rationalities, and practices, and that primarily has "as its target population, as its principal form of knowledge political economy, and as its essential technical means apparatuses of security."[2] Through this new ensemble of modern political apparatuses that modified, if not entirely abolished, the preceding sovereignty mode, population became reconfigured as the end of the government for the first time in history.

This chapter will delve into three strands of inquiry, which will add concrete historical dynamics to Foucault's notion of governmentality and enrich the dialogue on intersecting modes of power: first, population both as a multifaceted problem and the target of governance; second, the roles of scholars who contributed to the making of both population science and population policies; and last, the intersection of governmentality and imperialism.

The goal of the first inquiry on population is to investigate how the interwar blueprint for population governance prepared for the governmentalization of the state, which eventually materialized during wartime with the establishment of Kosei-shō (Ministry of Health and Welfare) and a series of population policies under the total war regime. While the wartime population policies will be examined in detail in the next chapter, this chapter will focus on the construction of *population science*, which paved the way for the institutionalization of population governance. The close relationship between population science and population policy leads to the next point about the roles of social scientists who cooperated with the interwar government. The think tank scholars' emphasis on "scientific" approaches to population governance exemplifies the nexus between policy and science, that is, a process in which scientific knowledge and modern governance are *co-produced*.[3] Using the approach of science and technology studies to the co-production of science and policy, I will articulate the roles of the think tank scholars in legitimizing the "scientific" governance of the Japanese population, and further, the relationship between interwar population science and wartime population policies.[4] Lastly, my inquiry on the intersection between governmentality and imperialism is intended to critique the absence of a discussion about imperialist desires as intrinsic to the operation of biopolitical power in Foucault's account. The development of biopolitical rationalities and practices that may appear to center around a population within a domestic context, in fact, necessitates colonial populations and territories to ensure the well-being of the metropole population at the expense of colonized bodies.[5] As will be elaborated in this chapter, the growing ascendancy of settler colonialism as an outlet for the overpopulated metropole after the foundation of Manchukuo point to an imperialist solution to what Alison Bashford calls the "standing room only" issue, that is, Malthusian and Darwinian imaginaries of shrinking space for survival.[6] The entanglement of imperialist ambitions and population discourse as embodied in the Manchurian migration policy was not coincidental but instrumental in the biopolitical maintenance of the Japanese population.

In what follows, I will trace the development of population science and its visions for population governance. The principles laid out by the think tank scholars range from social scientific reconfigurations of population to the necessity of a permanent national institution to regulate and manage the Japanese population. The primary bodies that laid down such principles during the interwar period include Jinkō shokuryō mondai chōsakai (Population and Food Problems Investigation Committee), established in 1927 and dissolved in 1930, and Jinkō mondai kenkyūkai (Population Problem Research Society), established in 1933. In addition to these two governmental research organizations, this chapter will focus on leading scholars who mediated between population science and policy, including social policy expert Nagai Tōru (1878–1973), diplomat and agricultural economist Nitobe Inazō (1862–1933), and agricultural economist Nasu Shiroshi (1888–1984). These scholars led governmental institutions in their pursuit of scientific research on various population issues and designed a comprehensive agenda for population governance.

The Making of Population Science and Population Governance

The population problem had been a buzzword among intellectuals and social reformers since the late 1910s in Japan. Neo-Malthusian reformers such as Abe Isoo and Ishimoto Shizue initiated a public discussion about overpopulation in Japan. These reformers interpreted the extended economic downturn and growing social unrest after the end of the temporary economic boom during the First World War as being caused by surplus population. Malthus's theory on the imbalance between population growth and food supplies was rearticulated by these Japanese reformers who reduced a series of social and economic problems into the "population problem." Meanwhile, pro–birth control activists and intellectuals such as Yamamoto Senji and Yamakawa Kikue saw overpopulation as a relative term. For these leftist critics, the cause of pressing social problems, particularly rising unemployment and poverty in urban and rural areas, was irrelevant to an absolute population size.[7] Instead, the fault undoubtedly lay in a capitalist system. While dismissing overpopulation as a mere illusion, they identified the essential problem as capitalism, or more specifically as the inherent flaw of the capitalist system that perpetuated the unfair distribution of resources.

The debate on the Japanese population problem between sociologist Takata Yasuma (1883–1972) and Marxist economist Kawakami Hajime (1879–1946) in the mid-1920s is another pivotal event that shows different or even conflicting interpretations regarding the population problem. The debate was triggered when Takata published his paper "Umeyo fueyo" (Be fruitful and multiply) in 1926. In the paper, Takata claimed that the vital issue at stake was the decrease in birth rates in Japan, foregrounding the value of population as the source of national power.[8] In opposition to both Malthusianism and Marxism, Takata adhered to a distinct view on what constituted the population problem while advocating for lowering the nationwide standard of living to address poverty.[9] Meanwhile, Kawakami Hajime criticized Takata's account of overpopulation in his article "Jinkō mondai hihan shūi" (Addendum: Critiques of the population problem) published in the same year, arguing that Takata's denialism resorted to exploiting wage workers further only to cater to capitalists' interests.[10] Moreover, Kawakami rebutted the ongoing neo-Malthusian discussions that reductively associated Japan's rapid population growth or high population density with the shortage of food resources. Taking a Marxist approach to the population problem, Kawakami claimed that "overpopulation is a product of capitalism that reached a dead end" and emphasized the historical, relative nature of the surplus population in a capitalist society due to immensely enhanced productivity.[11]

The debate between Takata and Kawakami in the late 1920s illuminates their different underlying views on the population problem. Whereas Takata put the survival of the Japanese nation to the fore from his ethnonationalistic approach to the conception of the Japanese population, Kawakami defined the population as a social construct and in a similar vein, identified the population problem with the essential feature of capitalism.[12] Scholarly debates on essentially how to problematize the Japanese population had ensued for nearly two decades, as a group of social scientists including Yanaihara Tadao, Ueda Teijirō, Minami Ryōzaburō, Ōuchi Hyōe, and Yoshida Hideo resituated the persistent Malthusian-Marxist debate in the contemporary context of Japan and took their discussions further into how to translate Japan's distinctive demographic trends into scientific knowledge.[13]

While a group of leading economists and sociologists developed various theoretical—that is, Malthusian, Marxian, synthetic, and nationalist—approaches to the Japanese population problem, Tanaka Giichi's new administration created Jinkō shokuryō mondai chōsakai, (Population and Food Problems Investigation Committee, hereinafter referred as PFIC) in July 1927.[14] The foundation of the PFIC as a research institute directly responsible to the cabinet was the first step toward conducting scientific research on the Japanese population under the government's leadership. Although the PFIC remained a temporary body, it played an initiating role in outlining the primary agenda of population policies from 1927 to 1930. The PFIC was largely divided into two parts: Jinkō-bu (Department of Population) and Shokuryō-bu (Department of Food). Both consisted of bureaucrats, politicians, businesspeople, and scholars in a range of academic disciplines including sociology, labor economics, social policies, animal science, agricultural chemistry, agricultural economics, and education.[15] As an advisory group to the government, the members of the PFIC created a bridge between research and policies.

As its name suggests, the PFIC was primarily in charge of investigating the pressing issues related to population growth and food security. Given a marked lack of consensus in social and intellectual realms regarding the definition of the population problem, it is worth looking closely into how the PFIC reconfigured the population problem in their own way. Nagai Tōru, a leading researcher of the Department of Population, along with agricultural economist and diplomat Nitobe Inazō and economist and professor at Tokyo Higher Commercial School (today's Hitotsubashi University) Fukuda Tokuzō, provides a revealing glimpse into the committee's idiosyncratic view, not only of the population problem but more fundamentally of population itself.

> Population problems in a nation lie in whether or not its society enhanced its productive forces sufficiently to sustain the population. A society, formed by its ethnic nation [*minzoku*], is divided regionally, and natural resources available in each region—both surface and subsurface resources—determine the productivity of the society. Productivity is also regulated by social organizations formed among the people, particularly economic organizations. In addition, other factors such as national mentality and social traditions combine to condition and determine productivity. In this light, population problems not merely arise between the productivity of society as a whole and the size of the population who composes the society. The causes and conditions of the population problems also lie in different factors such as natural resources, social organizations, and national mentality.[16]

As an economist specializing in social policy, Nagai shed new light on the complexity of the population problem in society. The complex causes of the problem included environmental and socioeconomic structures, national productivity, and characteristics of a population, all of which combined to affect social relations and economic practices. Nagai's distinctive view of the population problem is also salient in his critique of both Malthusian and Marxian framings of the problem. Despite ostensible differences between the two groups, Nagai pointed out that neither Malthusian nor Marxist advocates penetrated the essence of the population problem but merely replaced the problem with something secondary. While Malthusians equated the problem with food resource issues or simply poverty under the rubric "overpopulation," Marxists reduced the problem to unemployment by employing the reductive law of the relation between wage labor and capital.[17] Instead, Nagai turned to "social scientific" (*shakai kagaku-teki*) or "sociological" (*shakaigaku-teki*) approaches to population.[18] His emphasis on the social complexity of the population problem marks a sharp break from both Malthus's absolute law of population and Marx's ideological critique of capitalism.[19]

The reframing of the population problem as a set of complex social problems was groundbreaking in two senses: First, addressing the population problem no longer meant removing a single cause of the problem—whether the cause was overpopulation or capitalist exploitation. Instead, the population *per se* became the target of government. In other words, the population had to be problematized in multiple ways and intervened by bureaucratic, scientific, and technological apparatuses so that it could be managed at an optimal level. It was imperative for Nagai to use "population problems" in the plural to indicate a wide range of elements in human lives—from the tangible to the intangible and from the environmental to the biological. Second, insofar as population "problems" occur due to complex social relations, each society has its own problems that are different from those of other societies. Nagai highlighted the nation-state as a necessary condition for a society to exist. He argued that "contemporary population problems normally concern the entire society within a nation-state—meaning, the state comprised of a certain ethnic society [*minzoku shakai*]—and its ethnic nation [*minzoku*] or citizens [*kokumin*]."[20] For Nagai, insofar as a society's border was drawn along the national border, the population problems had to be demarcated along its national territorial line. In other words, the presence of the national border was a precondition for the theory of the Japanese population problem to exist.

Nagai's ideas for reframing the population problem were crystallized in the PFIC. Nagai participated in the special committee formed within the Department of Population to draft investigation reports on a range of population issues from 1927 to 1930. The special committee comprised of social scientists (Nagai Tōru, Fukuda Tokuzō, Ueda Teijirō, and Nasu Shiroshi), bureaucrats (Nitobe Inazō), physicians (Nagai Hisomu), politicians (Fujimura Yoshirō), and businesspeople (Shimomura Hiroshi and Inoue Masaji). Among them, Nagai took the lead in drafting investigation reports for the Department of Population submitted to the government.[21] Given Nagai's crucial role in formulating the primary agenda of the PFIC and drafting reports for submission to the government, it is no exaggeration to say that the agenda and activities of the committee were closely aligned with Nagai's interest in the sociological framing of the Japanese population. The special committee of the Department of Population prepared a total of eight official reports on a wide range of population problems in both Japan proper and its colonies. The subjects of the official reports are as follows: (1) domestic and overseas migration policy, (2) the control of supply and demand for labor, (3) population policies outside Japan proper, (4) population control measures, (5) increases in productivity, (6) the distribution of resources for living and the rationalization of consumption, (7) the establishment of a permanent body for the investigation of population problems, and (8) the establishment of Shakai-shō (Ministry of Social Affairs).[22]

Among the varied pressing issues and solutions proposed by the Population Department, the report on population control measures ("Jinkō tōsei ni kansuru sho hōsaku") embodied an effort to integrate different modes of knowledge needed for the government of the population. In the preliminary drafting process, Nagai Tōru and Nagai Hisomu submitted their individual report to the special committee. Whereas Nagai Tōru highlighted the need to implement social policies and improve public hygiene to address the problem of high fecundity and high mortality in Japan, eugenicist Nagai Hisomu outlined the government's active approaches to marriage and birth control to improve the quality of the Japanese population. Based on these two versions, Fukuda drafted the final report that incorporated both social policy–oriented approaches and eugenic intervention to the population problem to improve people's living conditions and "thereby create a healthy population both in quantity and quality."[23] In the final version of the report, the committee made the following suggestions to tackle pressing population issues in Japan.

1. To put efforts in advancing social hygiene and improving national health to prevent tuberculosis

2. To put extra efforts in improving hygiene and health-related facilities in both rural areas and workers' residential districts in urban areas

3. To promote physical training among women and improve women's nutrition levels

4. To give guidelines to working women on public hygiene

5. To spare no effort to protect female and young workers and to prevent child labor exploitation

6. To increase general social facilities for the protection of motherhood and childrearing

7. To establish appropriate facilities to provide medical consultations regarding marriage, childbirth, and contraception

8. To regulate illegal activities related to the distribution, sale, and advertisement of devices and medicines for contraception

9. To research on various facilities relevant to eugenics[24]

The PFIC diagnosed Japan's population problems by adopting the language of modern scientific disciplines that valorized specific ways of problematizing a population. The abovementioned suggestions indicate that the scholars involved in the PFIC situated the population problem at the nexus of statistics, medicine, labor science, public and home hygiene, nutrition science, and eugenics. These different branches of modern knowledge determined particular ways in which the population was problematized rather than merely functioning as a toolkit for analyzing the actual problems. Among the demographic challenges to which the PFIC closely attended, high fecundity and high mortality were defined as distinctively Japanese problems by the PFIC researchers. They employed statistical data on the Japanese population to demonstrate Japan's relatively high fecundity and mortality issues compared to major European countries, which presumably affected other demographic indicators such as low life expectancy and low working-age population ratio. All these demographic indicators highlighted peculiar patterns of the Japanese population that were not only different from other nation-states, but also legitimized the state's control of its population to address its national issue.

Therefore, the notion of "population control" in the title of the report did not necessarily refer to measures for decreasing the population size. The PFIC proposed multiple scientific measures for population control, which indicates their synthetic, knowledge-based approach to the lives of the Japanese people. According to the report on population control, recommended measures ranged from developing hygiene infrastructure and public welfare services to improving individual physical and reproductive health. These various measures to integrate social reforms with biological betterment and associate individuals' health with the quality of population as a whole embody "governmentality." With this notion, Foucault highlights the purposes of modern government as "the welfare of the population, the improvement of its condition, the increase of its wealth, longevity, health, etc."[25] In other words, the primary role of the modern state lies in the meticulous governance of a population. The report on the population control measures was the blueprint for the government of the Japanese population—more specifically, for regulating, managing, and optimizing the lives of the Japanese population in order to meet its ultimate aims: to "create a healthy Japanese population both in quality and quantity."[26]

The target population for the state control was not only *nationalized* but essentially *gendered*. Women's physical and reproductive health was of particular concern in the blueprint for the government of the Japanese population. As indicated in the report on population control measures, the PFIC showed great interest in improving women's physical and reproductive health as a primary source of the health of the Japanese population. The production of motherhood and female workers and the improvement in women's health and nutrition are strongly reminiscent of the contemporary feminist and birth control advocates' discussions in interwar Japan. However, the gendered dimension of this government blueprint was distant from the radical voices in the social sector, as marked by the fact that the PFIC researchers maintained a defensive attitude toward birth control.

The two main reasons for their skeptical, if not entirely hostile, view are worth noting. First, their aim was neither decreasing birth rates nor reducing the population size but decreasing mortality by improving socioeconomic conditions. The second reason, which is not irrelevant to the first, is that the scholars in the PFIC stressed the welfare of the population and their physical and mental health. Unlike the birth control advocates who defined women's bodies merely as a means of controlling population size and improving population quality, the PFIC's scholars regarded women's health as the target of the government itself in the assumption that women's reproductive health determines the overall health of the nation. Nagai Tōru's cautious approach to the use of birth control exemplifies such viewpoints. In the preliminary draft of the report on population control, Nagai argued that since birth control was merely a stopgap measure, there must be more fundamental ways of controlling the quantity and quality of the population in order to address Japan's unique demographic issues such as high birth rates and death rates, and high marriage rates and divorce rates. Nagai highlighted the role of the state in regulating, if not completely prohibiting, the use of contraceptive measures to prevent potential adverse outcomes and ultimately to ensure the health and welfare of the population. By the same logic, the PFIC attempted to limit the use of birth control to only eugenic grounds or hereditary reasons, and apply stringent restrictions on the illegitimate sale and promotion of contraceptives.[27] The latter idea came to fruition when the Home Ministry issued the Harmful Contraceptive Devices Control Regulation in 1930.[28] On the other hand, the former idea concerning eugenics became incorporated into the National Eugenic Law enacted in 1940, as discussed in Chapter 4.

Considering this, the PFIC not only laid the groundwork for the reframing of population problems but also reconfigured a population itself. The health and welfare of the Japanese population became a high priority in the goal of population governance. In addition, a population as the object of state control was inherently gendered due to the reconfigured link between women's reproductive health and the health of the nation. Building on these presumptions, the PFIC stated that population problems, or the effects of various state apparatuses for problematizing the lives of its people, must be addressed by each nation-state on the basis of a comprehensive understanding of its peculiar population patterns. Hence, for the researchers in the PFIC, long-term, scientific research of various demographic phenomena and research-based policies to govern its population rationally were the two most crucial principles to be implemented at the state level. Among the Department of Population's reports, a report on the establishment of a permanent body for the investigation of population problems particularly stressed such principles. Since the PFIC was set to expire by the end of March 1930, leading researchers on the committee explored ways to carry out the initiative to increase the state's roles and advance scientific knowledge on the *nationalized* and *gendered* dimensions of the population.

Ironically, the blueprint for nation-oriented—thus, *Japanizing*—knowledge and policies for population governance reflected an international trend toward foregrounding scientific research on populations in its time. The birth of the International Union for the Scientific Investigation of Population Problems (hereinafter referred to as IUSIPP) in 1928 was a milestone event in the growing international cooperation for accumulating demographic data and integrating scientific knowledge into the governance of populations.[29]

The IUSIPP was first conceived at the World Population Conference in Geneva (1927) where the League of Nations and leading birth control activist Margaret Sanger discussed the need for a permanent organization for international cooperation in the scientific investigation of population problems. The resolution on an international research institution came to fruition in the following year with the establishment of the IUSIPP. The initial members of the IUSIPP comprised of twelve nations, including Belgium, Denmark, France, Great Britain, Greece, Holland, Italy, South America (as a whole), Spain, Sweden, Switzerland, and the United States. Raymond Pearl (1879–1940), an American biologist who developed a research program focused on human population biology at Johns Hopkins University, was elected as the first president. As articulated in its statutes, the IUSIPP aimed to promote "international cooperation" to initiate scientific research on populations and to establish "common standards for the collection, tabulation, and analysis of data regarding human populations, including not only demographic, but also agricultural, economic, sociologic, and biologic data in the broadest sense."[30]

Both the title of the organization and its statutes clearly demonstrate that the IUSIPP sought a scientific approach to the investigation of each nation's population issues and "international" benchmarks for such scientific knowledge. The two key notions, namely *scientific* and *international*, that remain undefined in the ISUIPP's documents, are worth noticing as both terms were situated in their historical context. The term "science" encompassed different forms of knowledge, including sociology, economics, agriculture, demographics, and biology, and, more importantly, embodied the neutrality of modern knowledge as opposed to "religious, moral, or political discussion" of population problems.[31] Meanwhile, scientific data of each nation's demographic phenomenon was assumed to function as raw data for the *inter-national* collection of national population issues, which reiterates an inherently nation-based approach to a population as emphasized by the PFIC. The IUSIPP's vision reaffirms the consensus among population scientists worldwide to normalize extensive scientific investigations of population phenomena at both national and international levels.

Agricultural economist, diplomat, and politician Nitobe Inazō paid great attention to this growing international cooperation for facilitating the scientific study of populations. After having studied at the Sapporo Agricultural College, Johns Hopkins University, and later, the University of Halle in Germany, Nitobe pioneered the fields of agricultural economics and colonial studies (*shokumingaku*) in Japan beginning early in the twentieth century. Starting in 1903, he lectured on colonial developments and policies at the Kyoto Imperial University, and in 1906, at the Tokyo

Imperial University where he taught Yanaihara Tadao, who eventually assumed Nitobe's position as professor of colonial studies at Tokyo University. The establishment of the League of Nations in 1920 marked a turning point in Nitobe's career from a scholar to a diplomat. He served as the under-secretary general of the League of Nations for six years since 1920. After he retired from the position at the League of Nations, Nitobe returned to Japan and became a member of the House of Peers while also serving as the Japanese chairman of the Institute of Pacific Relations (IPR) until his sudden death in 1933.[32]

Nitobe's involvement in the PFIC as a member of a population science think tank in the Japanese government lies at the intersection of his scholarship and political career. Utilizing his expertise in the studies of colonial governance and internationalism, Nitobe took the initiative to establish a permanent organization for scientific research about the Japanese population and proposed developing a liaison between the permanent organization and the IUISSP in support of the IUISSP's internationalist approach to population science. In his recommendation to the government, submitted in February in 1928, Nitobe stressed the necessity for an academic institution consisting of experts in demographic research to contribute to communicating with the IUISSP and resolving domestic population problems.[33] The Department of Population officially adopted Nitobe's suggestion and submitted a proposal to establish a standing research institution to the Hamaguchi cabinet in January 1930. According to the proposal, the primary purposes of the permanent organization centered on extensive scientific investigations and activities on the Japanese population, including basic demographic research, scientific research on population control, investigation of solutions to population problems, theoretical studies of the population and its related problems, presentations and publications about research findings, lectures on population issues, and the appointment of Japanese delegates to the IUISPP.[34] Although the Hamaguchi cabinet approved the proposal and brought it to the Imperial Diet to assess the budget, the plan for a standing population research institute fell through due to the political turmoil in the early 1930s.[35] As discussed later in this chapter, it was not until 1933 that Nitobe's initiative was actually implemented. After securing funds from both the government and private sectors, Jinkō mondai kenkyūkai (Population Problem Research Society, hereinafter referred as PPRS) was founded as a quasi-private organization.

The continuity between the PFIC and the PPRS lay in the long-term pursuit of scientific investigations on population problems. The PFIC's leading researchers—including Nagai Tōru, Ueda Teijirō, and Nasu Shiroshi—continued to serve as researchers in the PPRS to undertake sociological and scientific research on population issues. Although having received private funds, the PPRS still mediated between population policies and population science. However, changing domestic and international political conditions beginning in the early 1930s played a considerable role in designing and implementing population policies. In particular, in terms of potential sources of food and land supply for Japanese settlement, the Manchurian Incident of 1931 and the establishment of Manchukuo in 1932 as the puppet state of the Japanese empire created new conditions for the population problems in Japan proper.

The changing geopolitical landscape begs the following questions: How did the scholars in population science view Japan's growing colonial expansionism into Manchuria? What were the impacts of the territorial and economic expansion of the Japanese colonial empire on the population policies in the metropole? To what degree did the scientific blueprint for population control reckon with the Japanese colonies? Or simply, were the colonized peoples under Japanese rule considered the target of the government, namely, a *population*? In what follows, I will delve into the intersection between governmentality and imperialism by focusing on the scholars' changing ideas of population policies in the 1930s. By focusing on Nitobe's conception of Japan's colonial expansion, I will first explore how population scientists conceived the roles of Japan's colonies in resolving the population problems in Japan proper before the Manchurian crisis arose. I will then proceed to examine the remaking of population policies after the founding of Manchukuo in 1932 to illuminate the complexity of executing the blueprint for the "governmentalization" of the Japanese state.

The Political Dilemma of Population Science

Despite controversy over the definition of the population problem, the increase in the absolute population numbers in Japan proper had been an undeniable fact from the late Meiji period onward. According to the national census, the population of Japan proper had grown by more than 700,000 to 800,000 every year since 1926. Ueda Teijirō, professor of economics at Tokyo Higher Commercial School, estimated that the population in Japan proper would increase from 60 million in the late 1920s to 90 million in the late 1950s, given the consistent tendency of the population to grow.[36] Moreover, a high population density in relation to insufficient arable land in Japan was another pressing concern for those who demanded scientific population policies. Ueda argued for industrial and commercial development as imperative to addressing the issue of high population density.[37] Although proposed solutions varied, researchers in population science essentially shared a view that Japan's rapid population growth and high population pressure should be tackled from a socioeconomic angle. Nasu Shiroshi, Ueda's fellow researcher at the PFIC and professor of agricultural economics at Tokyo Imperial University, also stressed the increase in agricultural and industrial productivity and the promotion of Japanese emigration to relieve population pressure in Japan proper.[38] Socioeconomic solutions to the high population density marked a departure from the Malthusian theory of population. Put another way, population growth was no longer an inexorable law of nature but a social condition to be addressed by institutional interventions.

Among various possible solutions to population growth and the high population density in Japan proper, emigration (*imin*) was often debated in the 1920s. The Immigration Act of 1924 in the United States that effectively banned all immigration from Asia created a new challenge for Japan.[39] As the American outlet for Japan's overflowing population was blocked amid growing anti-Asian racism, destinations for Japanese emigrants were largely limited to the Japanese empire's spheres of influence, particularly North China and the islands of the South Seas (Nan'yō), and to Latin America.[40] Immediately after the PFIC was founded in 1927, the think tank scholars launched an investigation into the economic and demographic conditions of Japan's colonies and foreign territories under military occupation to determine the effectiveness of emigration for relieving the population problems in Japan.[41] The 1927 report titled "Naichi igai sho chihō ni okeru jinkō taisaku" (Population solutions outside of Japan proper) provides a glimpse into the think tank scholars' initially negative outlook on Japanese emigration. In the report, the PFIC researchers articulated the practical difficulty of promoting mass emigration and the risk of fomenting instability in native societies in Japan's colonies.[42] The statistical data on the number of Japanese immigrants in Japan's official colonies suggested that colonies heretofore failed to absorb surplus population in the metropole. In colonial Korea, for example, despite long-term efforts by the Government-General of Korea and Tōyō takushoku kabushiki gaisha (Oriental Development Company) to encourage Japanese farmers to settle in the Korean peninsula after the annexation, the number of Japanese settlers increased by merely 17,000 per year and reached a total number of 440,000 as of 1926.[43] Likewise, as of 1926, the number of Japanese settlers in colonial Taiwan was 180,000, out of which only 4,000 settlers were farmers; the rest were either directly or indirectly involved in the government of Taiwan.[44] The fact that the colonies had not heretofore functioned as an outlet for the Japanese labor population, due to differences in the standards of living and labor costs between the metropole and colonies, was obvious proof that buttressed their pessimistic projection on emigration.[45]

Given these practical barriers to encouraging Japanese migration to the colonies, the PFIC researchers concluded that the role of the colonies in resolving the population problems in the metropole should be limited to an increase in Japan's productivity and the use of available resources through the development and utilization of economic resources in the colonies. The following comments in the report sum up the PFIC's preference for colonial economic development over mass emigration.

> There are many factors that need to be carefully considered with regards to population problems in territories outside of Japan proper, particularly Chōsen [sic] and Taiwan. The population problems in exterior territories cannot be overlooked; not only because of their effects on the population problems in Japan proper, but also because planting [ishoku] many Japanese people in the territories outside Japan proper might cause insecurity among local people, and in fact, mass settlement is impossible to fulfill. Moreover, the goal of taking measures for population policies in other territories such as Manchuria, Mongolia, Siberia, and the South Islands is not to curb Japanese population growth but to improve national productivity through reclaiming land, developing natural resources, and advancing industries in those territories.[46]

The PFIC researchers' skepticism about Japanese settlement in the colonies speaks to the fundamental question around various forms of colonialism. In particular, the question of whether the colonies ought to be integrated into the Japanese colonial empire only as a resource provider or as a destination for long-term settlement became a crucial factor to be addressed in developing population control measures in Japan proper. Drawing upon Robert Young's accounts of types of colonialism, the former type of colonies is referred to as "exploitation colonies" in which "trade, resource extraction, or port facilities were primary." In contrast, the latter type of colonies points to "settler colonies" in which the colonizers permanently settle in with political and cultural baggage from the metropole.[47] Whether an empire pursues exclusively economic exploitation from its colony or seeks to convert a colonial territory into a settlement for colonizers is historically contingent. Yet, such division in the concept of colonialism should not blind us to the fact that colonies were indispensable for solving the population problems facing Japan proper. The PFIC researchers' justification for prioritizing economic development in the colonies over Japanese colonial migration hardly reflects anti-imperialism. On the contrary, their idea of associating colonial development with population control in the metropole exemplifies biopolitical rationales for imperial expansion. In other words, the scholars upheld imperialism by making the growth of the Japanese colonial empire essential for the population's survival in the metropole.

Nitobe was an especially prominent figure who opposed settler colonialism while acknowledging the importance of Japan's colonial expansion in relieving the population problems. As a founder of colonial studies, or the scientific study of the principles of the colonial government, Nitobe lectured on the evolving system of colonial rules at the Tokyo Imperial University. In his view, the terrain of colonial policies ranged from political and militarist expansion into foreign territories to the diffusion of advanced cultural values to the colonized peoples. His well-known phrase "colonialism is the spread of civilization" (*shokumin wa bunmei no denpa*) reflects his firm belief in colonization as a civilizing mission to be fulfilled in Japanese colonies.[48]

Although the ways in which Nitobe justified imperialist expansion appear to be couched in the language of social Darwinism, he by no means advocated militaristic nationalism. From his holistic approach to international relations, Nitobe maintained that colonization is a nation's self-assertion and that "the international mind is the expansion of the national."[49] This suggests that, in his view, imperialism is part and parcel of the international order that harmoniously and peacefully accommodates different powers' desire to expand. Nitobe's idealistic viewpoint about internationalism, or "the coordination of many powers of mind—of intellect, emotion and will" by his definition, not simply endorsed imperialism but legitimized it as a valid principle of international order.[50] In the same vein, Nitobe noted that although social Darwinist doctrine already prevailed among the nineteenth-century Western powers that rationalized colonial expansions, international order manifested in international legal and diplomatic practices made colonial expansions legitimate in the twentieth century.[51] Given that, imperialism and internationalism were harmoniously embedded in Nitobe's view of geopolitical relations.

While Nitobe firmly justified colonization under the rubrics of civilization and internationalism, the question as to which form of colonial expansion Japan should adopt remained debatable. For Nitobe, the high population density and resultant social issues in Japan proper were indispensable factors to be considered in shaping the policies of colonial government. Although colonization (*shokumin*) originally referred to "planting people," Nitobe often conveyed skepticism about settler colonies as the preferred option for the Japanese empire. There were essentially two reasons for Nitobe's opposition to Japanese settlement in the colonies: his critical view of Malthusian overpopulation concerns and the infeasibility of a mass migration large enough to solve social problems in the metropole. The former reason was undergirded by many examples of what European nations had done: for instance, Belgium, with a relatively small population, still colonized Congo in pursuit of its commercial interests; or Italy and Ireland, which, because of their high population density, became countries that sent migrants, mainly to the United States, at the turn of the twentieth century. Nitobe used these European cases as references to support his point that there was no essential link between overpopulation and colonization.[52] With regard to the second reason, Nitobe noted that the promotion of Japanese settlement in the colonized territories was only a temporary and passive measure that proved ineffective in relieving the Japanese people of the population pressure in Japan proper. Nitobe's persistent skepticism about the promotion of colonial settlements is well exemplified in his statement at the IPR Conference in 1929 that "emigration afforded no possible aid to the nation's problem."[53]

If settler colonialism was not the ideal solution for Japan's multifaceted population issues, what did Nitobe envision as a way of tackling the population issues? Throughout his long-term career as an expert in colonial studies, Nitobe prioritized economic development in the colonies over establishing Japanese settlements. Moreover, his experience as a colonial officer serving for the Government-General in Taiwan in the 1900s provided him with an opportunity to lead successful colonial government policies. During his stay in Taiwan, Nitobe initiated a series of economic development policies ranging from the industrialization and mechanization of sugar production to market expansion for the sugar trade. Nitobe's efforts to promote the sugar industry influenced his thoughts on the principles of colonial government. One of the principles was that the process of integrating the economy of the colonies into that of the empire—by investing capital, reforming agriculture, rationalizing production, exploiting native resources and workers—was crucial for Japan proper to overcome the limits of productivity and sustain the livelihoods of its population.[54] In his view, colonization was a part of the economic planning of the metropole and, more fundamentally, its population policies.[55]

The idea of integrating colonial development policies into the population policies of Japan proper did not remain a minority view but was reflected in the reports of the PFIC and resonated with Nitobe's contemporaries. As shown above, the report on population solutions outside of Japan proper outlined an agenda for developing resources in colonial and foreign territories. The priority goal of developing Japan's colonies and semi-colonies was to sustain the Japanese population or even advance their lives in the metropole while the living conditions of the colonized populations were largely ignored. The 1929 report titled "Seisanryoku zōshin ni kansuru tōshin-an" (Report on Productivity Growth) also included an agenda for increasing the supply of natural resources both in domestic and foreign territories, which echoed the idea of incorporating colonial economic structures into imperial governmentality.[56]

Meanwhile, Yanaihara Tadao (1893–1961), who was a disciple of Nitobe at Tokyo Imperial University and followed in his footsteps by assuming the chair in colonial policy between 1923 and 1937, held a similar view and echoed Nitobe's solutions for the population problems in the metropole. Inspired by Marxist thoughts, Yanaihara emphasized that the central issue of the population problems lay in unemployment while criticizing the Malthusian concern about food supply as a fear-mongering tactic. Although Yanaihara took account into various possible options for relieving the population problems in Japan, ranging from industrial and technological development to Japanese emigration or settlement in the colonies, he concluded that the primary solution was the improvement of socioeconomic systems. Notably, in regard to the human mobility within the Japanese empire, Yanaihara noted that emigration had limited effects on the decrease in the absolute population size, and furthermore immigrants from the colonies outnumbered Japanese emigrants. Yanaihara's initially skeptical attitude toward the promotion of emigration and settlement in the colonies as a feasible solution for population problems culminated in his opposition to the mass migration program to Manchuria in the mid-1930s.[57]

In September 1931, the Kwantung Army invaded Manchuria following the Mukden (Manchurian) Incident. The Japanese military operations in Manchuria lasted more than a year and resulted in the founding of the puppet state of Manchukuo in February 1932. The continued aggressive policy and military operations in the Manchurian region in the early 1930s put Nitobe, who had foregrounded international cooperation while denying Japan's interest in colonizing Manchuria and Mongolia, in a troubling position. Between 1932 and 1933, he traveled throughout the United States on a lecture tour, en route to the IPR conference in Alberta, Canada. A series of lectures Nitobe gave to American audiences reveal the dilemma between his long-term aspirations for internationalism and the growing military expansionism in his home country. Despite this newly unfolding conflict in Manchuria, however, the question of incorporating the economic resources of the colonies into the government schemes for population control in the homeland remained unproblematic. In one of his lectures given in 1932, Nitobe's comment about Manchuria as the "lifeline of Japan" reveals his persistent effort to justify the fact that imperialism was essential for the lives of the Japanese population:[58]

> I have said, over and over again, that unless Japan can develop industries, she cannot exist. In the country itself there are not sufficient materials for industry, little coal, less iron, and a very small amount of oil. All these are found in abundance in Manchuria, and Japanese capital has developed the mines. Then, even for the prosperity of our agricultural industry, we must import fertilizers, and the best of them, soya bean cakes, are obtainable in Manchuria. This is why that region is called *the lifeline of Japan*.[59]

As discussed earlier, Japanese think tank scholars in population science prioritized colonial development to support the Japanese population in the metropole while the promotion of settlement colonies remained a contentious issue into the early 1930s. Although Japanese settlers did exist in Japan's overseas colonies (*gaichi*), primarily Taiwan and Korea, those imperial subalterns were by no means the product of institutional mobilizations but predominantly self-motivated entrepreneurs whose ties with the metropole and colonial administrations remained insufficiently established.[60] The creation of Manchukuo in 1932 marked a watershed in the discourse of population problems in Japan. The utopian image of Manchuria as fertile soil for Japanese settlers and as an outlet for an overflowing Japanese population gained ascendancy throughout the 1930s due to the impact of the Manchurian settlement campaign. How did researchers in population science respond to this new frontier? How did the establishment of Manchukuo create a new condition for Japan's population policies? With a focus on the PPRS, the next section delves into the remaking of population policies after the founding of Manchukuo.

Agrarian Imperialism and Revitalized Malthusian Rhetoric

The early 1930s was a turbulent period in Japan in both political and economic terms. The domestic political scene in Japan proper witnessed a succession of short-lived cabinets due to the growing military influence and the instability of the parliamentary system that symbolized the end of the so-called Taishō Democracy. Hamaguchi Osachi, who served as prime minister between March and April in 1931, was shot by a member of an ultranationalist secret society and forced to resign due to severe injuries. Wakatsuki Reijirō, who replaced Hamaguchi, was ineffective in controlling the military and eventually resigned after serving as prime minister for merely seven months. For another six months, from December 1931 to May 1932, Inukai Tsuyoshi was in office, but he also failed to control the growing power of the military. After Inukai was assassinated, Saitō Makoto, a former admiral in the Imperial Japanese Navy, served as prime minister from May 1932 to July 1934. From then, the cabinets were taken over mostly by military men until the end of the Asia-Pacific War.[61] In the meantime, the rise in militarism was more evident in international politics. A series of Japan's militarist and imperialist moves—ranging from Japanese territorial expansion into Manchuria in 1931 to the creation of Manchukuo in 1932 to Japan's withdrawal from the League of Nations in 1933—opened a rapid path toward Pan-Asianism, an imperialist vision that would replace internationalism.

Meanwhile, the Japanese economy between 1930 and 1932 was shaken by the repercussions of the worldwide Great Depression. In particular, the rural economy was more vulnerable than were urban industrial sectors due to the sharp decline in agricultural prices and income levels. For instance, compared to 1926, rice prices dropped by 50 percent in 1931, and annual agricultural income per household fell from 1,162 to 414 yen. In addition, sericulture was one of the most damaged parts of the Japanese rural economy during this period due to the sharp decline in demand for Japanese silk. The prices of raw silk dropped by one third between 1925 and 1929, and by another one third in 1931 alone. Therefore, rural problems (*nōson mondai*) emerged as a significant issue to be addressed during the Shōwa Depression.[62]

It was against this backdrop of political and economic turmoil that the PPRS was founded through cooperation between the government and private sectors. As mentioned above, the original decision to establish a standing research institution for the study of population problems was made in 1931 under the Hamaguchi cabinet. A series of replacements for the prime minister since then, however, impeded a budgetary allocation for the founding of the research institute. After three years of delays, the institute was finally founded with private funds on October 27, 1933, under the military government led by former admiral Saitō Makoto. The birth of the PPRS was an outcome of cooperation between the state, private, and academic sectors. The Home Ministry proposed the bill to form a research organization, while private foundations funded it by giving it 2,000 yen in the first year of its establishment. Its members included governmental elites who were previously involved in the PFIC, such as Nagai Tōru, Ueda Teijirō, Nasu Shiroshi, statistician and politician Yanagisawa Yasutoshi, and businessperson Inoue Masaji. Under the leadership of the first chairman Yanagisawa, the PPRS was involved in a wide array of activities: investigations of population problems and possible solutions, holding public lectures, publishing an official organ titled *Jinkō mondai* (Population problem), and attending international population conferences such as the IUISPP conference in Berlin in 1935.[63] The researchers of the PPRS served as a bridge between the government and academia and between policies and science through a variety of knowledge-producing activities.

It should be noted that the rise of militarism and the protracted economic crisis in the early 1930s, on both the domestic and international scenes, impacted the purpose of the PPRS. Although the PPRS carried on the legacy of the PFIC to pursue scientific and comprehensive research of population problems, there was a notable difference between the two organizations in the scope of their investigations. In contrast to the PFIC that maintained its negative outlook toward Japanese emigration and settlement in the colonies, its successor favorably considered the emigration and settlement option as a promising solution to the multifaceted population problems facing the metropole. Yanagisawa's speech at the first public lecture of the PPRS, held in Tokyo in December 1933, exemplifies the shifting opinion on Japan's colonial expansions. In his opening speech, Yanagisawa highlighted the two main goals of the PPRS from domestic and international standpoints: on the one hand, the PPRS pursued scientific investigations of solutions to population problems and general demographic phenomena; on the other, the PPRS sought to investigate colonial policies that would promote Japanese emigration and settlement into the colonies and contribute to the growth of the Japanese race.[64] Yanagisawa's idea of associating the metropole's population problems with colonial settlement policies marked a sharp departure from the previously dominant skepticism about colonization among the think tank researchers.

The increasing support among the PPRS researchers for emigration and settlement in colonial territories is also reflected in the scope and content of their investigations. In pursuit of the extensive study of population problems and their optimum solutions, the PPRS subdivided its research projects into five categories: demographic trends and their impact on industries; the distribution of population and agricultural resources; overpopulation and employment; emigration; and population control. For each subject, a team was responsible for undertaking research while different team directors were assigned in accordance with their field of expertise. Specifically, Nagai served as the director responsible for researching the impacts of overpopulation on employment and domestic living standards. Ueda Teijirō led the research on general demographic trends and possible solutions to overpopulation from a macro perspective. Meanwhile, Nasu Shiroshi, an expert on agricultural economics, headed the team investigating the distribution of population in rural and urban areas in relation to food resources, agricultural products, and land economy, while Shimomura Hiroshi, a journalist at *Osaka Asahi Shinbun* and former colonial bureaucrat in the Government-General of Taiwan, was in charge of investigating population control measures. Lastly, it was Inoue Masaji, president of Kaigai kōgyō kabushiki gaisha (Overseas Enterprise Co., Ltd.) who oversaw research into emigration policies.[65]

Japan's de facto acquisition of Manchurian territory in 1932, regardless of its official status as a sovereign state, brought a new vision to the researchers in population science. Among the abovementioned research projects conducted at PPRS, the subjects of emigration policies and food production were particularly pertinent to this imperialist vision embedded in the population discourse. Inoue, who had played a crucial role in promoting Japanese migration to Brazil and other Latin American countries in his capacity as the president of the state-subsidized overseas migration business company Kaigai kōgyō, strongly supported Japanese colonial and overseas migration. Although Inoue admitted that emigration would not be a direct solution to the overpopulation issue in Japan proper, he emphasized that migration and colonization would contribute to the development of natural resources and to the growth of agricultural and industrial productivity. As early as 1930, he submitted a proposal to the government to establish a policy of promoting overseas migration programs, supporting Japanese migrants' settlement in a new territory by providing subsidies and building infrastructure and educational facilities.[66] In his view, Manchuria and Mongolia would play a vital role in Japan's productivity growth mainly as a source of food and natural resources. In the meantime, Nasu was another quintessential figure of the pro-emigration researcher at the PPRS. Nasu advocated agrarianism (*nōhonshugi*), a nationalist idea foregrounding farming as the mainstay of Japanese political, economic, and cultural life.[67] Based on this ideological view, he had demanded Japanese farmers' emigration to the colonial territories as a solution to the lack of arable land, even before Manchukuo was founded. His initial support for Japan's colonial expansionism lay in the assumption that the exploitation of land, the intensity of labor utilization, and the supply of fertilizer had already reached their limits in Japan.[68] Both Inoue's and Nasu's imperialist outlook on Japanese emigration did not need to wait long to be materialized due to Japan's acquisition of what Nitobe called the "lifeline of Japan" in 1932.

As migration and colonial development increasingly drew attention from the PPRS members, the Malthusian theory of population gained its ascendancy back in the population debate in the early 1930s. The Malthusian population theory that had reduced a multidimensional population issue into a formula between population size and agricultural products was rearticulated in the context of growing imperialism in Japan. This revised Malthusian formula echoed with the Katō group's agrarian imperialism. The Katō group was a group of ideologues who advocated an agrarian ideology under the leadership of right-wing agrarianist Katō Kanji (1884–1967), who had been an active promoter of youth education in rural areas to revive a self-sufficient farm economy in Japan since the mid-1910s. Nihon kokumin kōtō gakko (Japan National High School), which Katō opened in Yamagata and later Ibaraki prefectures, was a vehicle for spreading Shinto-based nationalist ideology that equated farming with the essence of Japanese civilization. As the agricultural sector was severely affected by the Great Depression, Katō took his nationalist agrarianism further to embrace an imperialist vision and supported the "agricultural colonization" (*nōgyō shokumin*) of Manchuria and Mongolia (*manmō*) for the sake of the Japanese farmers.[69] The Katō group that endorsed Katō's idea of the Japanese farmers' migration to the *manmō* region included Nasu, Hashimoto Denzaemon of the Kyoto University Department of Agriculture, Ishiguro Tada'atsu of the Ministry of Agriculture and Forestry, Ikoma Takatsune of Takumu-shō (Ministry of Colonial Affairs), Sō Mitsuhiko, the head of the agricultural training center affiliated with Mantetsu (South Manchuria Railway Company), and Yamazaki Yoshio of the Fuji Kōgyō Company in Colonial Korea.[70] The foundation of Manchukuo provided these agrarianist ideologues with an opportunity to promote the mass migration of Japanese farmers to the new frontier of the empire.

A trial peasant emigration plan in 1932 resulted from coordination between the agrarian imperialist elites, the Kwantung Army, and the Ministry of Colonial Affairs. In February 1932, when the Kwantung Army planned to establish a puppet state in Japan's newly acquired territory, Nasu and Hashimoto—the brains of the Katō group and prominent professors of agricultural economics in the Tokyo and Kyoto imperial universities, respectively—consulted with the Kwantung Army about the promotion of Japanese emigration to Manchuria. In their consultation, Nasu and Hashimoto underlined the core purposes of promoting peasant emigration, including the protection of land ownership through land reclamation and policymaking, mass emigration for security reasons, and coordinated efforts to train Japanese immigrants in Manchuria.[71] The blueprint for promoting Japanese peasants' emigration and settlement in Manchuria, suggested by these two brains of the Katō group, was endorsed by the Kwantung Army, which attempted to utilize the peasant population primarily for military and security reasons—in other words, for security against anti-Japanese guerrilla forces in the region.

Meanwhile, the Katō group also contacted the bureaucrats of the Ministry of Colonial Affairs that initially objected to the emigration campaign. Katō, along with Ishiguro and Sō, initiated "Manmō rokusenjin imin an" (a plan for the emigration of 6,000 people to Manchuria and Mongolia). This plan not only sought the promotion of peasants' mass emigration but also specified regions for the mass emigration campaign. The main targets were Tōhoku (northeastern part of Japan), Hokuriku (northwestern part), and Kantō (east-central part), in which peasant populations struggled with land shortages and poverty.[72] The Ministry of Colonial Affairs eventually accepted the Katō group's proposal for relief of poor peasants through the promotion of mass emigration. Both the Kwantung Army and the Ministry of Colonial Affairs, regardless of the different goals they embraced, joined forces to execute the trial plan for Japanese peasant emigration and settlement in Manchuria between 1932 and 1935. Over four years, a total of 1,667 households, recruited on a nationwide scale, moved to and resettled in Manchuria.[73] The relative success of the trial emigration campaign eventually evolved into the Kwantung Army-launched campaign called "Manshū nōgyō imin hyakuman-ko ijū keikaku" (a plan for Manchurian agricultural migration of 1 million households) in 1936.[74]

As the advocates for the promotion of peasant emigration to Manchuria gained ascendancy among bureaucrats, military authorities, and agrarianist ideologues, the PPRS jumped on the Manchurian-solution bandwagon. In April 1936, when the Kwantung Army and the Army Ministry of Japan were drawing up a five-year plan for the Manchurian agricultural migration of 1 million households, the leading members of the PPRS submitted two proposals to the Hirota Kōki's cabinet: one proposal addressed the promotion of emigration and settlement in general while the other specifically focused on the issues of emigration to Manchuria. Both proposals manifested the think tank's concerted effort to terminate the protracted controversy over emigration and to place a high priority on the promotion of Japanese emigration and resettlement to solve the population problems in Japan proper. The specific demands of the PPRS to promote emigration as a fundamental solution for population growth were as follows: (1) the establishment of national migration policies; (2) diplomatic efforts to build amicable relationships with host countries: (3) the revision of Imin hogo hō (Migrants' Protection Act), passed in 1896; (4) the development of new settlements; (5) the installation and management of economic and social facilities to help Japanese migrants settle and stabilize their livelihoods; (6) the protection of Japanese migrants; (7) the promotion of economic relations between settlements and Japan proper; and (8) education and advertisements about migration.[75] All these demands converged on a single goal: the establishment of comprehensive national migration policies to replace comprehensive population policies.[76]

Meanwhile, another proposal by the PPRS titled "Manshū imin ni kansuru kengi" (a plan on migration to Manchuria) confirmed the growing importance of Manchuria as an outlet for Japan's overflowing peasant population. Unlike the abovementioned proposal that addressed population problems in general, the proposal on Japanese migration to Manchuria mainly dealt with the problems of rural areas and supported the extension of the campaign to promote collective peasant emigration to Manchuria. The logic underlying this proposal was that overpopulation was the main cause of rural poverty, which reiterated the agrarian imperialist argument in favor of peasant migration. This overpopulation theme was a rhetoric of displacement in two senses. On the one hand, the theme displaced the pressing agricultural crisis and increasing interregional disparities and reduced complex actual socioeconomic issues into merely the problem of population size. As Louise Young pointed out, Manchurian emigration was promoted to address the "unevenly felt agricultural crisis" suffered by rural areas across the nation, far from "distress caused by overpopulation."[77] On the other hand, the rhetoric focused on overpopulation simultaneously displaced the agenda for a comprehensive government of population, and it revived a Malthusian panacea—that is, the control of population size. The think tank's proposal to promote emigration and settlement in Manchuria symbolizes the resurrection of Malthusian logic in conjunction with increasing agrarian imperialism.

Seen in the broader context of the shaping of population policies during the interwar period, the goal for these policies drastically shrank from the optimization of life to that of population quantity. In comparison to the agenda for the comprehensive government of the population set by its predecessor PFIC, the PPRS limited its function to the regulation of population size in proportion to the production of food resources and arable land areas.

This changing agenda, though, cannot simply be understood as a regression. The government's changing perception of the Japanese population and its aim toward quantifiable resources for the sake of Japan's imperialist expansion not only intervenes into a linear narrative of the Foucauldian notion of governmentality, but also shines a new light on the population in a state of flux, in other words, the malleability of the population at the nexus of governmentality and imperialism. The mobilization of Japanese peasants for the promotion of collective emigration and settlement in Manchuria indicates an overdetermined life of the population, namely, a form of life oscillating between a quantified population and an essentialized ethnic group (notably, *minzoku*) or between the target of biopolitical governance and an imperial national subject. The following statements illuminate how the think tank scholars redefined the Japanese population as, on the one hand, an entity subjected to control to achieve a balance between the population size and productivity, and on the other, a mobilizable labor resource to construct Japan's settler colony in Manchuria:

> When considering the origin of Manchukuo, there is no question about the importance of Japanese migration to Manchuria in establishing the social and cultural basis for consolidating and developing a special relationship between Japan and Manchuria. Notwithstanding, it is of urgent necessity to pay special attention to the issue of migration to Manchuria in terms of a solution for population problems. . . . There are a few things to keep in mind when it comes to agricultural migration to Manchuria—particularly preparing Japanese farmers sufficiently for a different climate, culture, and style of living from Japan to prevent a

"brilliant but vain attempt," and to make full use of our farmers' superior technology, management skills, and civilized life to achieve coexistence and co-prosperity between Japan and Manchukuo, as well as to lead cultural improvement in rural areas in Manchuria.[78]

When in 1936 the military regime took over the government after the February 26 Incident, a coup d'état launched by young Imperial Japanese Army officers, the role of the PPRS became highly limited to a supporting role in implementing national policies. The scholars who once pursued governmentalizing the state by mobilizing a wide range of state apparatuses for the welfare of the population now shifted toward mobilizing the population—in particular, its health, labor force, fertility, and daily lives—in conformity with the national population policies. These scholars' pro-migration stance in the mid-1930s was a harbinger of this transition of population policies from social and welfare reforms to the mobilization of human resources.

It should be noted that the researchers of both the PFIC and the PPRS cannot simply be considered as victims or passive supporters of escalating militarism. Given the goal to centralize population policies under the national policy initially set by the PFIC, the scholars in population science themselves laid a steppingstone to integrating various bureaucratic, social, and scientific measures into a unified national policy for population control. As a successor to the PFIC, as soon as the Sino-Japanese war broke out, the members of the PPRS also strongly demanded a comprehensive system of population policies in preparation for a protracted war.[79] As a result, Jinkō mondai kenkyūsho (Institute of Population Problems), an affiliated organization with the Ministry of Health and Welfare, was established in August 1939. After its establishment, the institute took charge of population research and advanced the imperial-nationalist rhetoric of population control by foregrounding the Yamato race in population discourse and promoting a pronatalist policy to mobilize the workforce for war efforts.[80] Despite the different directions of the population policies of the interwar and wartime regimes, the interwar plan to establish a comprehensive, scientific system for population control survived and even came to fruition under the total war regime.

Entanglements Between Science and Policy, Governmentality, and Imperialism

Through the lenses of population discourse deployed by the think tank scholars, this chapter traced the process of the co-production of population science and policies during the interwar period. The trajectory of interwar population science and policymaking reveals the leading role of scholars, especially social scientists in designing and establishing a comprehensive and scientific approach to controlling, optimizing, and managing the Japanese population. The narrative surrounding the emergence of governmentality in Japan, though, by no means unfolds linearly. The close reading of population discussions made by the researchers in the PFIC and the PPRS allows us to understand the historical entanglement between governmentality and imperialism. Especially, the fact that the scholars who were involved in the PPRS ended up embracing emigration and settlement as part of their solution to the population issues in Japan proper reveals the indispensability of colonial expansion in the development of biopolitical population governance in the metropole. As the blueprint for the governmentalization of the state becomes entangled with the imperialist vision, the notion of the population remained in a state of flux. As discussed above, the creation of Manchukuo in 1932 resulted in the reordering of the Japanese population both as human resources and as the Japanese race. In sum, the life of the population continued to be problematized due to complex geopolitical conditions that required the population not only to be quantified and mobilized but also to be racialized and gendered.

In July 1937, the Second Sino-Japanese War began, and Japan entered a state of war that lasted until August 1945. The total war system (*sōryokusen taisei*) integrated various political, economic, and social apparatuses into a unified and rationalized system that required full-scale mobilization of resources.[81] Human resources, whether they be military forces or labor forces, were not an exception. The Ministry of Health and Welfare established in January 1938, played a pivotal role in integrating the population policies into a unified national policy with the aim of mobilizing, managing, and reproducing human resources. Under the total war system, the focus of population control shifted from addressing overpopulation to producing "healthy soldiers and healthy citizens" (*kenpei kenmin*). Neither poverty nor unemployment, allegedly caused by the overflowing population in the metropole, was a pressing concern for the bureaucracy, the military, and scholars in population science during wartime. This sudden shift certainly does not imply that the nation's war effort finally cured the longstanding overpopulation problem. As the wartime slogan "healthy soldiers and healthy citizens" symbolizes, the redefining of the Japanese population as mobilizable human resources invalidated the resurrected Malthusian logic. In what follows, I will look into the wartime population policies to discuss how the total war regime consummated, rather than abandoned, the interwar blueprint for governmentalizing the state and illuminate why the gendering of the population was indispensable in reordering the population as human resources mobilized for war efforts.

FOUR

Building a Biopolitical State

THE MOBILIZATION OF HEALTH FOR TOTAL WAR

> Total Mobilization is far less consummated than it consummates itself; in war and peace, it expresses the secret and inexorable claim to which our life in the age of masses and machines subjects us. It thus turns out that each individual life becomes, even more unambiguously, the life of a worker; and that, following the wars of knights, kings, and citizens, we now have wars of workers. The first great twentieth-century conflict has offered us a presentiment of both their rational structure and their mercilessness.
>
> ERNST JÜNGER, "Total Mobilization" (1930)

> The National Mobilization Law prescribes the control and management of human and material resources during wartime (including a quasi-state of war) to maximize the effective use of every element of national power needed for national defense.
>
> CABINET OF JAPAN, Kokka sōdōin hō [National Mobilization Law] (1938); translation is mine

Questions of Welfare, Fascism, and Biopolitics

As the Second Sino-Japanese War turned into a protracted conflict, Prime Minister Konoe Fumimaro's administration was geared toward total war (*sōryokusen*).[1] Kokka sōdōin hō (National Mobilization Law), enacted in March 1938, inaugurated a new era of total mobilization that officially lasted until August 1945. As clearly indicated in Article 1 of the law, its primary goal was to control and manage "human and material resources" efficiently as part of wartime mobilization efforts.[2] In particular, human resources (*jinteki shigen*) were rendered, from a functionalist perspective, as an integral element for strengthening national defense during wartime. In this age of total mobilization, every aspect of human faculty, ranging from physical strength to reproductive health to moral values, became the target of planning, rationalization, and mobilization to maximize military capabilities and workforce productivity both on the battlefields and the home front. What Ernst Jünger (1895–1988), a German philosopher and a leading figure in the national conservative movement in the Weimar years (1918–1933),[3] expected to come to pass following the end of World War I began to transpire in the Japanese empire in the late 1930s: human lives were integrated into the readily mobilizable workforce under the slogan of total mobilization.

At first glance, Japan's population policy during the wartime period (1937–1945) appears to be a marked departure from the interwar population discourse that were primarily deployed in social and academic realms. The difference between the interwar and the wartime population discourse can be summed up in terms of two factors: first, a change in the central actors of population discourse—from social reformers and intellectuals, who had aimed to address the population problems with scientific and medical solutions, to the government, which institutionalized various population policies. Second, a shift in the main goal for problematizing the population in Japan proper, from solving social issues to mobilizing human resources for total war. As seen in the previous chapters, the interwar population discourse—including birth control movements, eugenics, and population science—was primarily focused on the social impact of the population problem no matter how it was defined and strove to tackle a series of problems including unemployment, poverty, class inequalities, and the economic gap between rural and urban areas. Meanwhile, the wartime policy redefined the population as a human resource from the vantage point of the state and overturned the hitherto dominant claim about an overpopulated Japan proper. In the wake of war, the core of the state policy promptly shifted toward promoting population growth as well as improving workforce productivity. In other words, the wartime government became the main stakeholder in population discourse, reshaping the approach to population management that had merely been a means of responding to modern crises into the ultimate end of government.

However, this seemingly marked difference between interwar and wartime population discourse cannot be simply seen as a complete discontinuity. When it comes to the integrated and scientific intervention into demographic issues, the wartime policy reflects continuities rather than discontinuities with the interwar blueprints for governing the population. In particular, the creation of Kōsei-shō (Ministry of Health and Welfare, hereinafter MHW) in January 1938 and the resultant process of formulating population policies under the leadership of the MHW provide a revealing account of the emergence of a biopolitical state in the wake of total war. By the notion of "biopolitical state," I emphasize the integration of population discourse into the state systems and practices that seek to optimize both the quantity and quality of a selected population. The ways in which the total war state orchestrated knowledge and institutions to rationalize the management of the Japanese population under the quintessential slogan of "healthy soldiers and healthy people" (*kenpei kenmin*) indicate that the wartime regime materialized the interwar initiatives to governmentalize the Japanese state.

The narrative stressing the continuity between interwar and wartime periods in Japanese history challenges the conventional plot of Japanese fascism as a marker of deviation from modernity or of incomplete modernity. As J. Victor Koschmann sharply points out, the postwar historiography of Japan was premised on a binary of "premodern particularism and modern universalism," according to which the fascist regime in wartime Japan was seen as a residue of feudalism and, thus, a symptom of a failed modernization.[4] Accordingly, Japan's total war history between 1937 and 1945, or even the history of the prolonged Asia-Pacific war between 1931 and 1945, was interpreted as a complete break from both the preceding history of so-called Taishō Democracy and the postwar history centered on peace and democratization. Since the late 1990s, this postwar historiography that placed wartime Japan in a dark valley has been challenged by a group of historians who have sought to decolonize and de-essentialize the heretofore Western-centric, universalized conception of modernity. According to their decolonizing view of modernity, Japanese fascism was by no means a lack of or an antithesis to the ideal path of modernization. On the contrary, the fascist regime of Japan emerged *within* the process of modernization and further maximized modern rationalities and systems to address the crisis of modernity manifested in the Great Depression.[5] My analysis of the wartime population policies in this chapter echoes the critical approach to Japanese fascism. By looking into how the wartime fascist regime *consummated* the interwar blueprint for biopolitical rationalities and institutions, I emphasize the maximization of modern systematic and scientific intervention in the population, as opposed to the blind equation of fascism with an irrational, regressive form of power. In so doing, I aim to dissociate Japanese fascism from a culturalist—hence, particularist—account and instead situate it among various inflections of biopolitical modernity that valorized the systematic, scientific management of bodies.

It does not mean, though, that the fascist regime of Japan was immune from historical changes. A specific historical context during the total war years is worth examining, for the goal of redefining Japanese fascism is not to make it fit into another misleadingly universal theory of biopolitics but to elucidate under what circumstances and specifically in which forms biopolitical power was manifested in wartime Japan. There are two questions to be addressed in relation to the nature of the biopolitical state in wartime Japan. First, what were the impacts of the wartime situation in rearticulating the state and the population? The creation of the MHW and its leading role in establishing population policies throughout the wartime years allows us to understand the simultaneous construction of warfare and welfare systems, under which a selected population was integrated into human resources and governed by the entangled rationalities of biopower and necropower. According to Achille Mbembe, "necropower," or power of death, refers to different modes of power that manifest themselves in violent and destructive forms such as resistance, war, and terror.[6] The notion of necropower is essential to understand the other, if not opposite, side of biopower, as Mbembe argues that "to be sovereign is to exert one's control over mortality and to define life as the deployment and manifestation of power."[7] It is worth noting that biopower and necropower hardly cancel each other but conjointly constitute the modern forms of power in a Jekyll-and-Hyde fashion. The simultaneous making of warfare and welfare regimes under which life was redefined as a population in need of the state protection on the one hand and human resources subject to total war mobilization on the other exemplifies this entanglement of biopower and necropower. Meanwhile, the second question to be examined is who, which population, was to be subjected to the institutional care of the biopolitical state? As I will discuss in this and the next chapter, the wartime population discourse did not merely function to optimize bodies to produce healthy soldiers and healthy people but also assigned a limit to bodies to be optimized, namely, *a population*. Given this, it is of utmost importance to investigate where the line was drawn between the population worthy of biopolitical protection and the undesirable bodies excluded from institutional care. To elucidate the politics of inclusion and exclusion embedded in the wartime biopolitical regime, close attention will be paid to how race and gender were factored into the wartime population discourse.

To that end, this chapter explores the process by which the Japanese wartime population policies were established under the banner of total mobilization. The historical trajectory from the creation of the MHW to the establishment of Kenmin-kyoku (Healthy People Bureau) under the MHW in November 1943 provides a glimpse into the transformation of the Japanese state into the primary agency of population discourse and the intertwined relationship between welfare and warfare systems. By revisiting the nature of Japanese fascism through the lens of the biopolitical state, this chapter aims to challenge the conventional distinction between the interwar and the wartime periods and between the warfare state and the welfare state.

Multiple Paths Toward an Integrated Welfare Policy

As the Marco Polo Bridge Incident[8] in July 1937 led to a full-scale war between the Japanese empire and the Republic of China, the Japanese government reorganized its system of governance in pursuit of two interlinked objectives: the formation of the warfare and welfare state. The relatively swift endorsement by the cabinet council to establish a central government institution in charge of public health merely three months after the Sino-Japanese war broke out and the eventual creation of the MHW in January 1938 are symbolic events revealing how instrumental an integrated welfare policy was for the state to wage a full-scale war. As the first national body that unified labor policies, welfare programs, and public health systems in modern Japan, the MHW marked the birth of the biopolitical state, namely, the state that aims to optimize its people's lives by means of various governmental apparatuses to rationalize human bodies and health at both the collective and individual levels. Within the broader context of Japan's prewar population discourse, it was during wartime that the Japanese government, which had maintained a passive approach to population health management and fragmented public health policies during the interwar years, became the central actor for governing various population and welfare issues to meet the wartime demands for labor.

As studies of the history of welfare have shown already, the close link between welfare and warfare in twentieth-century history is a well-known inconvenient truth. For example, Richard Titmuss's classic study of British social policy reveals the effect of World War II on the development of universal welfare policies in Britain.[9] When it comes to German *Sozialpolitik*, the authoritarian social policies initiated by Otto von Bismarck, the first chancellor of the German empire, in the late nineteenth century, Götz Aly argues that the Nazi regime reinforced Bismarckian *Sozialpolitik* by prioritizing full employment, progressive income taxes, and universal pension schemes while confiscating Jewish property to implement such redistributive policies.[10] The Japanese military regime during wartime also exemplifies the historical association between warfare and welfare policies, as explored by Gregory Kasza. As opposed to the dominant hesitation in existing studies to credit wartime policies with the development of postwar welfare policies, Kasza highlights the continuities between wartime and postwar welfare policies in terms of universal health insurance, workers' pensions, and public healthcare programs.[11] Despite differences in the concept of welfare, along with different sociopolitical structures, there has been a scholarly consensus about the impact of war, and World War II in particular, on the emergence and development of welfare systems across nations.

In the meantime, however, the continuities between the interwar and wartime periods with respect to social and welfare policies have not been thoroughly examined in the history of welfare in modern Japan. While the total war played a decisive role in establishing and integrating welfare policies under the leadership of the MHW, warfare was not the *sole* push factor that gave rise to such universalized and centralized welfare schemes. The question at stake here is whether the launching of the new ministry governing health and welfare was merely a reaction to the Sino-Japanese War. The close examination of the process of establishing the MHW allows one to grasp the fact that not only did a plan for a unified governmental institution for public health and social policy precede the outbreak of the Sino-Japanese War, but also that the plan bore the imprints of the interwar population discourse. If the creation of the MHW was not a direct reaction to the war, what was the initial purpose for creating the new central government institution? Who were the main actors initiating and formulating the plan for integrated health and social policies? What policies embraced the interwar population discourse, and what role did the total war play in rearticulating the goal and scope of welfare policies? These questions provide a way to revisit the wartime welfare policies as an extension of the interwar population discourse and to clarify the historical link between warfare and welfare through the lens of the biopolitical state.

The path toward the creation of the MHW reflects the multiple conceptions of welfare as different governmental agencies envisioned them. The most vocal advocates for a new administrative institution for social and health policies even before the war broke out included Rikugun-shō (Ministry of Army) and Kikaku-chō (Planning Agency) under the cabinet in the governmental sector, and Chūō shakai jigyō kyōkai (Central Association for Social Work, hereinafter CASW) in the social sector. Against the backdrop of a prolonged economic depression, chronic poverty, and public health issues both in urban and rural areas, and escalating political unrest in the mid-1930s, both the government and the social sectors strove to address the ongoing socioeconomic issues by developing a state-led, integrated, and rationalized welfare system. However, it should be noted that the concept and the goal of welfare were envisioned differently by the Ministry of Army, the cabinet, and the CASW. Their different conceptions of welfare ultimately reflected their different ideas about the state *per se*.

In May 1937, the Ministry of Army took the initiative in formulating a specific plan for a new welfare ministry, which the army named Eisei-shō (Hygiene Ministry).[12] In particular, Koizumi Chikahiko (1884–1945), head of the Ministry of Army's Imukyoku (Medical Bureau) and later the minister of the MHW (1941–1944), is credited with forming a framework for the Hygiene Ministry.[13] Since the mid-1920s, Koizumi had highlighted the significance of military hygiene (*gunjin eisei*), practical science that aimed to improve the physical fitness of soldiers through optimizing clothing supplies, nutritional support, and living conditions. For him, military hygiene was not simply a military problem, but a national one as it would ensure national security and preserve the lives of the "Yamato people" (*minzoku*).[14]

As the leader of hygiene and health administration in the army beginning in 1934, Koizumi had advocated the necessity of systematic and rational approaches to improving the physical strength of the Japanese people (*kokumin tairyoku*). Koizumi's understanding of people's physical strength was distinctive in three regards: first, his notion of physical strength encompassed three dimensions of human capability including physique (*taikaku*), work capacity (*kinōteki nōryoku*), and mental faculties (*seishinryoku*); second, such standards for people's health were derived from the military's physical examinations for conscripts (*chōhei kensa*); and lastly, hygiene was broadly defined as a rational way of improving not only the physical strength of male soldiers but ultimately that of the Japanese population, which reiterated his earlier argument on the potential contribution of military hygiene to the prosperity of *minzoku*.[15] In particular, Koizumi lamented the physical deterioration of the Japanese male youths (*sōtei*) who were subjected to military conscription. Echoing Koizumi's lamentation, Terauchi Hisaichi, army minister, also worriedly pointed out a drastic increase in the number of failures in the military physical examinations for conscripts in the mid-1930s.[16] In response to growing concerns over national security, Koizumi rationalized the need to develop hygiene policies at the state level primarily to increase the number of able-bodied males who would potentially become Japanese imperial soldiers.[17]

The plan for the Hygiene Ministry clearly reflects Koizumi's conception of hygiene as a scientific means for improving physical strength and national defense. This should come as no surprise because Koizumi drafted the plan for the Hygiene Ministry on behalf of the Ministry of Army in May 1937. The first draft for the plan outlined the structure and function of the new ministry, which comprised nine bureaus including hygiene, physical strength, education, industry, social work, insurance, transportation, migration, and medical affairs.[18] This all-encompassing approach to public hygiene and health revealed marked differences from the existing health administration. As opposed to the heretofore fragmented and uncoordinated administration, the plan for the Hygiene Ministry sought to consolidate different administrative institutions within one body. Furthermore, hygiene that had merely fallen under the control of the Ministry of Home Affairs became the heart of government policy. In other words, hygiene lay at the intersections of individual bodies and national security, physical capabilities and national productivity, and biopolitical and geopolitical goals.

The plan for the Hygiene Ministry provoked adverse reactions from both inside and outside the Ministry of Army. Amid sharply escalating tensions between the cabinet and the Ministry of Army after the February 26 Incident, the Ministry of Army was hesitant to take a political risk by encroaching upon public hygiene, which was considered to be the responsibility of the Ministry of Home Affairs.[19] Despite a growing consensus concerning the need for integrated social policies, the cabinet and the Ministry of Home Affairs, in particular, were wary of the Ministry of Army taking the initiative in reforming the public hygiene and health system. As a result, the Ministry of Army submitted a revised plan for Hoken shakai-shō (Ministry of Public Health and Social Affairs) to Konoe's new cabinet in June 1937. Besides the name of the new ministry, there were a few differences between the first and the second versions in terms of its structure: the second draft outlined fewer bureaus, this time including hygiene, physical strength, childcare, rational living (*seikatsu gōri*), medical affairs, social affairs, and insurance. Among these, the bureau of rational living incorporated and reorganized the industrial, transportation, and migration affairs that were separately laid out in the previous version.[20] However, there was little difference between the two versions in the fundamental aim of integrated social policies: to enhance people's physical health as a primary way to reinforce national defense.

On July 9, 1937, the Konoe cabinet approved the Planning Agency's proposal to establish the Ministry of Public Health and Social Affairs.[21] Although the two proposals formulated by the Ministry of Army and the Planning Agency respectively shared the same title, there was a noticeable discrepancy between these two administrations in terms of centralizing the social and public health systems. From its inception, the cabinet under the leadership of Konoe emphasized its role in initiating a state-directed welfare system. Its immediate action to formulate and approve the proposal for the Ministry of Public Health and Social Affairs provides a glimpse into the cabinet's attempt to restrain the Ministry of Army from interfering with the governmental system, including public health administration. In addition to the tug of war between the cabinet and the army, a crucial difference is noted between the two plans in their conceptions of welfare. As seen above, the army's plan reduced the bodies of the Japanese population, particularly their physical strength, into a means to national security. Moreover, hygiene represented a scientific vehicle for optimizing human bodies and mobilizing healthy bodies for national defense. The absence of any reference to welfare in the army's plan contrasts with the fact that the cabinet prioritized the welfare of the population to improve the people's physical health (*kokumin taii*).[22] The following statement in the Planning Agency's proposal spells out the cabinet's emphasis on the state's responsibility for its people's welfare to improve their physical health.

> Improvements in people's physical health require far more than health policies. With the aim of reforming irrational elements of people's daily lives, the policies must be concerned with various social issues including occupations, labor, social relief and welfare facilities, and the social security system, which form the basis of daily lives. Providing fundamental solutions to such social issues is a crucial step to completing the improvements to people's physical health.[23]

As seen above, the Konoe cabinet rearticulated welfare, which had been substantially left in the hands of local governments and civil sectors, as the key responsibility of the state. According to the Planning Agency's proposal, physical health was located at the complex intersection of economic, social, and biological factors. Through this reframing of physical health in a comprehensive way, the Konoe cabinet highlighted the need for a state-directed welfare system. In light of this, its plan to "consolidate multiple administrative institutions concerning physical education, public health, hygiene, labor, social affairs" into the Ministry of Public Health and Social Affairs reflects shifting ideas of the state itself.[24] This rearticulated welfare system required the state to function as the primary institution for reproducing desirable bodies rather than merely addressing social problems. In other words, the state-directed welfare system was not only *preemptive*, but, more importantly, it was *productive*.

This transition in the conception of welfare leads to the question of what propelled Konoe's cabinet to undertake state intervention in the welfare of the population. It is worth noting that the idea of the comprehensive government of bodies preceded an official declaration of total mobilization. As seen in the previous chapters, the Japanese government, from the late 1920s onward, increasingly paid attention to the overpopulation issue and its allegedly resultant social problems. As the economic depression deepened and incidents of political and social unrest increased, the interwar government worked in tandem with social scientists to develop population studies as a groundwork for addressing pressing social issues. This groundwork predates the Planning Agency's plan for maximizing the state's role in securing the welfare of the population. As discussed in the previous chapter, the interwar blueprint for governing the Japanese population laid down some basic principles including the establishment of Shakai-shō (Ministry of Social Affairs) and a permanent body for the scientific investigation of population problems.[25] However, because Manchuria appeared to offer a promising place to relocate the surplus farming population in Japan proper, the plan for establishing a new ministry for welfare and social affairs was not implemented until January 1938. As mentioned above, the February 26 Incident of 1936 raised the alarm that the prolonged economic depression, particularly rural poverty and increasing social stratification, would lead to the rise of political radicalism, whether it be ultra-nationalism or communism. Given this, Konoe's cabinet was instrumental in executing the plan for a centralized and integrated welfare system, which had been deferred because of an imperialist expectation that Manchuria would function as an outlet for Japan's surplus population.

This cabinet-directed plan for the new ministry was endorsed by the private sector, particularly, the CASW. When the army's second proposal was submitted to the cabinet in June 1937, the CASW put forward its recommendation to the government for prioritizing social policies over hygiene policies. As a nationwide organization for social work agencies, the

CASW put significant emphasis on developing social policies that aimed at promoting people's welfare and securing their living standards. Despite its acknowledgment of the importance of physical fitness, the CASW echoed the cabinet's disapproval of the army's plan and emphasized the implementation of social policies as a necessary condition for improving the people's physical fitness.[26] The CASW also proceeded to formulate its own plan for the Ministry of Social Affairs, which was submitted under the name of its president Kiyoura Keigo to the cabinet, the Planning Agency, and the authorities of the army and navy on June 19, 1937. This proposal reflects the CASW's efforts to integrate social and public policies into a unified national welfare system and, furthermore, to expand the boundaries of welfare to include the entire Japanese population. The most salient point in the CASW's proposal, which charted the organizational structure of the Ministry of Social Affairs, is the establishment of Jidōkyoku (Children's Bureau).[27] Using a broad definition of child welfare, the CASW put the social protection and healthcare of the population of mothers and children at the center of its welfare policies. This plan for the Children's Bureau under the Ministry of Social Affairs aimed to institutionalize the state's responsibility for reproducing its population. As described later in the next chapter, although the plan for the Children's Bureau was not eventually implemented, its goal to promote the health of mothers and children was integrated into the MHW's campaign for "healthy people" (*kenmin*).

In view of this, the MHW was a product of the policy discussions around solutions for the population problem in the preceding years. Even prior to the outbreak of the Sino-Japanese War, there was already a growing consensus among both governmental and private sectors on the need for an integrated welfare institution. Although the motivations for and the conceptions of welfare varied among the Ministry of Army, the Konoe cabinet, and the CASW, they invariably agreed on the state's central responsibility for the people's welfare and the pressing need for a comprehensive approach to welfare policies—ranging from labor relations and insurance policies to medical and health services—to promote the health of the population in Japan proper.

If the historical conditions for the creation of the MHW already existed, what were the effects of warfare on the ministry? It is undeniable that the Sino-Japanese War acted as a catalyst. Nevertheless, even more significant was the redirection of the goals of the welfare policies in response to the escalation of the initial war between Japanese and Chinese troops into a protracted full-scale war. As soon as the Sino-Japanese War broke out, the cabinet accelerated the process of creating a new welfare ministry. After going through the negotiation process among existing ministries about the realignment of roles and responsibilities, the final touch was added by the Privy Council, which refused to use the term "social" because the term connoted socialism.[28] Instead, conservative leaders within the Privy Council employed *Kōsei*, a notion originating in one of the scriptures of Confucianism, the *Book of Documents* (*Shūjīng*).[29] In the original Confucian text, *Kōsei* referred to enriching people's lives by providing the necessities of life. The modern translation of *Kōsei* under the wartime regime in Japan would mean enriching people's lives by providing far more than bare necessities. As the era of *Kōsei* unfolded after the creation of the MHW in January 1938, *Kōsei* acquired a new meaning, that is, enriching the lives of the Japanese population under the state control of broad-ranging aspects of human lives, especially productive and reproductive capacity. The term *Kōsei* represented the comprehensive conception of welfare as it was envisioned by different proposals for establishing an institutional body during the interwar years. At the same time, *Kōsei* reflected the shifting goal of welfare against the backdrop of a full-scale war. In other words, warfare contributed to redirecting the underlying goal of state-run welfare policies: reproducing a healthy population whose bodies were required for mobilization as human resources at the state's discretion.

Wartime Population Research and Planning

The MHW took the initiative in formulating and executing population policies throughout the total war. The development of wartime population policies is largely divided into two periods: in the first period (1938–1941), the MHW established and operated affiliated bodies, including Jinkō mondai kenkyūsho (Institute of Population Problems) and Minzoku eisei kenkyūkai (Race Hygiene Research Society) to undertake policy-related research and planning. In the second period (1941–1945), the MHW proceeded to execute various population policies that collectively aimed at increasing the population size and improving the health of the Japanese population. The cabinet's endorsement of Jinkō seisaku kakuritsu yōkō (Guidelines for Establishing Population Policy, hereinafter Population Guidelines) in January 1941 marked a turning point in the wartime population policies. As a point of transition from planning to implementation, the Population Guidelines represented a systematic effort to optimize the quantity and quality of the Japanese population throughout the wartime period. In what follows, I trace the trajectory of wartime population policies to explore how the wartime government appropriated the existing population discourse in the remaking of the entire Japanese population into labor resources.

As stated in the previous section, the MHW was established in January 1938 to replace the existing Bureau of Social Affairs and centralize tasks related to national health, social work, and labor issues. The new ministry was initially organized into five bureaus including physical strength, hygiene, preventive healthcare (*yobō*), social affairs, and labor affairs, and two subsidiary organizations called the Temporal Department of Military Assistance and the Insurance Center (*hokenin*).[30] The initial structure of the MHW primarily reflected the Planning Agency's initial plan for the Ministry of Public Health and Social Affairs, particularly its goal to consolidate previously separate social and health policies into a unified system. The creation of the MHW thus required the realignment of roles and responsibilities that had been heretofore assigned to different governmental authorities, including the Ministry of Home Affairs and its affiliated bureaus overseeing social affairs and hygiene, Monbushō (Ministry of Education), Teishin-shō (Ministry of Communications), and Shōkō-shō (Ministry of Commerce and Industry). The five bureaus and two subsidiary organizations of the MHW replaced the preceding social welfare administration and assumed a wide array of responsibilities, namely, health policy, public hygiene, prevention of epidemics and diseases, eugenic practices, social welfare, maternal and child healthcare, employment, labor affairs, military aid, and national insurance.

Aside from the consolidation of welfare administration, the MHW played a pivotal role in transforming the structural foundation of welfare programs. In other words, the state became the primary agency for fashioning different modes of welfare and defining the scope of national subjects for determining whose lives mattered in the state-led welfare programs and whose did not. The enactment of Kokumin kenkō hoken hō (National Health Insurance Law) in April 1938 exemplifies how the imperial state set a national boundary of welfare. The main purpose of the National Health Insurance Law was to universalize health coverage for illnesses, injuries, childbirth, and deaths by extending the entitlement to insurance benefits to a more significant portion of the Japanese population.[31] This universal healthcare system was preceded by the Employer's Health Insurance Law of 1922, which facilitated the advent of social insurance to provide benefits exclusively to factory workers and miners. The National Health Insurance Law then extended coverage to farmers, fishers, and self-employed people, and added a community-based regular subscription plan to the existing employment-based plan. As a result, this wartime insurance reform led to an increase in the number of insured people from 578,759 in 1938 to 40,745,624 in 1945, and to the coverage of more than 95 percent of towns and villages across Japan proper.[32]

The universalization of health insurance in the metropole is sharply contrasted with the situation in colonies, especially the two formal colonies of Japan—that is, colonial Korea and Taiwan—where health insurance was commercialized and even used as exploitation tools. In colonial Korea, the Ministry of Communications of the Government-General of Korea introduced Simplified Life Insurance in 1929 and maintained the same policy throughout the war. This colonial insurance policy was designed to simplify the subscription process so as to maximize the number of subscribers and use revenues for colonial enterprises and eventually Japan's war efforts.[33] Meanwhile, the Government-General of Taiwan had maintained a hands-off approach to life insurance throughout the colonial period, which resulted in the commercialization of life insurance in colonial Taiwan.[34] The absence of universal health insurance in colonial Korea and Taiwan reveals how the discourse of welfare was differently deployed throughout the Japanese colonial empire. Considering this, the national form of welfare does not simply characterize a welfare state, a notion that conventionally refers to a state that plays a leading role in offering social services and economic benefits to promote its citizens' well-being.[35] Essentially, the wartime development of welfare policies was expressed in the form of imperial nationalism, which demonstrates the substance of the biopolitical state. By incorporating biopolitical rationalities into its social policies, the wartime state expanded the entitlement of social welfare from the lower class to a larger portion of its population to govern the bodies of national subjects. At the same time, the state decided which bodies were to be defined as the population that deserved protection from the state, and which modes of welfare were to be allocated to the bodies that mattered to the state. Toward the end of the war, the colonial governments in both Korea and Taiwan eventually implemented a series of public health policies primarily to meet the urgent need for workforces.[36] The recalibration of colonial strategies during wartime reflects what Takashi Fujitani calls "polite racism," an inclusive form of racism that entails practices of integrating colonized and racialized populations into the regime of biopolitics.[37] Although parts of, if not full, public health benefits were granted eventually to selected colonized populations, the enlarged entitlement hardly indicated the disavowal of racism but the advance of governmentality to make more worthy bodies readily mobilizable.

The dynamics of inclusion and exclusion of bodies in the making of health and welfare policies intertwined with racial ideologies in the Japanese empire. The schema of race was constructed in a dual way: the formation of the Japanese race on the one hand and the categorization of other races in its colonies on the other. These two modes of racial construction in the Japanese empire worked in tandem to reify the idea of the Japanese race in virtue of racialized colonial others. The so-called Yamato race that evoked the idea of the biological unity of the Japanese people was only sustainable by labeling colonized bodies as racial others. Biopolitical rationalities valorized by the wartime regime in Japan reinforced this logic of the Japanese race as the state would now take the lead in improving the quality of the race by employing welfare measures. Considering that, from the outset, the MHW exclusively aimed at promoting the health of the Japanese population, and the wartime regime distinguished the Japanese population from the colonized peoples whose bodies were deemed unworthy, or less worthy of the protection of the imperial state. Although the imperial state vigorously promoted Pan-Asianism at an ideological level, as exemplified in the declaration of New Order in East Asia in November 1938, its rhetoric of Asian solidarity did not necessarily mean that all the colonized populations would be included in the category of worthy bodies. The biopolitical state prioritized the Japanese race over other racialized populations, and, thereby, race served as a self-evident criterion for determining worthy and unworthy bodies in the context of the colonial empire.

Notwithstanding, race is by no means a transcendent, fixed category of bodies but an ideological product that requires constant reification to be sustainable. Accordingly, the biopolitical state during the wartime years invested persistent efforts in forging scientific knowledge to represent different types of bodies and to attribute different qualities to the racialized bodies. For this endeavor, two governmental institutions served primary roles in producing knowledge on bodies under the auspices of the MHW. One was the Institute of Population Problems (hereinafter called IPP), which played a crucial role in conducting a wide range of studies of the Japanese population during the wartime period; the other was the Race Hygiene Research Society (hereinafter called RHRS), a think tank group responsible for investigating eugenics-based measures and sterilization laws. Both governmental institutions illuminate how the biopolitical state meticulously constructed scientific knowledge of bodies and how such knowledge rationalized political and medical intervention in the bodies of the population with the dual object of maximizing the capacity of human resources and improving the quality of the Japanese race.

The IPP was established in August 1939 within the MHW as a research body responsible for investigating a wide range of population issues and solutions. As examined in the previous chapters, interwar policy discussions regarding population issues were led by two think tank groups: the PFIC and the PPRS. Although the IPP appears to have been built on these earlier efforts to construct comprehensive, scientific knowledge about Japan's demographic phenomena, the fundamental goal of population science was rearticulated during wartime due to the pressing need to repurpose knowledge to lay the groundwork for mobilization. As the National Mobilization Law in March 1939 heralded an era of total mobilization, the question arose as to how to mobilize and deploy human resources effectively. According to the plan for forced labor mobilization in 1939, the state needed an additional 1.1 million male and female workers to meet the burgeoning demand for labor in various fields of industry, including munitions factories, coal mining, construction, transportation, and farming.[38] The role of the IPP was to devise effective population policies that primarily aimed at supplying enough able-bodied workers to serve the state's wartime needs. Furthermore, under the total war regime in which forced mobilization became normalized, long-range policies were required not only to meet the need for labor, but more fundamentally to transform the entire population into healthy and productive workers. When the plan for creating the IPP was released, the news media endorsed the importance of population policies in waging war. For example, the *Tokyo Asahi Shinbun* commented that "it is urgent to build national population policies, an integral part of the permanent plan for the forced labor mobilization, in order to wage a protracted war and support the long-term [wartime industrial] construction."[39] This editorial gives a glimpse into a growing consensus on the normalization of wartime emergency and the need to transform the population into labor resources.

To that end, the IPP launched a set of population research projects to build a scientific foundation for a long-term plan to mobilize forced labor. The Research Bureau of the IPP was largely divided into four sectors according to research areas that included demography, ethnic and racial studies, the social sciences (i.e., sociology, economics, social policies, and geography), and the biological sciences (i.e., social biology, pre-clinical and clinical medicine, and race hygiene). The following list presents the seven major research topics that the Research Bureau of the IPP embarked on in November 1939:

1. The effects of war on demographic phenomena (quantity-wise, quality-wise, and socioeconomic dimensions)
2. Ways to raise birth rates (dynamic statistics, causes for low fertility, and government solutions)
3. Ways to decrease death rates (dynamic statistics, leading causes of death and diseases, and government solutions)
4. The relationship between social environments and the quality of the population
5. Carrying capacity (the relationship between changing industrial structures and population size in Japan proper, colonies, and China, respectively)
6. Demographic phenomena of neighboring peoples and Japanese settlers in other countries
7. Demographic phenomena and policies in foreign countries[40]

Four research sectors under the Research Bureau worked in coordination to accumulate data regarding each major research subject. Reproduction was their top priority among the demographic subjects the Research Bureau examined. Notably, the Research Bureau focused on conducting statistical surveys on fertility and reproductive health as a first step towards developing a pronatalist policy. This priority is exemplified by the first statistical survey of the IPP on fertility (*shussanryoku*). Although the national census had been carried out every five years since 1920, detailed statistical data covering socioeconomic and biological causes of demographic transition was still absent. Okazaki Ayanori, demographer and one of the chief researchers of the IPP, noted that the purpose of statistical research on fertility is "to collect statistical data clarifying the correlation between fertility among married couples and social or environmental conditions, which is integral to establishing population policies and laying out evaluation criteria for the policies."[41] Okazaki's emphasis on the direct link between statistical data and population policies reflects a specific mode of knowledge production, that is, the co-production of demographic knowledge and wartime policymaking. On the one hand, statistical data quantified complex population phenomena to cater to the specific needs of the wartime regime. On the other, the total war policies that aimed at increasing the size of the able-bodied population intervened in the process of knowledge production by not only shaping questions to be addressed—particularly on fertility—but also by determining the social boundaries within which such questions were valid—namely, the family and the nation-state.

This correlation between statistics and policies was manifested in the fertility research of 1940, particularly in terms of how survey subjects were categorized, how the questionnaire was organized, and how data were analyzed. The fertility researchers studied over 80,000 married couples nationwide and conducted a comprehensive survey on age-specific and occupation-specific fertility rates.[42] Its analysis covered socioeconomic and biological impacts on different fertility rates among four occupational groups that included salaried workers, wage workers, farmers, and medium- and small-sized traders and manufacturers, between urban and rural areas, and between wealthy and poor people. Even more significant was that the collected data functioned at the state level as objective criteria for regulating the socioeconomic and biological conditions conducive to boosting fertility rates. For example, the analysis of statistical data on the relation between the marital age of women and fertility led to the conclusion that early marriage for women (between the ages of 18–20), regardless of social status, contributed to improving fertility.[43] It is worth noting how families formed through marriage were brought into focus in connection with population management. The underlying assumption was that the family was the basic unit for reproduction as well as the medium for administering the population. The reordering of the family as the normative unit for procreation was central in shaping prenatal policies under the banner of "give birth and multiply" (*umeyo fuyaseyo*).

The normalization of the family as a legitimate unit for procreation in the wartime regime exemplifies the redefined value of the family as the "privileged instrument for the government of the population," as Foucault puts it.[44] Foucault argues that with the emergence of population, the family that used to function as a model embodying moral and symbolic values previously became an "element internal to population" to enable various techniques of government to be deployed among individual bodies.[45] Foucault's idea on the shift of the family from a model to an instrument, though, falls short of elucidating the dual nature of the family in the biopolitical state in wartime Japan. The total war regime not only instrumentalized the family to collect demographic data and promote its pronatalist policy, but also shaped its normative value by legitimizing a family formed through marriage and childbearing exclusively. Families formed outside of marriage and those who failed to contribute to fertility rates would be considered illegitimate or deviant according to the normalized form of the family. This suggests that the family functioned as a model and an instrument simultaneously in the Japanese biopolitical state, which required the former to strengthen state control over individual bodies and thereby increase the instrumentality of the family further. As further examined in Chapter 5, the family remained as a crucial instrument as well as a symbolic unit for the government of the Japanese population throughout the wartime years.

In the meantime, the RHRS, created in November 1938 within the Eugenics Bureau of the MHW, also played a leading role in designing the wartime population policies focusing exclusively on the quality of the population. As its name indicates, the RHRS was responsible for investigating race hygiene (*minzoku eisei*) and promoting eugenics ideas as a preliminary to enacting a eugenic sterilization law. The concept of race hygiene originated from a German notion *Rassenhygiene* popularized by German physician and anthropologist Alfred Ploetz (1860–1940) in the early 1900s.[46] Although both eugenics and race hygiene shared the same vision of achieving human progress through selective reproduction, the ways in which the ideas and practices of race hygiene were deployed in Germany were particularly geared toward the betterment of the Nordic race through the extermination of presumably inferior elements.[47]

The selective and destructive mechanism embedded in the notion of race hygiene was ironically supported by a group of Japanese eugenicists despite its explicit racism against non-white races. Nagai Hisomu, professor of physiology at Tokyo University, was a leading proponent of race hygiene in Japan. Having trained in physiology in Göttingen University in Germany, he led the promotion of eugenic ideas and called for support from the state to popularize eugenics. Nagai's effort culminated in the foundation of Nihon minzoku eisei kyōkai (Japanese Association of Race Hygiene) in 1930 and the publication of a journal entitled *Race Hygiene* since 1932.[48] Similar to the German race hygiene movement, the Japanese Association of Race Hygiene under Nagai's leadership also stressed the betterment of the Japanese race by means of the extermination of inferior traits within the race. Such an exclusionary principle of race hygiene was clearly reflected in the draft of the Law for the Protection of Race Hygiene drawn up by Nagai to legalize sterilization on eugenic grounds. This draft of the Law for the Protection of Race Hygiene was submitted to the

Imperial Diet in 1934, which resulted in failure. Although the legislative attempts that were made three more times in subsequent years between 1935 and 1938 ended up failing to come to fruition, Nagai and his fellow eugenicists in the Japanese Association of Race Hygiene contributed to creating an academic and legal discussion regarding the enforcement of sterilization in Japan.[49] With the birth of the MHW, the race hygiene movement, previously mainly led by medical scientists, became subsumed into state-led population policies. Especially, the launching of the RHRS as a subordinate research body of the MHW indicates that the wartime regime would actively incorporate exclusionary principles of race hygiene into its population control measures.

The primary responsibility of the RHRS was to conduct a preliminary investigation required to enact a eugenic sterilization law in Japan. From its inception, the RHRS justified its role in preparing for the establishment of sterilization policies as part of the national policy for improving people's physical fitness and human resources.[50] The doctrine of the race hygiene movement that the extermination of inferior traits is indispensable for improving the quality of the population underlaid the rationale for the state's aggressive intervention into individual reproduction. In its reports on race hygiene, the RHRS highlighted the three primary goals of the eugenics sterilization law, which included biological benefits on eugenic grounds, alleviation of socioeconomic burdens, and crime prevention.[51] These three goals indicate that the wartime population policies would not only concern the increase in the population size by offering social and welfare benefits to the Japanese population but also focus on the improvement of the quality of the Japanese race by implementing reproductive control. By eradicating allegedly inferior elements of the Japanese race, the state would achieve race betterment in both biological and social senses.

The RHRS's emphasis on sterilization for the benefit of the quality of the race brings us to the question of who, then, were those bodies labeled as inferior elements to be exterminated. The following statements from the RHRS's report on existing sterilization laws worldwide suggest that "inferiority" was an arbitrarily defined concept conflating medical diagnosis with social norms and national values:

> The reason why those with hereditary mental disorders are considered the most important target of the sterilization law is that their illnesses are deeply related to eugenics, socioeconomic, and crime issues. In contrast, hereditary physical disabilities are less crucial targets because those with hereditary physical disabilities are unlikely to be antisocial despite their lack of ability to make a living. Thus, their socioeconomic

impacts are not as substantial as those with hereditary mental illnesses. Also, alcohol addicts are normally included in the category of hereditary mental disorders due to their lack of aptitude. Considering the toxic effect of alcoholism on a fetus, alcoholism is significantly poisonous to a nation. Fortunately, in Japan, the issue of malignant alcoholism is unusual, compared to foreign countries. In a similar vein, paraphilia is rare in Japan whereas there are tons of sexual deviants or hideous sexual perverts in foreign countries. For syphilis and tuberculosis are not hereditary diseases, it goes without saying that different measures are required to control them. Additionally, it is no wonder that there are few countries that sterilize serious criminals. A crime itself is not hereditary but its root cause, that is, a mental disorder is.[52]

As the report shows, the RHRS paid keen attention to hereditary diseases as the potential target of sterilization laws. Especially, mental illnesses and physical disabilities that were supposedly inheritable were considered undesired traits on both medical and socioeconomic grounds. According to the principle of race hygiene, those bodies labeled as undesirable ought to be denied their reproductive freedom and subjected to sterilization procedures enforced by the state. The RHRS justified the enforcement of reproductive deprivation by arguing that a sterilization law would serve as a preventive measure for racial degeneration on eugenic grounds and for poverty and crime on social grounds.[53]

Such logic of differentiation embedded in the RHRS report on race hygiene laid the foundation for Kokumin yūsei hō (National Eugenic Law) promulgated in May 1940. The law conferred powers on the central and local governmental authorities and medical practitioners to govern the sterilization of those with (or potentially with) mental or physical hereditary diseases. The types of hereditary diseases specified in the law included hereditary mental disorders, hereditary mental retardation, severe or malignant hereditary personality disorders, severe or malignant hereditary physical illnesses, and severe hereditary deformities.[54]

Since those with the aforementioned diseases were neither forced nor coerced into sterilization but recommended to apply for sterilization operations under this law, it is fair to say that the consequence of the enforcement of the National Eugenic Law was less destructive than that of the Law for the Prevention of Offspring with Hereditary Diseases under Nazi Germany or that of American sterilization programs.[55] Nevertheless, the fact that only 538 cases of sterilization[56] were carried out under the National Eugenic Law should not blind us to the essentially violent logic underlying race hygiene—that is, inferior elements of the population, however arbitrarily defined, should be wiped out for the sake of the race. Indisputably, the enactment of the sterilization law during wartime indicates nothing but the rationalization and institutionalization of exclusionary politics under the guise of science.

Toward the Reproduction of Healthy People and Superior Race

As the Sino-Japanese war dragged on for two years due to China's tenacious resistance against the Japanese military forces, with support for its military action by the United States and the Soviet Union, the Japanese government braced for a protracted war by reorganizing the entire territory and resources within the Japanese empire. The reorganization of the empire began with the declaration of Dai tōa kyōeiken (Greater East Asia Co-Prosperity Sphere) on June 29, 1940, an imperialist war propaganda that rendered the ongoing war as a racial war between the East and the West, and a just war for "peace and order within the [Greater East Asian] Sphere."[57] This imperial manifesto exemplifies an ideological effort to emphasize "geographical, historical, racial, and economic" unity within all the regions of the Japanese empire under the euphemism of the "co-prosperity and co-existence" of the sphere.[58]

This ideological effort was soon followed by a series of governmental, military, and economic actions to realign both human and material resources within the empire. The passing of Kokudo keikaku settei yōkō (Outline for the Establishment of National Land Planning, hereinafter National Land Planning) in September 1940 was the first step toward a comprehensive and efficient plan to distribute industries, infrastructures, and the workforce to meet regional variations and, ultimately, to integrate different regions of the Japanese empire into an organic economic community.[59] The National Land Planning marked a milestone in wartime policies in modern Japan in various senses: first, it aimed at expanding the system of total mobilization to include colonies and semi-colonies under the banner of a "Japan-Manchuria-China plan."[60] Second, its ultimate goal was to perpetuate the wartime governmental system by developing "comprehensive and scientific schemes" of land development throughout the Greater East Asian Sphere.[61] Last, its all-encompassing scheme integrated existing welfare and social policies into wartime economies, which led to the molding of populations into workforces. In view of this, the National Land Planning was indicative of the perpetuation of the wartime regime throughout the empire.

Needless to say, this process of normalizing the war had a critical impact on population policies. The National Land Planning laid down the guidelines for "population distribution planning" to place wartime workers in suitable areas and positions, just as industrial, logistical, and cultural infrastructures were expected to be properly distributed according to regional needs.[62] The underlying logic behind this distribution plan was that the life of the population, along with the material resources necessary to wage war, would be incorporated into the warfare system. Shortly after the government imposed the principle of population distribution planning, the PPRS held a conference in support of the new principle of population policies. The fourth national conference of Jinkō mondai zenkoku kyōgikai (National Council for Population Problems), which took place November 14–15, 1940, centered around the themes of "population, ethnic nation, land" (*jinkō, minzoku, kokudo*).[63] With Kanemitsu Tsuneo, the head of MHW, and chief researchers of the IPP in attendance, the national conference included more than 130 presentations that addressed solutions for pressing wartime population issues. In particular, the rational and efficient distribution of population in accordance with the principles of National Land Planning was discussed in consultation with the Konoe cabinet. Shimojō Yasumaro (1885–1966), economist and head of the advisory committee of the National Council, highlighted the importance of integrating population policies into broader land planning. According to Shimojō's view, both human and material resources had to be allocated differently according to each region's specific needs for labor, types of industry (i.e., heavy industry or agriculture), and levels of economic and infrastructure development throughout the Greater East Asian Sphere.[64] His blueprint for the reorientation of wartime population policies can be summed up as the "fit-for-purpose" distribution of human resources.[65] As a result of this governmental effort to mobilize and distribute resources using the euphemism of land planning, population policies were swiftly subsumed into land development policies.

By the end of 1940, the initial population policies that had focused on population research and planning gave way to a new emphasis on executing policies for human resource reproduction and allocation. The Population Guidelines endorsed in January 1941 marked the beginning of a new phase of wartime population policies. Following the principles of the National Land Planning, the Population Guidelines primarily aimed at integrating population policies with a mission to "build and advance the East Asia Co-Prosperity Sphere" by increasing the size of the Japanese population, improving its quality, and adequately deploying labor forces throughout the sphere.[66] This primary aim required specific objectives to be fulfilled through various population policies, which were largely categorized into four sections. The objectives of the Population Guidelines are articulated as follows:

> The population policies of our nation must place priority on the following objectives with the aim of increasing the population in Japan proper to one hundred million by 1960. Separate provisions apply for populations outside Japan proper: (1) to ensure the long-lasting development of the population; (2) to surpass other countries in terms of the fertility and quality of the population; (3) to build up military forces and the workforce to sustain the state's high level of militarization; and (4) to secure the leadership of the Japanese population among Asian peoples through proper distribution of the population.[67]

Just as the goal of the National Land Planning was to perpetuate the wartime economy through the rational distribution of resources, the Population Guidelines aimed at constituting the ground for the perpetuation of a wartime mode of life. Here, the wartime mode did not necessarily mean a state of emergency as opposed to normal peacetime, but the expression of "a state of exception," as Giorgio Agamben argues, that [would become] "a lasting practice of the government."[68] Agamben points out the fictitious yet productive nature of the state of exception that generates a condition where life and law can no longer be distinguished. According to him, this specific fiction according to which "anomie ... is still related to the juridical order and the power to suspend the norm has an immediate hold on life" does not remain conceptual, but becomes *practical*, as in the case of many Western countries that had witnessed after World War I how life and law "[were] bound and blurred together, [became] the rule, then the juridico-political system [transformed] itself into a killing machine."[69] Agamben's notion of the state of exception provides critical insight into the total war regime under which state sovereignty enabled the state's ability to determine the limit of the law as well as the border between worthy and unworthy life.

The permanent progress and co-prosperity of the Greater East Asian Sphere was not merely a rhetorical euphemism but an expression of the juridico-political order regarding life in the state of exception. What was at stake here was that the wartime regime in Japan allowed life to prosper only to deprive individual bodies of the right to life. In other words, precarious life served as a necessary condition for the state's biopolitical apparatuses to operate. Here, precarity does not derive from the deprivation of state protection, but the state's arbitrary power to define life as a readily mobilizable resource, and thereby wield its exclusive right to valorize the life and the death of the population. The perpetual wartime mode of life, as envisioned by the Population Guidelines, was nothing but precarious life situated in a murky zone where biopower and necropower became entangled to reinforce each other. Therefore, the lines between life and death, and between welfare and warfare, became indistinguishable through the state's arbitrary power over individual bodies.

Various systemic approaches articulated in the Population Guidelines to govern the population exemplify this precarious mode of life, the very product of the biopolitical state during wartime. To a great extent, the ways in which the guidelines addressed pressing population issues—including fertility, mortality, and physical and mental capability—embraced the interwar population discourse. The continuity between interwar welfare planning and actual wartime population policies primarily concerns the problematization of the population in terms of quantity and quality, the emphasis on the state's responsibility for welfare, and a comprehensive and scientific approach to administering the population. In addition to such general principles, the Population Guidelines provided detailed plans to increase birth rates, decrease death rates, and improve the health of the people, all of which would materialize under the guidance of the MHW. The irony was that the interwar blueprint for population and welfare—whose primary aim was to allow people to live well—had to be subsumed into the biopolitical state—which exercises power over both life and death to valorize selected bodies—in order to materialize fully.

Six months after the cabinet endorsed the Population Guidelines, the MHW underwent restructuring with an eye to implementing detailed plans for increasing the population's size and improving its health. The establishment of Jinkō-kyoku (Population Bureau) that replaced Tairyoku-kyoku (Bureau of Physical Strength) demonstrates the wartime government's commitment to extensive population policies.[70] Following the Population Guidelines, the Population Bureau was entirely in charge of governing both the quantitative and qualitative aspects of the population. In regard to the quantitative dimension, the Population Bureau focused on approaches to increase fertility, such as marriage promotion, and medical and financial assistance programs for pregnant women and children. Meanwhile, positive eugenics, namely, a set of scientific discourse aiming to encourage reproduction among those with desirable traits, underlay the bureau's effort to raise the population's quality. The ambiguity in the criteria for "desirability" hardly presented an obstacle but provided ample room for pursuing multiple paths—physical, mental, acquired, and

Building a Biopolitical State • 127

congenital—toward race betterment. Just as the arbitrary criteria applied to the categories of inferior traits, the idea of desirable bodies was malleable to the extent that it justified the biopolitical state to take both preemptive and reactive measures to control individual bodies.

There are two quintessential examples of preemptive and reactive measures employed by the total war regime. As for the former, the promotion of eugenic marriage (*yūsei kekkon*) to control body-as-nature through interventions into procreation exemplifies a preemptive approach to the management of the population. With the promulgation of the National Eugenic Law in 1940, the MHW launched a campaign to promote eugenic marriage through the operation of Yūsei kekkon sōdansho (Eugenic Marriage Consultation Office) in Tokyo (Figures 4.1 and 4.2).[71] Yasui Hiroshi,

Figure 4.1 The Eugenic Marriage Consultation Office opened in Mitsukoshi department store, Tokyo, 1940.
Source: *Shashin shūhō* 116 (May 1940): 4.

Figure 4.2 Yasui Hiroshi (left) and a female visitor to the Eugenic Marriage Consultation Office to seek advice on the inheritability of color blindness.
Source: *Shashin shūhō* 116 (May 1940): 5.

psychiatrist and eugenicist, was appointed as a director of the Consultation Office. Before his appointment, he participated in Yūsei kekkon fukyūkai (Eugenic Marriage Popularization Society), a group founded in 1935 as an affiliate with the Japanese Association of Race Hygiene, and served as an editor of *Yūsei* (Eugenics), the monthly journal of the Eugenic Marriage Popularization Society.[72] As a vocal advocate of eugenic marriage, Yasui was invited along with other eugenicists and feminists to the RHRS roundtable discussion on eugenic marriage in 1939, which led to the announcement of Kekkon Jikkun (Ten Maxims for Marriage) outlining principles to fulfill a desirable marriage on eugenic grounds (Figure 4.3).[73]

With the opening of the Eugenic Marriage Consultation Office, the eugenic marriage campaign that eugenicists in social sectors had previously promoted became fully incorporated into the state's population policies. Employing the existing eugenic marriage advocates such as Yasui, the MHW operated the consultation office to offer advice about marriages and procreation and organized exhibitions to popularize eugenic knowledge especially among female clients. The MHW's emphasis on eugenic

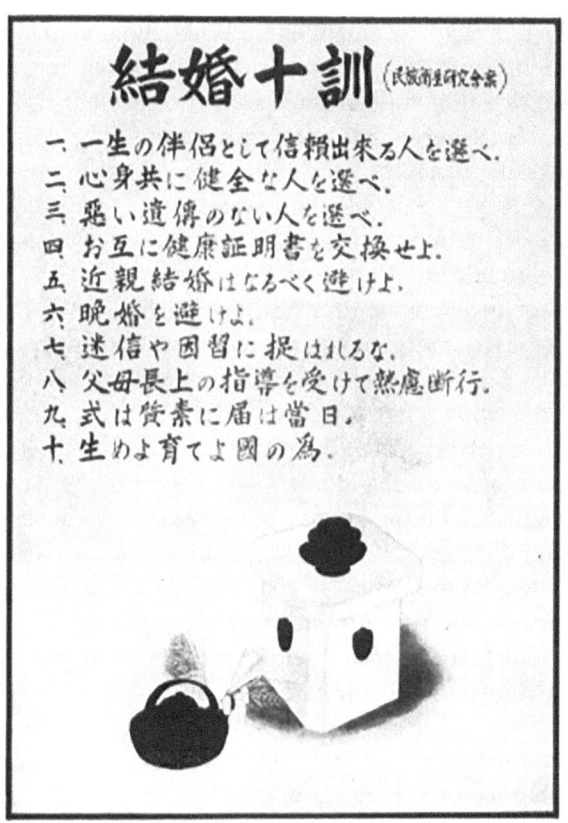

Figure 4.3 Ten Maxims for Marriage: (1) select a trustworthy other half; (2) select a mentally and physically healthy person; (3) select a person who has no inferior inheritable traits; (4) exchange health certificates with each other; (5) avoid a consanguineous marriage; (6) avoid a late marriage; (7) do not fall into superstitions or old customs; (8) take guidance from parents and older members of the family and carefully consider a marriage; (9) have a simple wedding and file a marriage certificate on the same day; (10) give birth and raise children for the nation. Translation of the maxims is mine.

Source: Kōsei-shō yobō-kyoku [The Bureau of Prevention, Ministry of Health and Welfare], *Kokumin yūsei zukai* [Illustrations of national eugenics] (Tokyo: Kokumin yūsei renmei, 1941), 63.

principles in marriage was essentially intended to encourage people of healthy stock to procreate while discouraging those with so-called unhealthy, inferior traits from producing their offspring. The Population Bureau's pamphlet "Kekkon sōdan ni okeru kenkō mondai ni kansuru shidō shishin" (Guiding principles for marriage counseling regarding health issues) offers a revealing look at the state's effort to increase the population with so-called superior traits on eugenic grounds by decreasing those with inferior traits, including infertility, tuberculosis, sexually transmitted diseases, leprosy, and hereditary diseases.[74]

Meanwhile, Kenmin undō (Campaign for Healthy People) was a reactive solution through the institutional nurturing of healthy bodies. The MHW launched the campaign for healthy people from 1942 forward to encourage physical activity and cultivate nationalism and rational living skills among its people. Under the banner of "healthy people" (*kenmin*), the MHW led a wide-ranging reform movement that encompassed the promotion of imperial nationalism, the encouragement of procreation and marriage, healthcare for mothers and children, the development of physical strength, the rationalization of everyday life, and the prevention and eradication of tuberculosis and sexual diseases.[75] Such a comprehensive approach to the government of the population was essentially geared toward the production of desirable laborers whose mode of life would fit well into both battlefront and home front. Notably, various state-led programs that aimed to boost physical fitness, such as Rajio taisō (Radio Calisthenics) (Figure 4.4) and Dai nihon kōsei taisō (Welfare Calisthenics of Great Japan) indicate how the state power permeates individual lives through disciplining their bodies and instilling the idea of desirable physicality in the people.[76]

The state's efforts to rationalize people's daily lives focusing on frugality and home hygiene also suggest the deployment of biopolitical techniques on an everyday level. By disciplining bodies and reorganizing daily lives, the campaign ultimately aimed to "perpetuate the prosperity of the imperial nation [*kōkoku minzoku*] and the development of the co-prosperity sphere through the ceaseless growth of the imperial nation both quantity- and quality-wise."[77] Indeed, the wartime population policies established under the leadership of the MHW mobilized a wide range of measures, both preemptive and reactive, to optimize both the quantity and quality of the Japanese population. Ironically, the optimized life resulting from biopolitical interventions was achievable only at the expense of, or potential expense of life throughout the wartime period.

Figure 4.4 "Twenty Thousand People's Radio Calisthenics," 1941.
Source: *Shashin shūhō* 181 (August 1941): 17.

Implications of the Biopolitical State

Toward the end of 1943, Japan fought a losing war against the Allied powers. While struggling with the shortage of war supplies and workers, the military government abolished the Planning Agency and the Ministry of Commerce and Industry, and it established Gunju-shō (Ministry of Munitions) in September 1943 to make every effort to produce munitions and war materials and to control conscripted workers directly.[78] Two months after this realignment, the MHW also underwent restructuring. The Population Bureau was replaced with Kenmin-kyoku (Healthy People Bureau) while the Social Affairs Bureau was abolished. As opposed to the preceding bureau, which concerned fertility and population size, the Healthy People Bureau emphasized physical training and disaster and emergency relief at the local level.[79] The shifting emphasis away from long-term, constructive population policies to temporary relief measures implied that the losing war effort was impeding the imperial nationalist endeavor to increase the population size and improve its quality. It was only after the protracted war ended and the empire collapsed that the postwar government established Jinkō mondai shingikai (Population Problem Inquiry Council, founded in 1949) and resumed discussions about population and welfare policies at the policy level. Although postwar population policy is beyond the scope of this book, it is worth noting that the postwar history of the welfare state is situated within the broader scope of population discourse. As this chapter has highlighted by using the notion of the biopolitical state, warfare hardly undermined welfare, but instead *reconfigured* it as a state-directed, comprehensive scheme for improving human resources.

In sum, the emergence and development of the biopolitical state expose the interwoven relationship between welfare and warfare and illuminates the central role of population discourse, especially eugenics and race hygiene, in reifying the idea of race(s) and normalizing biopolitical interventions in the interwar and wartime periods and even afterwards. What is at stake here is that population discourse facilitated differential politics to improve the lives of a selected population at the cost of others. In the next chapter, I will turn to the construction of motherhood during wartime to discuss further the gendered and racialized politics inherent in the biopolitical state.

FIVE

"Fertile Womb Battalion"
THE GENDER AND RACIAL POLITICS OF MOTHERHOOD

In the current circumstance, what is increasingly considered as the most important role of women is to use their innate motherhood qualities to serve the nation as a mother and raise many outstanding future citizens.

> TAISEI YOKUSANKAI [IMPERIAL RULE ASSISTANCE ASSOCIATION], *Bosei no hogo* [The protection of mothers] (1944); translation is mine

If we apply the notion of class in the relations of production to the relations of reproduction, men would be called the ruling class whereas women would belong to the ruled class. Although women have a means of reproduction, namely a womb, the fact that a womb belongs to a woman's body hardly indicates that women "own" a womb. The scheme of patriarchy has sought to put the means of reproduction called the womb under its domination and control. The ruling class in the relations of reproduction has aimed to let women stay ignorant about their bodies, have men control over women's bodies, and deprive women of their contraceptive freedom and reproductive self-determination.

> UENO CHIZUKO, *Kafuchōsei to shihonsei: Marukusu shugi feminizumu no chihei* [Patriarchy and capitalism: the horizon of Marxist feminism] (1990); translation is mine

From Voluntary Motherhood to Nationalist Motherhood

As the Japanese fascist regime actively incorporated biopolitical rationalities and measures into its wartime policies to optimize human resources, it became clear that the bodies of Japanese nationals were subject to state control and surveillance institutionalized in the form of welfare policies. Hence, the emergence of the biopolitical state during the wartime indicates a shift in the concept of family-state (*kazoku kokka*) that was once propagated to transform the people into the children of the nation-state ideologically in the Meiji period.[1] While the essentials of the family-state ideology were still inculcated into the mind of Japanese nationals during wartime, the biopolitical state expanded the spiritual kinship between individuals and the nation-state to include their imagined biological unity called race and amalgamated the Meiji nationalist ideology with population policies.

It was precisely because of the renewed family-state ideology that gender was an integral apparatus of the biopolitical state in wartime Japan. In view of the Meiji family-state ideology, the ideal virtues of women were defined as "good wife, wise mother" (*ryōsai kenbo*). The emphasis on women's leading roles in families and households reflects the modernization process facilitating the gendered division of labor primarily to confine women within the sphere of social reproduction. The domestication of women was thus aligned with the modern national ideology that normalized gender segregation in society. Yoshiko Miyake argues that this Meiji gender ideology encapsulated in the slogan "good wife, wise mother" was promoted by the wartime state as "women's reproductive roles were integral to the preservation of the family system."[2] While acknowledging the wartime state's effort to revitalize the gender ideology and family system in the Meiji era for war efforts, I argue that women's reproductive roles were rearticulated to meet the needs of the biopolitical state. In other words, women's reproductive roles were no longer merely ideologically defined but revalidated for biological and eugenic reasons and actively supported by the state institutions in the form of protection (*hogo*).

Japan's wartime welfare benefits and legal aid seeking the protection of motherhood, thus, affirm the gendered nature of governmentality. Specifically, gender was an integral part of state management of bodies not because of fundamental biological differences between the two sexes informing women's gender roles, but conversely, gender was instrumental in naturalizing women's reproductive roles—both biological and social reproduction—and thereby, legitimizing state intervention in the quantity and quality of the population. The increased discourse on motherhood during wartime to encourage women to produce as many healthy children as possible epitomizes the instrumentality of gender in the biopolitical management of the population. A set of wartime population policies that specifically targeted mothers and women of childbearing age in the name of the protection of motherhood served to essentialize women's reproductive bodies not only as a natural instinct but also as a sole medium through which women's political agency was recognized in the nation-state. Thus, motherhood was not an innate identity of women, but a constructed site where the biopolitical regime and various stakeholders in population management facilitated the gendered division of labor both in families and in larger society so as to maximize female reproductive function.

In Chapter 2, I discussed that the feminist birth control movement in interwar Japan heralded a new era of feminism by rearticulating women's political agency in relation to their maternal duties and reproductive labor. The feminist concept of "voluntary motherhood" embodied this vision of maternal feminism with which Japan's pioneering feminists promoted women's gendered agency as opposed to male-dominated political subjectivities. The feminist advocates for birth control even furthered the discussion of maternal feminism by highlighting how women's reproductive autonomy would contribute to addressing complex socioeconomic issues and improving the health of the nation. In particular, Ishimoto Shizue was a quintessential spokesperson for voluntary motherhood that would liberate women from involuntary procreation and enable them to become mothers serving in the interest of the nation in her eugenics-inspired feminist vision.

Ironically, while feminist birth control advocates who promoted voluntary motherhood by means of contraceptives were suppressed by the state authority due to their radical thoughts, the core idea of voluntary motherhood was co-opted by the wartime regime and incorporated into its population policies.[3] The wartime government's co-opting of feminist thinking was less concerned with the empowerment of women than with the reinforcement of gender roles by glorifying women's reproductive roles as their inborn vocation and adopting policies for the protection of motherhood on eugenic grounds. This irony leads us to the question regarding the instrumentality of motherhood both in feminist politics and in the biopolitical operation of the state. Scholars of Japanese feminist history have answered this question, mainly focusing on the ideological consensus made between anti–birth control feminist leaders and the wartime government on the eugenic cause.[4]

The trajectory of the maternal feminist movement—specifically, the anti-venereal disease campaign of Shin fujin kyōkai (New Woman Association) in the early 1920s to the foundation of Bosei hogo renmei (Motherhood Protection League) and the Eugenic Marriage Popularization Society in 1935—reveals the strategy of what Ueno Chizuko called "gender segregation," a feminist thought foregrounding fundamental differences between male and female.[5] This movement was led by prominent female figures such as liberal feminists Hiratsuka Raichō, Yamada Waka, Ichikawa Fusae, and Kaneko Shigeri, physician Takeuchi Shigeyo, and psychologist Kōra Tomiko. The segregation strategy was aligned with the wartime state's pronatalist and eugenics-motivated population policies as both considered motherhood to be essentially women's privileged vocation. While this chapter adds to the body of research that discusses the ideological intersection between maternal feminism and the state gender ideology, I seek to illuminate the construction of nationalist motherhood as a vital instrument for the state's population control during wartime. In so doing, I highlight the underlying ideological homology between eugenic feminism and the state's motherhood protection policies and, furthermore, to cast light on gender politics situated in the center of population discourse, far from being peripheral.

The instrumentality of motherhood in the biopolitical state epitomizes the gendered division of citizenship whereby women are rendered reproductive instruments. Here, the gender binary was not the only mechanism for differentiation deployed by the wartime regime. The gendering of citizenship intersected with racial and class lines to differentiate women who were entitled to be mothers from those whose motherhood ought to be denied and hence, who were excluded from state protection and assistance. So-called comfort women, or military sexual slaves mobilized across the Japanese colonial empire, were deemed to be women unfit for reproduction and instead were forced to serve for "comforting" tasks, namely, sexual instruments for the purpose of satisfying masculine-imperialist desires. The latter half of this chapter discusses the mobilization of comfort women as disposable sexual resources as a supplementary, rather than antithetical narrative to the history of the construction of nationalist motherhood in imperial Japan. It is not my intention to defend the motherhood—or potential motherhood—of the colonized women by contrasting them with the state's treatment of Japanese women. While bearing in mind that motherhood is not an inborn identity of women but a product of gender politics just as much as objectified sexuality, this chapter argues that the biopolitical state in wartime Japan deployed differential modes of body politics that intersected gender, race, and class lines.

Healthy and Fertile Mothers in the Interest of the Imperial State

The protection of motherhood was a longstanding feminist agenda in modern Japan. The debate on motherhood protection in the Taishō period indicates Japanese first-wave feminists' efforts to reconfigure motherhood as a public issue and a political identity exclusive to biological women. Since the mid-1930s, feminists who foregrounded women's maternal roles and responsibilities in families made a concerted effort across the feminist political spectrum to enact a law providing welfare aid to financially struggling mothers. As part of legislative efforts, maternal feminist Yamada Waka, leading suffragists Ichikawa Fusae and Kaneko Shigeri, leftist feminist Sakai Magara, and other feminist activists organized a group called Bosei hogo hō seitei sokushin fujin renmei (League for the Promotion of the Legal Protection of Motherhood) in 1934, which was renamed Bosei hogo renmei (Motherhood Protection League) in the following year.[6] As its name suggests, the league led a campaign to demand that the state provide financial assistance for impoverished mothers and lobbied the Diet for legislation.[7] In March 1937, the legislative efforts finally came to fruition when Boshi hogo hō (Mother-Child Protection Law) was enacted. The main thrust of this law was to ensure financial assistance to a mother and her child (under 13 years old) who were in poverty or if a father was absent or incapable of working.[8] Expectedly, the passage of the Mother-Child Protection Law was applauded in feminist circles as the first legislation that directly addressed mothers' issues in the legal history of Japan. For instance, progressive women's publication *Shūkan fujo shinbun* (Weekly women's newspaper) gratifyingly commented in its editorial that "enacting a law to protect mothers raising children is a cause of celebration as it indicates that the distinctive nature of motherhood has come to be recognized nationally."[9] The underlying premise of this comment echoes maternal feminists who deemed motherhood to be a women's divine duty that needed national assistance and protection.

The Mother-Child Protection Law of 1937 may have been the first law that acknowledged the state's responsibility for relieving vulnerable mothers, but it was not until the wartime population policies took shape that the state recognized the instrumentality of motherhood. The wartime state's policy for motherhood was sharply distinguished from the preceding approach focusing on the relief of the poor. Under the wartime biopolitical regime, it was mothers in general, regardless of their financial status, who became subject to the care and control of the government in the name of protection. The increasing institutional interest in motherhood during wartime begs the question as to the fundamental goal of the state's paternalist approach to the maternal body—whether it referred to an actual or a potential mother. As seen in what follows, a series of policies implemented to support mothers' reproductive responsibilities contributed more to *gendering* women as mothers than to resolving gendered challenges faced by mothers. Essentially, the wartime regime's paternalist protection of mothers aimed at taking advantage of women's reproductive function and labor to address the pressing need for human resources. Precisely because of this instrumentality of motherhood, the protection of mothers in general became one of the vital agendas for wartime population planning.

The slogan "fertile womb battalion" (*kodakara butai*),[10] which was used by the wartime government to promote its pronatalist policy, clearly illustrates the increasing government intervention into reproduction during the wartime period. In May 1940, the MHW released an outline for Yūryō tashi katei hyōshō (National Commendation for Families with Many Healthy Children). According to the outline, the purpose of this commendation was to recognize those who contributed to cultivating the foundation of the state by maintaining a sound family and raising healthy children.[11] Similar to the *Mutterkreuz* (Mother's Cross of Honor) under Nazi Germany, the MHW's plan for the commendation for large and healthy families was intended to valorize the reproductive role of the family unit and to set normative standards regarding reproductive activities that were worthy of recognition and protection.[12] To be eligible for the MHW's commendation, the applicant family should be comprised of both parents bound by a lawful marriage, their children should be at least 6 years old, and all the children should be physically and mentally healthy. The criteria were not simply to determine whether a family was eligible for the national commendation for its contribution to population growth, but also to dictate which forms of family as well as which bodies needed to be deemed normative. Needless to say, a family with both legal parents and multiple "healthy" children, as the title of the commendation suggests, was an ideal form of the family unit the MHW envisaged to promote population growth. On November 3, 1940, a national holiday called *Meiji-setsu* established to commemorate the Meiji emperor's birthdate, the MHW awarded commendations to 10,336 families across the nation to celebrate the nation in their own way.[13] All the families chosen for the award had more than ten children, and among those, four families were commended for having fourteen children in each family.

These large families were invariably named the "fertile womb battalion" and praised for their "patriotic fertility" (*kodakara hōkoku*) by the wartime media. Not only metropolitan media including newspapers and magazines, but also local newspapers, reported on the fertile womb battalion, with detailed coverage on the largest families in their region.[14] In so doing, the media in general, deliberately or not, served as a vehicle for promoting the state's pronatalist policy by eulogizing large families for their patriotic contribution to the nation. The repeated coverage of the Shiroto family, which was known as being the largest family in wartime Japan, gives a revealing look into the media's propaganda role in publicizing the government's pronatalist policy. For example, the women's magazine *Fujokai* (Women's world) and the militarist propaganda magazine *Gahō yakushin no nihon* (The advance in Nippon) covered the Shiroto family from Nagasaki, which was commended for having sixteen children in 1940; they were praised enthusiastically for being "Japan's best family blessed with many children" (*nihon ichi no kobukusha*) or "Japan's best fertile womb battalion" (Figure 5.1).[15]

The media coverage of the Shiroto family also paid close attention to the mother, Shiroto Kimi, who gave birth to many children during her marriage over two decades. Shiroto Kimi's story was included in the propaganda book *Nihon no haha* (Japan's mothers) published by Nihon bungaku hokokukai (Patriotic Association for Japanese Literature), a centralized literary organization sponsored by the Information Bureau.[16] In a piece titled "The Commander of Japan's Best Fertile Womb Battalion" in *Nihon no haha*, novelist Tatsuno Kyūshi recalled his visit to the Shiroto family and described Shiroto Kimi as an "outstanding Japanese mother."[17] The rationale for praising Shiroto as an exemplary mother of Japan was her extraordinary fertility—that is, having seventeen children as of 1943—and her mothering responsibility in protecting her children perfectly from illness. Using a military metaphor, namely the "battalion commander" who was in charge of leading a fecund family, the author reframed the gendered division of labor on patriotic terms and thereby reaffirmed that women were recognized as rightful citizens only through reproductive bodies and responsibilities. As Ruth A. Miller sharply comments on the gendered nature of citizenship in the modern biopolitical system by arguing "reproduction as a political duty is one of the most

Figure 5.1 A family portrait of the Shiroto family with sixteen children.
Source: Tanaka Mitsuko, "Nihon ichi no kodakara butai, jyūroku no shiroto-ke, Nagasaki" [The best fertile womb battalion in Japan, Shiroto family with sixteen children from Nagasaki], *Gahō yakushin no nihon* 5, no. 12 (1940).

basic attributes of citizenship,"[18] under Japan's wartime biopolitical regime, the role of producing healthy offspring became identical to the civic duty of motherhood. Put simply, the wartime discourse reconstituted women as imperial citizens who possessed a fertile womb.

Shiroto Kimi was one of the many idealized Japanese mothers due to their extraordinary reproductive abilities and devoted childcare. As each year the government commended more families for having more than ten children, more stories of exemplary motherhood filled the pages of both government propaganda and popular magazines throughout the wartime period. The continued coverage of fertile womb battalions in these paper media, regardless of whether the government had direct control or not, contributed to popularizing the idea that having many healthy children and raising them to be proper Japanese citizens was a way of fulfilling patriotic duties. Through the media coverage, these patriotic mothers with fertile wombs shared their childrearing methods—such as how to feed and educate children, how to lead a frugal life, and how to manage busy caretaking. The media's praise for their mothering abilities was often supported by family portraits of happy, smiling people or photos of vibrant children (Figures 5.2 and 5.3). The children's good health and potential to contribute to the nation were commented on in a celebratory manner.[19] This indicates a nationalist desire projected onto Japanese women—that is, women have a lifelong duty to be mothers and to reproduce laborers for the nation's prosperity.

While the "fertile womb battalion commendation" aimed to popularize nationalist norms of motherhood by displaying exemplary families, subsequent population policies since 1942 sought to proactively manage and intervene into women's reproductive bodies in order to address the wartime needs for human resources. From the view of the state, the maternal body represented the locus of the intersection between nature and nurture. In other words, the wartime population policies equated women with their reproductive bodies, which were presumed to be the embodiment of natural and hence transcendent motherhood. Simultaneously and ironically, the state also sought to implement welfare and administrative

Figure 5.2 A family portrait of the Shino family with eleven children.
Source: Tsuchiya Hidemaro, "Onna bakaride jyūichinin kyōdai, nakayoshi kodakarabbutai hōmon" [Eleven siblings, all female: a visit to a fertile womb battalion with strong bonds], *Fujokai* 62, no. 6 (1940): 221.

Figure 5.3 Photos of the Tsunoda family with twelve children. The photo on the bottom right features the family performing Radio Calisthenics at 6 am, which appears to highlight the physical fitness and patriotism of the family.

Source: "Kodakara ikka no sōryoku atsumete" [Pull everyone together from the fertile womb battalion], *Shashin shūhō* 298 (November 1943): 16–17.

intervention into maternal bodies to optimize their fertility, which was instrumental in improving the quantity and quality of the Japanese population ultimately.

The nationalist norms of motherhood as typified in the media discourse were further reified through various concrete policies on maternal bodies, whether their fertility is actual or potential. The MHW's campaign for "healthy people" launched in 1942 to improve people's physical strength and boost their nationalist sentiment at the local and individual level showcases the state's increasing instrumentalization of maternal bodies to optimize its population. As the following outline of the "healthy people" campaign reveals, the wartime state legitimized its specifically gendered population policies using the norm of ideal motherhood:

> whereas men go to the battlefields or serve in the industrial workforce to fulfill the duty of national defense with brave hearts, the primary duties of mothers are to keep their homes safe, to produce as many superior and healthy citizens as possible, and to raise them as good imperial subjects.[20]

In view of this sentiment, it was not the female body in general but the *reproductive* body that the biopolitical state problematized to secure the welfare of the population and ultimately strengthen the workforce.

The particular attention to maternal bodies in the wartime biopolitical regime led to the ordinance regarding "Ninsanpu techō" (Handbook for the Expectant Mother, hereinafter Handbook) in July 1942.[21] The ordinance intended to provide medical and material resources to pregnant women in order to protect and improve their health. To do so, the central government mandated local governments to publish and distribute the Handbooks to pregnant and postpartum women and to advise them regarding health checkups. In the meantime, expecting mothers were required to consult care providers, including physicians and midwives, to confirm their pregnancy, seek medical care and health advice throughout the pregnancy and postpartum period, and fill in various forms appended in the Handbooks to keep track of the pregnancy. The range of information mothers were required to provide through the Handbooks included mothers' personal information and due date, mothers' and newborn babies' health examination results, birth certificates, and details on childbirth (including miscarriages, preterm births, and stillbirths) (Figures 5.4 and 5.5).[22] If a pregnancy determination turned out to be false or a mother died while pregnant, the already-distributed Handbook needed to be returned to the local government. Given the requirements imposed on mothers who received it, the Handbook essentially served to collect data regarding birth rates at the local authority level and, more importantly, to keep individual mothers under state and medical surveillance.[23] In other words, the meaning of the protection of mothers manifested in the Handbook policy was nothing but the surveillance of mothers to ensure their fertility.

In addition to enforcing the monitoring of expecting mothers in administrative and medical domains, the Handbook policy also aimed to discipline pregnant women to develop daily healthy habits and seek medical care during pregnancy and postpartum. In particular, "Ninsanpu no kokoroe" (Guidelines for expectant mothers) included in the Handbook spelled out specific rules for women to follow to ensure the care of their health and the birth of healthy offspring.[24] The guidelines encompassed developing a healthy routine while avoiding physically strenuous activities, maintaining a balanced diet, having regular checkups with care providers (namely, physicians and midwives) and seeking medical treatment if a mother has any abnormal symptoms or preexisting health conditions, delivering a baby with the help of care providers, and keeping away from any superstitions after birth. Such emphasis on the medicalized care

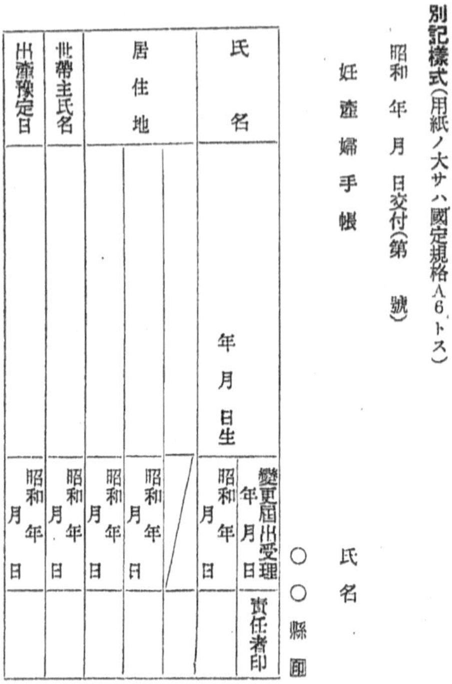

Figure 5.4 The personal information form included in the Handbook for the Expectant Mother. The range of information required to be provided by mothers included name, address, householder's name, and due date.

Source: "Ninsanpu techō kitei no seitei" [The establishment of the ordinance in the Handbook for the Expectant Mother], *SPP* 3, no. 8 (August 1942): 32.

Figure 5.5 The form for the pregnant woman and newborn health examination included in the Handbook for the Expectant Mother. The information to be supplied in the form included previous experiences of childbirth (including miscarriages and stillbirths), mother's occupation, dates and details of prenatal checkups, and care provider's signature.

Source: "Ninsanpu techō kitei no seitei," *SPP* 3, no. 8 (August 1942): 33.

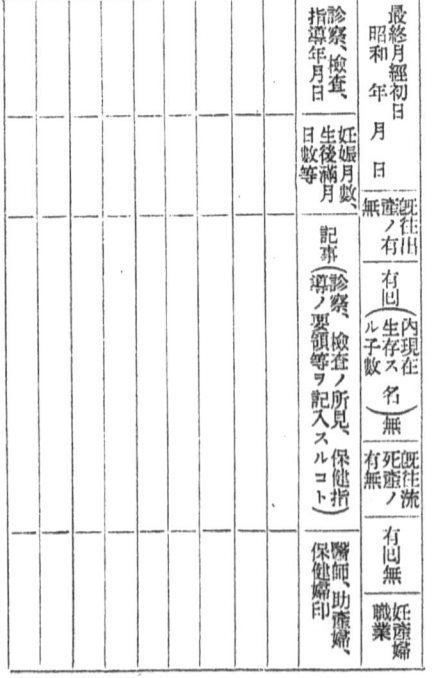

of expectant mothers indicates the state's effort to rationalize the process of childbirth by mandating the intervention of medical experts and knowledge into individual mothers' birth experiences. Moreover, mothers were expected to have the self-discipline to follow medical instructions to ensure their health and, more importantly, their newborns' health. Considering the shortage of medical personnel and resources during the wartime, it is reasonable to conclude that the guidelines were devised as ideological tools rather than as a feasible plan despite the state's endeavor to recruit medical practitioners and train students to fill the gap in medical resources throughout the wartime years.[25] The ideological dimension of the guidelines is pronounced in its nationalist statement that "expectant mothers ought to serve for the nation by being mindful of taking care of themselves during pregnancy and giving birth to an excellent child."[26] Given this, the Handbook policy aimed less to protect expectant mothers *per se* than to protect the imperial nation essentially through disciplining them to conform to the gendered ideology of motherhood.

Such ideological propagation of nationalist motherhood was assisted by medical experts and patriotic women's associations. Nihon bosei hogokai (Society for the Protection of Mothers) and Dai nippon fujinkai (Greater Japan Women's Association), both of which were founded in February 1942 coincidentally, served as active agents in the enforcement of maternal policies during the wartime years. The Society for the Protection of Mothers was a state-sponsored group consisting of obstetricians and gynecologists across the nation. In close conjunction with the Population Bureau of the MHW, the members of the society took the initiative to provide healthy guidance to expecting mothers, promote medical knowledge on pregnancy and childbirth, and address reproductive issues under special circumstances, including the protection of expecting mothers at workplaces or during air raids.[27] The prospectus of the society gives a revealing glimpse into the nationalist motivation of medical experts in the group including Kinoshita Seichū (1869–1952), an ob-gyn and the first chief director of Sanikukai that had provided medical relief to poor mothers and children since 1918.[28] According to the prospectus, the ob-gyns in the group aimed at the "reinforcement of national power" (*minzoku-ryoku*), for which the promotion of maternal health was integral.[29] Considering the rhetoric that aligned itself with the state's motherhood protection policies, it is noted that the society was not merely a medical unit providing expert knowledge and skills on reproductive health. The ob-gyns in the society rather repurposed their obstetric and gynecologic expertise in the interest of the nation and thereby became one of the active vehicles for the propagation of the nationalist ideology of motherhood. "Ninpu-kun" (Maxim for expecting mothers) was drafted and distributed by the Society for the Protection of Mothers, signifying this propaganda role of the medical professionals in enforcing the wartime maternal policies.

Maxim for Expecting Mothers

- Giving birth to and raising a baby is women's vocation.
- Having many children may cause hardship temporarily but brings pleasure afterward and serves the nation.
- A healthy child comes from a healthy mother.
- If you think you are pregnant, have a checkup; if your pregnancy is confirmed, submit the form for expecting mothers.
- Have a checkup once a month.
- Expose yourself to sunshine and air and do moderate exercise.
- The basic rule of nutrition is to have a balanced diet.
- Since most miscarriages happen in the second and third months of pregnancy, be careful during this period.
- Extreme morning sickness should not be ignored.
- Be extra careful about major house cleaning, moving, walking up and down a staircase, going out in the rain, laundry, crowds of shoppers, vehicles, etc.
- Those who experienced miscarriages or stillbirths need a blood test (it is even better that everybody gets a blood test).
- Swelling and numbness should not be taken lightly; symptoms like headaches, eye paralysis, and blurred vision require immediate medical care from doctors.
- Avoid overdoing it while eating sufficiently during postpartum; postpartum recovery takes twenty days and complete recovery takes forty days.
- Follow the breastfeeding rule precisely.[30]

Similar to the guidelines for expectant mothers, the maxim set disciplinary guidelines for expecting and postpartum mothers to allow medical and administrative interventions to be normalized in women's reproductive experiences. As noted previously, such gendered guidelines were essentially geared toward a nationalist cause, that is, producing as many healthy children as possible to enhance the national power.

Meanwhile, the Greater Japan Women's Association, a state-sponsored women's organization that amalgamated existing women's groups including Aikoku fujinkai (Patriotic Women's Association) and Kokubō fujinkai (Women's National Defense Association), was another primary agent in the propagation of motherhood ideology and the execution of the state's maternal policies.[31] The Greater Japan Women's Association, or *Nippu*, recruited members from married women aged 20 or older, which enabled *Nippu* to grow into an organization consisting of 20 million women nationwide as of 1945 and to further expand into the colonies including Korea, Taiwan, and the South Sea Islands.[32] As a result, *Nippu* served as the most significant liaison between the state and the home front and between national and local bodies—that is, Taisei yokusankai (Imperial Rule Assistance Association) at a centralized national level and Tonarigumi (Neighborhood Associations) at myriad local levels. As Sandra Wilson keenly observes, *Nippu*'s liaison role was oriented towards not only gendered but also racialized principles.[33] Its emphasis on the appropriate duties and virtues of "Japanese women" (*Nihon fujin*)[34] in service to the nation dictated its activities of mobilizing women on the home front for patriotic duties. The patriotic activities promoted among "Japanese women" encompassed boosting nationalism and womanly virtues, rationalizing daily lives, providing support to soldiers while practicing drills needed to protect the home front, and most notably, raising children who would become future citizens of Japan.[35]

Among various home front activities *Nippu* carried out during the wartime years, the protection of the health of mothers and children was a primary task that aligned with the state's pronatalist policies. *Nippu* took the initiative in providing health guidance to expecting mothers and mothers with small children on commission from local governments. In each town association (*chōnaikai*), *Nippu* appointed a supervisor in charge of health guidance for mothers and children (called *kenmin shunin/bosei hodō i'in*) and carried out public health activities, primarily focusing on expecting mothers and young children.[36] Whereas the role of healthcare providers mainly concerned the medicalization of childbirth using their professional authority, *Nippu* played an auxiliary role for the state's surveillance capacity by taking advantage of its fine-mesh local networks across the nation. All health guidance supervisors were in charge of ensuring that expecting mothers receive the Handbook and see a care provider for a regular checkups, and they supported mothers in poverty by distributing medical vouchers. In addition to the care of expecting mothers in their area, *Nippu*'s health guidance supervisors were also responsible for the health of infants and young children. They worked in close liaison with local governments, public health agencies, and welfare and healthcare providers such as district commissioners (*hōmen i'in*) and public health nurses (*hokenfu*) to make sure that infants and small children went through physical examinations and maintained proper nutrition. For families who needed extra support for childcare, the supervisors instructed Neighborhood Associations to assist the families in need so that their local community could share the responsibility for childcare.[37]

With impending air raid threats in the last two years of the war, *Nippu* increasingly emphasized expectant mothers' emergency preparedness to assure their safe delivery despite the potential absence of medical resources. Such an approach unveils a chilling aspect of the state's population policies that pushed forward with the production of as many children as possible even though there was a bleak outlook on those children's survival. Women's bodies, especially bodies of expectant mothers, were merely an instrument for the Janus-faced biopolitical power. The wartime population policies intended to protect motherhood were essentially geared toward the defense of the nation at the potential expense of the lives of mothers and their children. In the view of the state, the protection of motherhood would be actualized only on the condition that female bodies served the purpose of reproduction to maximize the size of mobilizable human resources for war efforts. Undoubtedly, *Nippu* took part in this twofold exercise of biopolitical and necropolitical power: on the one hand as a surveillant that oversaw maternal bodies on behalf of the state, and on the other hand as an auxiliary authority that enabled the violent process of the mobilization of wombs to unfold throughout the wartime years.

As mentioned in Chapter 4, with the prolonging of the war, Japan's governmentality was recalibrated to mobilize colonized populations as human resources. The integration of male colonial bodies primarily from colonial Korea and Taiwan into military manpower along with Japanese soldiers unequivocally affected the colonial discourse of motherhood and reproduction. In colonial Korea, for instance, the establishment of Kōseikyoku (Bureau of Health and Welfare) within the Government-General of Korea in 1941 coincided with the extension of the mobilization of soldiers to Korean male imperial subjects, enabled by Rikugun tokubetsu shiganheirei (Army Special Voluntary System Law) of 1938 and the 1943 revision of Heieki hō (Military Service Law) to enforce the conscription of Koreans beginning in 1944.[38] Ishida Sentarō, the first director of the Bureau of Health and Welfare, assigned colonial Korea the role of a logistics base for the prolonged war, and accordingly, promoted a pronatalist policy to ensure the supply of human resources.[39]

The pronatalist measures implemented under the aegis of the colonial government included the commendation of mothers with more than ten children, campaigns for eugenic marriage, free medical consultation for expectant mothers, as well as prioritization for egg rationing.[40] Such measures taken in line with the slogan of "deliver, increase, and raise,"[41] though, did not develop into a full-fledged policy to protect motherhood unlike the campaign in Japan proper. As An T'ae-yun rightly notes, the wartime pronatalist policy in colonial Korea focused more on rhetorical propaganda to imbue colonial female citizens with maternal nationalism rather than establishing concrete public health measures to protect the health of mothers.[42] In addition, the abolition of the Bureau of Health and Welfare within a year after its creation indicates that governmentality in the Japanese empire maintained the logic of differentiation between Japanese and colonial bodies, and in the same vein, colonial mothers were not fully integrated into the zone of imperial mothers entitled to the state's protection. The illusory aspects of the wartime ideology of imperialization (kōminka) that legitimized differentiation along gender and race lines are demonstrated more clearly by the ways in which the wartime regime distinguished reproductive bodies from exploitable bodies. The following section will delve into the structure of violence against female colonial bodies who remained in the "zone of indifference"[43] with little anticipation of inclusion.

Comfort Women: Female Bodies Unworthy of Protection

The instrumentalization of motherhood during wartime reveals a historical process through which Japanese women were reduced into their reproductive bodies, or, put more simply, their wombs. This suggests a particular way of gendering women's political subjectivity under the biopolitical regime: namely, the ideological construction of nationalist motherhood was the single legitimate path allowed to Japanese women to be acknowledged as proper citizens by the state. This gendered division of citizenship during wartime, though, can be further complicated when taking intersectionality and colonialism together into account. Intersectionality is a theoretical framework to critically engage with the multidimensionality of human experiences that are differently informed by sex, race, gender, class, and other identity categories.[44] Kimberlé Williams Crenshaw, a civil rights advocate and a pioneering scholar of critical race theory, developed the framework of intersectionality to illuminate the importance of accounting for differences in the experiences of Black women whose identity is situated at the complex intersection of race, gender, class, and other social factors.[45] Crenshaw sharply observes differences within a homogenized group by arguing that "the elision of difference in identity politics is problematic, fundamentally because the violence that many women experience is often shaped by other dimensions of their identities, such as race and class."[46] Echoing Crenshaw's emphasis on differences in experiences shaped by intersecting identity categories, I argue that women's experiences under Japan's biopolitical regime were differently conditioned along the intersecting lines of gender, race, and class. In the context of Japan's colonial empire, the ways in which the state mobilized female bodies were primarily legitimized by women's racial identity while class identity intersected with racial factors to complicate further the patterns of women's mobilization for war efforts. Precisely because of this particular historicity under Japanese colonialism that facilitated racial politics within the empire, it is integral to employ both lenses of intersectionality and colonialism to elucidate the heterogeneity of women's experiences during wartime.

In what follows, I will examine the experiences of Japan's wartime military sex slaves, or "comfort women," to navigate the instrumentality of women's bodies other than fertile wombs and thereby decolonize the wartime narrative of motherhood ideology. Particular attention will be paid to the following questions: What were women's wartime experiences under Japanese colonialism other than being mobilized as the wombs for the nation? What does the mobilization of Japanese women' ideal motherhood represent within the intersectional map of the instrumentality of female bodies? The complex lens of intersectionality and colonialism will allow us to reconnect scattered narratives around female bodies in the Japanese colonial empire to illuminate multifaceted historical experiences around gendered bodies under biopolitical control.

"Comfort women" (*ianfu*) is an imperialist masculinist euphemism referring to the military sexual slaves mobilized and imprisoned by the Japanese military during the wartime period.[47] It is estimated that approximately 200,000 women were forced to serve in military-run or military-sponsored quasi-brothel facilities called "comfort stations" (*ianjo*) during the Asia-Pacific War (1937–1945).⁴⁸ So-called comfort women mainly were minors who were rounded up from different regions under the Japanese colonial empire, including Japan proper, Korea, China, Taiwan, the Philippines, the Dutch East Indies (present-day Indonesia), French Indo-China (Vietnam, Cambodia, Laos), British Malaya (Malaysia), and Timor. Due to the absence of official statistics regarding the number and ethnicity of those comfort women, the proportion of different ethnicities that made up the enslaved women has been only conjectured based on pertinent hygiene and medical reports produced in local units and individual testimonies of victims.⁴⁹ The variety of circumstances women encountered—ranging from the abduction and relocation of unmarried young women to comfort stations outside their home countries to the forced mobilization of local women for sexual slavery in their home regions—adds further challenges to obtaining the complete picture of who the victims of Japan's military sexual slaves were.

Although acknowledging the importance of evidence on the size and ethnic backgrounds of military sex slaves under the Japanese colonial empire to redress the unresolved issue of comfort women, it is not my intention here to investigate and determine the precise number of victims by ethnicity. The primary focus here instead is why the system of military sexual slavery was needed in the first place and how local and central military authorities treated enslaved women who came from across the empire. Answering these two questions will allow us to understand what is mentioned above as the "intersectional map of the instrumentalization of female bodies" that were variously rendered under the biopolitical regime, namely, the bodies to procreate and the other bodies to be raped. Considering this, it suffices to mention here that a significant number of comfort women were Korean and Chinese, while the rest of the women were from Japan proper, Taiwan, and occupied regions in Southeast Asia and the Pacific Islands.⁵⁰ The inclusion of Japanese women in the demographics of enslaved victims does not necessarily invalidate my argument on the politics of race and ethnicity in facilitating the wartime military sexual slavery system. Instead, the fact that most Japanese comfort women were recruited among prostitutes and barmaids (*shakufu*) who were over the age of 21,⁵¹ whereas most enslaved women from Japan's colonial or occupied regions were minors and were not previously engaged in the sex industry, reaffirms the differentiation of women along racial lines. In addition, it should be noted that Japanese prostitutes and barmaids who eventually came to serve as comfort women during wartime were largely recruited in impoverished areas or victims of girl trafficking in the prewar period.[52] The existence of Japanese comfort women along with those from Japan's colonized and occupied regions suggests the intersection of racial politics and class stratification, both of which enabled the sexual exploitation of selected female bodies in an institutionalized way.

As Yoshimi and other scholars have already examined, the primary purpose of the operation of Japan's military sexual slavery system was to prevent the spread of sexually transmitted diseases (STDs) among the Japanese troops and to deter rapes of local women in the occupied areas.[53] Due to the rampant rape incidents committed by Japanese troops in occupied territories—notoriously, during the Nanjing Massacre of 1937–1938—as well as the Imperial Japanese Army's pressing concerns over the spread of STDs among Japanese soldiers (who presumably used civilian brothels), military leaders in the Ministry of Army and expeditionary forces agreed on the need to establish comfort stations and recruit women in tandem with the Ministry of Foreign Affairs and local police forces.[54] The military authorities' plan to supply women as sexual subjects to ensure a "safe sex" for Japanese forces indicates the prevalence of misogynist militarism in the military institutions. That is to say, the military sexual slavery system legitimized male sexual domination as a natural entitlement while instrumentalizing female bodies as exploitable sexual objects. Despite acknowledging the health risks accompanied by unbridled rapes, the military authorities sought to resolve the issue of rampant rape cases by introducing systematic "gang rapes" against a selected group of women in order to protect Japanese male bodies and satisfy their misogynistic masculine desire.

The ways in which enslaved women under Japan's military sexual slavery system were treated were in sharp contrast to how the Japanese government treated Japanese mothers and potential mothers in Japan proper. The major differences between the treatment of comfort women and that of Japanese mothers were first, the primary function of the former was to provide sexual services that did not, and should not, involve any reproductive functions, whereas the latter was considered exclusively the legitimate source of offspring; and second, precisely because of these different roles designated by the masculine empire, medical interventions in for comfort women were focused on the prevention of venereal diseases for the protection of Japanese male bodies whereas medical interventions in Japanese mothers and expecting mothers were aimed at assisting in producing healthy offspring for the sake of the nation's health.

The distribution of condoms (*sakku*) in comfort stations and the enforcement of the use of condoms by central and local military authorities are clear indications of the sexual instrumentality embodied by comfort women. As some remaining official documents substantiate, Japanese military authorities required Japanese military and civilian personnel who used comfort stations to wear condoms in order to prevent the spread of venereal diseases among them.[55] Testimonies from the victims of the Japanese military sexual slavery also support the fact that soldiers and civilian employees were required to use condoms in principle when visiting comfort stations. The late Kim Bok-Dong, a Korean survivor of Japan's military sexual slavery system, gave testimony as follows in the Women's International Tribunal on Japanese Military Sexual Slavery of 2000 (hereinafter Women's Tribunal):[56]

> Fifteen soldiers usually came each day, but on the weekend the number often exceeded fifty. The enlisted soldiers came between noon and 5pm on Saturdays and from 8am to 5pm on Sundays. They had to be gone by 5pm when the military police came to check on the station. Officers arrived after 7pm, many of whom slept there and then left. If my vagina was swollen and it was hard to penetrate, the soldiers put an ointment on the condom and forced themselves in. If I didn't know that my menstruation had started and a soldier saw the blood, he would get angry, and slap my face and hit me.[57]

Besides the repulsively violent scene of sexual assault recollected by Kim, her testimony reveals how such violence was accompanied by the goal of protecting male aggressors as explicitly symbolized by condoms and ointments for venereal diseases. The existence of regulation around the use of condoms, though, did not necessarily mean that the regulation was strictly observed by military and civilian employees during wartime. As the collected testimonies during the Women's Tribunal suggest, most users of comfort stations did not use condoms, and "thus, many comfort women became pregnant as a result of the repeated rapes."[58]

The pregnancy of comfort women was an unwelcomed consequence of the military sexual slavery system from the perspective of the Japanese military authorities. Unlike the Japanese mothers whose reproductive experiences were subjected to governmental and medical care for the sake of population governance, the bodies of military sexual slaves were completely excluded from bodies deserving the state's protection and were reduced into exploitable objects deserving physical and reproductive violence. The oral judgment of the Women's Tribunal poignantly sums up the magnitude of violence against the enslaved women at comfort stations as follows:

Most of the young girls or unmarried women lost their virginity when they were first raped. During their time in the facilities, the relentless violence and violations resulted, intentionally or incidentally, in a variety of reproductive harms, such as pregnancy, abortion, miscarriage, sterilization, sexually transmitted diseases, and sexual mutilation. The beatings, stabbings, burnings, and sexual tortures inflicted during the course of the rapes and enslavement caused enormous pain and suffering, as did the humiliating medical checkups forced upon the women.[59]

At the heart of the systematic violence inflicted on comfort women was the misogynistic desire of the empire to legitimize the instrumentalization of racialized and gendered bodies not as fertile wombs but as exploitable vaginas.

Meanwhile, the ways in which medical interventions penetrated the bodies of comfort women also showcase the systematic violence perpetrated by Japan's masculine empire. As the abovementioned oral judgment in the Women's Tribunal indicates, regular medical checkups conducted on enslaved women did not intend to protect their bodies from venereal diseases but aimed to ensure the protection of male aggressors' health by putting the women's bodies under surveillance. Although detailed regulations regarding medical checkups varied depending on military unit jurisdiction, regular checkups for venereal diseases were carried out in principle by military medical officers in each comfort station facility.[60]

The Allied Translator and Interpreter Section (ATIS) report published after the war by the Supreme Commander for the Allied Powers, General Douglas MacArthur, provides a revealing glimpse into how the imperial military authorities enforced and regulated medical examinations of comfort women in their controlled area.[61] The ATIS report includes a crucial document entitled "Rules for Authorized Restaurants and Houses of Prostitution in Manila" initially issued by Lieutenant Colonel Onishi in Manila District Line of Communication Squad in February 1943. The report did not use the term "comfort women" explicitly but referred to the women who served as sex slaves for soldiers and civilian employees as "hostesses (geisha and waitresses [*sic*])"[62] in its translated version. Notwithstanding, the fact that the military imposed direct control over the operation of pertinent facilities and regulation of employees strongly indicates the presence of comfort stations and comfort women in Manila during the wartime years. According to Onishi's document, "hostesses" under the jurisdiction of the army in Manila would "ordinarily be examined by army physicians once a week at a designated place."[63] The regular medical examinations did not only seek to diagnose venereal dis-

"Fertile Womb Battalion" • 155

eases but also included bacteria examinations and comprehensive checkups detecting contagious diseases and tuberculosis.[64] The regular medical examinations of employees fell under the responsibilities of the managers of comfort stations, who were also responsible for keeping their facilities sanitary and reporting the conditions of facilities to the army every month. If a "hostess" was diagnosed with any unfavorable diseases at a regular medical checkup, the person was banned from serving customers until permission was granted and was required to get treatment at shared expense between the hostess herself and a manager.

The detailed regulations by the Manila District Line of Communication Squad on medical checkups still leave a question mark as to whether such regulations were strictly observed under the harsh conditions of wartime. As seen in the abovementioned quote from the oral judgment of the Women's Tribunal, testimonies from the survivors of Japan's military sexual slavery system disprove the actual effectiveness of such measures in preventing STDs. Notwithstanding the gap between intended hygiene measures and actual effectiveness, the detailed regulations on the regular medical checkups of comfort women indicate the Japanese army's institutional efforts to put the women's bodies under surveillance with the aim of protecting the health of individual male aggressors. Although Japanese

BROTHELS

EXAMINATION REGISTER		House Name				
Date of Examination	Month	Day	From To	Hour Hour	Minute Minute	
Person Examined						
Decision	Passed Name	Diseased		Name		
Name of Diseased Person	Name of Disease	Remarks:				
YOSHIKO (Name used as example)	Stage Syphilis					
YASUKO (Name used as example)	Tracheal gonorrhea (気 管 淋)					
Other matter for reference						
Examining Medical Officer	Army Medical Officer ....Rank xxxxxxxxxxx Seal					

Figure 6—CHART NO. 2, MEDICAL INSPECTION REPORT FORM.

Figure 5.6 The Medical Inspection Report Form appended to the Allied Translator and Interpreter Section (ATIS) report. The form was reproduced based on "Rules for Authorized Restaurants and Houses of Prostitution in Manila" (1943).

Source: ATIS Report no. 120 (November 15, 1945), 15.

mothers in Japan proper were also under state and medical surveillance, there was a noticeable difference in the ultimate goal of surveillance. Whereas the bodies of Japanese mothers were seen as the source of the Japanese race, the bodies of comfort women were regarded as the source of venereal and other infectious diseases by military authorities. The contrasting images between mothers as a national womb and comfort women as carriers of venereal disease are explicitly represented by the contrasting medical approaches to women's bodies, namely the Handbook used among expectant mothers in Japan proper, on one hand, and the medical examination form used for Japan's military sexual slaves on the other (Figure 5.6). Unlike the former that intended to support the production of healthy offspring, the latter sought to pathologize women's bodies and deprive them of any reproductive functions. In view of this, Japan's imperial nation selectively facilitated different instrumentalities of women, that is, fertile wombs and exploitable vaginas to maximize its wartime labor sources. Fertility and exploitability were by no means inherent in the physicality of individual women but were forcibly legitimized by the intersecting forces of misogynistic and colonial oppressions.

Two Bodies: Mothers and Comfort Women

This chapter examined different instrumentalities embodied by female subjects of the Japanese colonial empire. On the one hand, Japanese mothers in Japan proper were placed under the paternalistic and meticulous gaze of the state and medicine during the wartime years due to pressing demand for human resources. The particular care of the maternal body, as exemplified by various population policies such as the commendations for families with many healthy children and the Handbook, illuminates how instrumental the gendered ideology of motherhood was for the wartime biopolitical regime to enforce its pronatalist and eugenics policies. In this process, the Meiji family-state ideology was revitalized and modified to emphasize the biological unity not only between a mother and her child but also between the state and family, and to redefine the ideal role of women as producing as many healthy offspring as possible in the interest of the imperial nation. A range of wartime policies implemented in the name of the protection of mothers, therefore, not only reinforced the gendered division of citizenship, but also reduced womanhood to its reproductive role. The maternal body was nothing but her womb: a potential source for healthy Japanese people.

In the meantime, Japanese military sex slaves, or comfort women, were other bodies subject to the gaze of the misogynistic empire. In contrast to Japanese mothers or potential mothers whose instrumentality concerned exclusively reproductive roles from the state's perspective, comfort women were regarded as bodies unworthy to procreate and thus exploited as sexual objects. Given the fact that the majority of enslaved women were colonized female subjects and those from the impoverished class, it should be noted that the Japanese military sexual slavery system lay in a mixture of gender, racial, and class oppression. Under the misogynist surveillance that embodied this multidimensional oppression against selected female subjects, colonized female bodies were reduced into sexually exploitable objects and constantly subjected to that imperial-medical gaze that diagnosed them as a source of venereal diseases.

However, the two contrasting bodies—mothers and comfort women—should not be deemed as representing a hierarchical relation. A simplistic interpretation focusing on racial differences between Japanese mothers and military sexual slaves may lead to a misleading conclusion that women in Japan proper benefited from the wartime biopolitical measures while comfort women did not. Although it is crucial to acknowledge the magnitude of violence suffered by Japan's military sex slaves during the wartime and afterwards, it is also important to understand the different instrumentalities deployed by the wartime regime against women's bodies as a whole. The biopolitical rationalities remade Japanese mothers into a womb for the Japanese nation while justifying the exploitative violence against comfort women in the name of the protection of male soldiers. For both bodies, surveillance was put into practice in the form of medical interventions, which did not intend to protect the health of women's bodies but to secure the health of male human resources. Given this, Japanese mothers and comfort women were not at opposite poles from each other but were constructed differently, as wombs and vaginas, by the differential modes of biopolitical intervention.

EPILOGUE

The Continued Politics of the "Population Problem"

IN THE FINAL FEW MONTHS OF the Asia-Pacific War, the territory of Japan proper suffered the deadliest attacks from the Allied forces. Tokyo was destroyed by a series of firebombing attacks on March 9 and 10, 1945, creating nearly 100,000 casualties and with over 2 million people who lost their homes. During the Battle of Okinawa between April and June 1945, also known as one of the bloodiest battles during the Asia-Pacific War, roughly 150,000 Okinawan civilians were killed. The atomic bombings of Hiroshima and Nagasaki on August 6 and 9, respectively, caused unprecedented destruction and loss of life in both cities. More than 200,000 deaths were reported in the two cities that were completely devastated by unheard-of atomic bombs, and many more casualties followed in the subsequent years due to the long-term effects of radiation exposure. Less than a week after Nagasaki was bombed by the United States, Emperor Hirohito announced Japan's surrender to the Allies through a radio broadcast on August 15, 1945. Not long after the Jewel Voice Broadcast, the Asia-Pacific War officially came to an end when the Japanese foreign minister Shigemitsu Mamoru signed the surrender document on September 2 aboard the USS *Missouri*. It was not only the war that ended with the signing of the Japanese Instrument of Surrender but also the Japanese colonial empire and the military regime. The formal defeat of Japan appeared to mark the new beginning of Japan as a democratic state under the guidance of the U.S. occupying forces.[1]

Japan's postwar historical narratives that foreground a complete break from the wartime fascist regime and imperialist ideology fail to recognize the continued practices of biopolitical power. The "population" that had been subjected to statistical analysis, scientific investigation, and government regulation since the prewar period remained the site of scientific inquiry and government intervention in the postwar years. The irony was that the wartime government aimed to increase its population under the slogan of "give birth and multiply" (*umeyo fuyaseyo*), whereas the postwar government shifted its ground and claimed that Japan was overpopulated. Statistically, it was true that Japan's population increased sharply from 1945 through the 1950s because of the repatriation of overseas Japanese, the decline in the death rate, and the postwar baby boom.[2] Especially during the first five years after the war, the rate of natural increase hovered above 20 percent. In addition, approximately 6.3 million demobilized Japanese soldiers and repatriates returned to Japan, which resulted in an increase of 5 million people, after accounting for the 1.2 million former colonial subjects who returned to their home countries.[3] Although postwar demographic statistics evidently indicated the issue of population quantity, what was really at stake was not population growth itself but an imbalance between Japan's economic capacity and the population size.[4] The Malthusian framing of population issues remained valid in postwar Japan, where the need to achieve economic recovery and national reconstruction was most urgent. As a result, the "population problem," no matter how protean or elusive the concept has been, was still a pressing issue with which government bureaucrats, demographic experts and social activists grappled in the postwar years.

Then, how did postwar Japan respond to overpopulation and its resultant issues? There were largely three main approaches deployed in addressing the population issues: first, the organization of administrative bodies that investigated and devised policy-level solutions; second, the government-initiated family planning program; and third, the enactment of the Eugenic Protection Law that legalized abortion under certain circumstances. These three main approaches were by no means new tactics but evolved out of the legacy of interwar and wartime population discourse. Insofar as the organization of administrative bodies is concerned, the two research bodies that had existed since the 1930s, namely, the quasi-private PPRS and the IPP under the MHW, continued to serve as primary organizations to investigate demographic issues and develop solutions. In 1953, Jinkō mondai shingikai (Population Problem Inquiry Council), previously founded in 1949 under the cabinet, was established under the MHW as the standing body to evaluate population policies and regulation programs. With the foundation of this new government body, the three organizations formed a collaborative relationship for addressing population issues while maintaining the division of labor between them: bureaucrats in the IPP were responsible for investigating general demographic factors while researchers in the PPRS developed policies based on the demographic reports created by the IPP. The Population Problem Inquiry Council then deliberated on proposed policies in the final stage of establishing population policies. Similar to the patterns of population discourse during the interwar and wartime years, policymaking procedures regarding population issues in postwar Japan involved the interplay between populations science and government bureaucracy. The continued roles of key researchers such as Nagai Tōru—appointed as the standing director of the PPRS in 1951 and the acting chairman of the Population Problem Inquiry Council in 1953—and Tachi Minoru—appointed as the director of the IPP in 1959—in working within and with the government to develop population policies illuminate the continuous interplay between science and policies in deploying population discourse.[5]

In the meantime, family planning was one of the critical solutions to the overpopulation issue faced by postwar Japanese society. As discussed in this book, birth control had been subjected to government oppression since the 1930s due to its pronatalist policy. In contrast, the postwar government took a positive stance on promoting birth control campaigns to achieve economic recovery by means of controlling population growth. In fact, the initiative to examine birth control as a possible solution to overpopulation was first taken by the General Headquarters of Allied Powers (GHQ). Between 1946 and 1949, GHQ invited two American scientists specializing in demography, Edward Ackerman and Warren Thompson, to lead the investigation of population solutions in conjunction with Koya Yoshio, director of Kokuritsu kōshū eiseiin (National Institute of Public Health).[6] In 1950, the National Institute of Public Health launched a seven-year pilot program to promote birth control in three selected villages, assisted by funds from the Rockefeller Foundation. These preliminary steps during the occupation period culminated in the cabinet's decision to popularize birth control in 1951, followed by the MHW's concrete action plans for birth control campaigns utilizing healthcare workers including midwives, nurses, and public health nurses.[7] In addition, Nagai, who had served as the standing director of the PPRS since 1951, was influential in the postwar government's launching of family planning campaigns.

As examined in this book, Nagai cast serious doubt on the efficacy of birth control in addressing population issues during the interwar years, but he became an advocate for family planning as part of Shin seikatsu undō (new life movement) in the postwar period.[8] From his renewed perspective, family planning was no longer a defensive approach to population issues but a vital means for rationalizing family life at a micro level and increasing national productivity at a macro level. In the meantime, Nihon kazoku keikaku renmei (Family Planning Federation of Japan), an affiliate of the International Planned Parenthood Federation (IPPF), was founded in 1954 to support birth control campaigns and to serve as the liaison between the Japanese government and the IPPF in carrying out the campaigns. Ironically, pioneering birth control advocates such as Katō (Ishimoto) Shizue, Majima Kan, and Ōta Tenrei, whose activism had been substantially restricted due to state oppression during the interwar period, came to play a significant role in establishing the Family Planning Federation of Japan; they worked closely with bureaucrats including Koya to support the government-led birth control campaign.[9] The complete shift in the government's position from the prewar pronatalist, anti–birth control approach to the postwar pro–family planning stance hardly indicates a sudden transition from the feudalistic, inhumane control over fertility to the democratic protection of reproductive rights. The postwar family planning campaigns rather carried on the legacy of preceding population discourse that problematized the quantity of population from the viewpoint of economic productivity. The feminist activism to strengthen the discursive association between women's reproductive rights and birth control would have to wait until the 1970s.[10]

It was not only family planning but also eugenics policies that reflected the continued discourse on population in transwar Japan. As discussed in the previous chapters, the wartime government implemented the eugenic sterilization policy under the National Eugenic Law. This Law was not abolished by the postwar government but replaced with Yūsei hogo hō (Eugenic Protection Law) in 1948. The postwar eugenic bill was drafted as early as 1947 by Katō and Ōta, both of whom were long-time birth control advocates and Nihon shakai-tō (Japan Socialist Party) Diet members, but their progressive approach to legalizing birth control and abortion ended up being diluted in the final version of the bill due to the opposition from the Diet.[11]

The Eugenic Protection Law that gained nonpartisan approval was geared toward enabling forced sterilizations and legal abortions to prevent the increase of inferior offspring on eugenic grounds and to protect maternal health. Specifically, the law prescribed that those with hereditary diseases, genetic disorders, leprosy, and mothers whose lives were at risk should be subjected to involuntary sterilizations.[12] As for abortions, the law initially restricted the eligibility for legal induced abortions to maternal health reasons and rape victims, but its eligibility was extended to include economic reasons in the 1949 amendment.[13]

Note that the postwar eugenic law differed from the wartime eugenic law in that the former introduced legal induced abortions for the protection of mother's health and welfare whereas the latter primarily concerned sterilizations for eugenic purposes. Notwithstanding this difference, the continued efforts to improve the quality of the Japanese population by means of eugenic measures should not be overlooked. The binary logic that distinguished the superior from the inferior remained the underpinning of eugenics policies in the postwar years. According to this logic, those who were considered to have inferior traits from a medical perspective, as well as the perspective of public interest, were denied their reproductive rights. In consequence, during the period when the Eugenic Protection Law was in effect (1948–1996, nearly fifty years), approximately 25,000 sterilizations were performed either with consent or forcibly.[14] The Eugenic Protection Law exemplifies postwar democracy's blind spot in which the principle of equality and freedom was selectively applied, and biopolitical logics rationalized the exclusion and discrimination of selected bodies. Although the central rhetoric of eugenics changed from race betterment in the wartime period to the public interest in the postwar period, biopolitical strategies of inclusion and exclusion remained intact in the blind spot of democracy.

The trajectory of population discourse in Japan during the period between the late 1910s and the 1950s reveals the evolving ideas and technologies of governing a selected population as an essential step towards reconstructing modernity. The interwar population discourse foregrounded the optimization of the quantity and quality of the Japanese population to tackle socioeconomic issues. To this end, various scientific and governmental tactics were mobilized, such as statistics, eugenics ideas, birth control, population science, colonial migration, and welfare policies. These tactics facilitated a social imaginary in which individuals formed a biological community called "population" and at the same time excluded the inferior, racialized others and disposable bodies. The wartime regime consummated the existing ideas and plans of building a centralized and systematic control of the Japanese population by maximizing governance and scientific interventions into productive and reproductive bodies. The wartime population policies collectively aimed to increase the number of human resources and improve their health by expanding the state's control over reproductive practices. The growing emphasis on ideal motherhood in the wartime population policies alludes to the instrumentality of the female body with a national womb in the governmentalization of the imperial state. The patterns of population governance in the immediate postwar years evolved out of these historical experiences of problematizing, regulating, and differentiating a selected population. The quantity and quality of the Japanese population was repeatedly subjected to government interventions and scientific inquiries, both of which operated according to the biopolitical rationalities that translated demographic phenomena into a problem, more specifically, a fundamental problem of political economy. The postwar family planning and eugenics programs were instrumental not only in reconstructing Japan's devastated economy and state system, but also in sustaining the discursive juxtapositions between biological and political life, superiority and inferiority, and inclusion and exclusion.

Fast forward to today: Japan is still facing a series of interconnected population issues such as low fertility, aging population, shrinking population size, and labor shortage. The ways in which the contemporary government institutions have dealt with these issues resemble the modern population discourse: the central government has worked to raise fertility rates by providing welfare benefits to families while local governments introduced AI-based matchmaking services to boost marriage and birth rates. In addition, the "womenomics" campaign promoted during the second term of Prime Minister Abe Shinzo (1954–2022) to address Japan's population issues and chronic deflation by empowering female citizens showcases the gendering impact of population discourse. The campaign reveals the government's desire to normalize heterosexual families as the basic unit for procreation, to naturalize motherhood, and by doing so, to control the population so as to address socioeconomic challenges. The contemporary patterns of population discourse beg the familiar question of how the "population problem" is associated with the national economy, gender politics, and reproductive science and technology. The historical narratives around population discourse in modern Japan are still relevant to the ongoing discussions of Japan's population crisis. "Population" has always been problematized to reorder life instead of being a problem itself.

GLOSSARY

American Birth Control League (ABCL)
Japanese Association of Race Hygiene: *Nihon minzoku eisei kyōkai*
Birth Control Research Society: *Sanji seigen kenkyūkai (Seigenkai)*
Birth Control Review: *Sanji seigen hyōron (Hyōron)*
Central Association for Social Work (CASW): *Chūō shakai jigyō kyōkai*
Eugenic Marriage Popularization Society: *Yūsei kekkon fukyūkai*
Family Planning Federation of Japan: *Nihon kazoku keikaku renmei*
Greater Japan Women's Association: *Dai nippon fujinkai (Nippu)*
Imperial Rule Assistance Association: *Taisei yokusankai*
Institute of Population Problems (IPP): *Jinkō mondai kenkyūsho*
International Planned Parenthood Federation (IPPF)
International Union for the Scientific Investigation of Population Problems (IUSIPP)
Japan Birth Control Clinic: *Nihon ninshin chōsetsu sōdansho*
Japan Birth Control League: *Nihon sanji chōsetsu renmei*
Japan Federation of Labor: *Nihon rōdō kumiai sōdōmei (Sōdōmei)*
Japan Labor Union League: *Nihon rōdō kumiai dōmei*
Japan Labor Unions Council: *Nihon rōdō kumiai hyōgikai*
Japanese Society for the Study of Birth Control: *Nihon sanji chōsetsu kenkyūkai (Chōsetsukai)*
Ministry of Health and Welfare (MHW): *Kōsei-shō*
National Institute of Public Health: *Kokuritsu kōshū eiseiin*
Ōhara Institute for Social Research: *Ōhara shakai mondai kenkyūsho*
Population and Food Problems Investigation Committee (PFIC): *Jinkō shokuryō mondai chōsakai*
Population Problem Inquiry Council: *Jinkō mondai shingikai*
Population Problem Research Society (PPRS): *Jinkō mondai kenkyūkai*
Proletariat Birth Control League (Pro-BC): *Musansha sanji seigen dōmei*
Race Hygiene Research Society (RHRS): *Minzoku eisei kenkyūkai*
Red Wave Society: *Sekirankai*
Society for Constructive Birth Control and Racial Progress (CBC)
Society for the Protection of Mothers: *Nihon bosei hogokai*
Studies of Population Problems (*SPP*): *Jinkō mondai kenkyū*
Women's Birth Control League of Japan: *Nihon sanji chōsetsu fujin dōmei (Fujin Dōmei)*

NOTES

Introduction

1. Muramatsu Yōko, "Funin chiryō no hoken tekiyō kakudai ni muketa ugoki" [A move towards the expansion of health insurance coverage for infertility treatment], *NLI Research Institute*, accessed February 14, 2022, https://www.nli-research.co.jp/report/detail/id=67353?pno=2&site=nli.

2. "Funin chiryō tekiyō, chakushōzenkensa wa handan miokuri, taigaijyusei nado taishō e, Kōsei-shō" [The Ministry of Health, Labour, and Welfare announced the health insurance coverage for infertility treatment including IVF while the plan to cover preimplantation genetic testing is shelved], *Asahi Newspaper* (December 15, 2021), https://digital.asahi.com/articles/ASPDH56YLPDHUTFL006.html.

3. Muramatsu, "Funin chiryō no hoken tekiyō kakudai ni muketa ugoki." Muramatsu cited the census data published by *Kokuritsu shakai hoshō/jinkō mondai kenkyūsho* (National Institute of Population and Social Security Research) in 2015.

4. Kawasaki Shigeru, "Nihon no tōkeigaku no rekishiteki hatten ni okeru kōteki tōkei no yakuwari" [Roles of official statistics in the historical development of statistics in Japan], *Nihon tōkei gakkaishi* 49, no. 2 (2020): 169–171.

5. Fujino Yutaka, *Nihon fashizumu to yūsei shisō* [Fascism and eugenic ideas in Japan] (Kyoto-shi: Kamogawa shuppan, 1998), 56–62; Honda Sōshi, *Kindai nihon no yūseigaku: "tasha" zō no seiritsu o megutte* [Eugenics in modern Japan: on the formation of images of "others"] (Tokyo: Akashi shoten, 2022), 28–36.

6. Michel Foucault, *Discourse and Truth: The Problematization of Parrhesia* (six lectures given by Michel Foucault at the University of California, Berkeley, October–November 1983), ed. Joseph Pearson, http://foucault.info/documents/parrhesia/index.html.

7. Existing research on the intertwining relationship between social policies and eugenics in modern Japan includes Sugita Naho, *Jinkō, kazoku, seimei to shakai seisaku* [Population, family, life and social policy] (Kyoto-shi: Hōritsu bunkasha, 2010); Sugita Naho, *Yūsei yūkyo to shakai seisaku: jinkō mondai no Nihonteki tenkai* [Eugenics, euthenics and social policy: the development of population problem in Japan] (Kyoto-shi: Hōritsu bunkasha, 2013); Sugita Naho, "Nihon ni okeru jinkō-shakai hoshōron no keifu" [A genealogy of population-social security theories in Japan], *Jinkō mondai kenkyū* [hereinafter *SPP*] 73, no. 4 (2017): 239–253; Takaoka Hiroyuki, *Sōryokusen taisei to fukushi kokka: senjiki Nihon no shakai kaikaku kōsō* [Total war system and the welfare state: Japan's wartime plan for

social reform] (Tokyo: Iwanami shoten, 2011).

8. On the historical trajectory of eugenics movements and policies with a critical approach to the political nature of scientific knowledge and its integral role in the social control of bodies and reproduction, see Fujino, *Nihon fashizumu to yūsei shisō*; Honda, *Kindai nihon no yūseigaku*; Yokoyama Takashi, *Nihon ga yūseishakai ni narumade: kagaku keimō, medhia, seishoku no seiji* [The history of eugenic society in Japan: scientific enlightenment, media, and politics of reproduction] (Tokyo: Keiso shobo, 2015). Also, there is a body of research that revisits Japan's biopolitical modernity—that is, the construction of the Japanese race in the process of nation-building—through the lens of eugenics, which includes Sumiko Otsubo and James R. Bartholomew, "Eugenics in Japan: Some Ironies of Modernity, 1883–1945," *Science in Context* 11, no. 3-4 (1998): 545–565; Sumiko Otsubo, "Between Two Worlds: Yamanouchi Shigeo and Eugenics in Early Twentieth-Century Japan," *Annals of Science* 62, no. 2 (2005): 205–231; Jennifer Robertson, "Blood Talks: Eugenic Modernity and the Creation of New Japanese," *History and Anthropology* 13, no. 3 (2002): 191–216.

9. The body of research examining state and social control over reproduction in modern Japan by employing gender analysis includes Sabine Frühstück, *Colonizing Sex: Sexology and Social Control in Modern Japan* (Berkeley: University of California Press, 2003); Ogino Miho, *"Kazoku keikaku" e no michi: kindai nihon no seishoku o meguru seiji* [The road to "family planning" politics over reproduction in modern Japan] (Tokyo: Iwanami shoten, 2008); Takeda, *The Political Economy of Reproduction in Japan: Between Nation-State and Everyday Life* (London: RoutledgeCurzon, 2005); Yuki Terazawa, *Knowledge, Power, and Women's Reproductive Health in Japan, 1690–1945* (Cham: Palgrave Macmillan, 2018); Fujime Yuki, *Sei no rekishigaku: Kōshō seido, dataizai taisei kara baishun bōshihō, yūsei hogo hō taisei e* [History of sex: from the system of licensed prostitution and abortion laws to the system of anti-prostitution and eugenics protection] (Tokyo: Fuji shuppan, 1997).

10. For the research on the continuity of population policies in transwar Japan, see Ogino Miho, "Shigenka sareru shintai: senzen, senchū, sengo no jinkō seisaku o megutte" [Bodies transformed into resources: on prewar, wartime, and postwar population policies], *Gakujutsu no dōkō* 13, no. 4 (2008): 21–26; Hiroshima Kiyoshi, "Gendai nihon jinkō seisaku-shi shōron: jinkō shishitsu gainen o megutte, 1916–1930" [An essay on the history of population policies in modern Japan: on the concept of the quality of population], *SPP*, no. 154 (1980): 46–61; Hiroshima Kiyoshi, "Gendai nihon jinkō seisaku-shi shōron (2): kokumin yūsei hō ni okeru jinkō no shitsu seisaku to ryō seisaku" [An essay on the history of population policies in modern Japan (2): policies on the quality and quantity of population according to the National Eugenic Law], *SPP*, no. 160 (1981): 61–77.

11. Although postwar population control is beyond the scope of this book, it is worth mentioning that a growing body of research—mainly in the fields of Japanese history and science and technology studies (STS)—has investigated the continuity of population discourse in transwar Japan and revealed a broader meaning of postwar population policies represented as family planning and the Eugenic Protection Law in relation to cold war geopolitics, nation-rebuilding, and demographic imaginaries. On research of postwar population discourse, see Aya Homei, "The Science of Population and Birth Control in Post-War Japan," in *Science, Technology, and Medicine in the Modern Japanese Empire*, eds. Philip C. Brown and David G. Wit-

tner (London: Routledge, 2016), 227–243; Aya Homei and Yōko Matsubara, "Critical Approaches to Reproduction and Population in Post-War Japan," *Japan Forum* 33, no. 3 (2021): 307–317; Astghik Hovhannisyan, "Preventing the Birth of 'Inferior Offspring': Eugenic Sterilizations in Postwar Japan," *Japan Forum* 33, no. 3 (2021): 383–401; Yōko Matsubara, "The Enactment of Japan's Sterilization Laws in the 1940s: A Prelude to Postwar Eugenic Policy," *Historia Scientiarum* 8, no. 2 (1998): 187–201; Tiana Norgren, *Abortion Before Birth Control: The Politics of Reproduction in Postwar Japan* (Princeton: Princeton University Press, 2001); Aiko Takeuchi-Demirci, *Contraceptive Diplomacy: Reproductive Politics and Imperial Ambitions in the United States and Japan* (Stanford: Stanford University Press, 2018).

12. For the research on discursive aspects of population, see Alison Bashford, *Global Population: History, Geopolitics, and Life on Earth* (New York: Columbia University Press, 2014); Matthew Connelly, "Seeing Beyond the State: The Population Control Movement and the Problem of Sovereignty," *Past & Present* 193 (2006): 197–233; Matthew Connelly, *Fatal Misconception: The Struggle to Control World Population* (Cambridge, MA: Belknap Press, 2008); Bruce Curtis, *The Politics of Population: State Formation, Statistics, and the Census of Canada, 1840–1875* (Toronto: University of Toronto Press, 2001); Susan Greenhalgh and Edwin A. Winckler, *Governing China's Population: From Leninist to Neoliberal Biopolitics* (Stanford: Stanford University Press, 2005); Susan Greenhalgh, *Just One Child: Science and Policy in Deng's China* (Berkeley: University of California Press, 2008); Carole R. McCann, *Figuring the Population Bomb: Gender and Demography in the Mid-Twentieth Century* (Seattle: University of Washington Press, 2017).

13. Curtis, *The Politics of Population*, 3.

14. As for the genealogy of demographic knowledge in the mid-twentieth century, McCann points out how the "population crisis" is "discovered" both socially and epistemologically not only to create a social imaginary regarding the normality of family planning but also to uphold U.S. imperialist hegemonic masculinity. McCann, *Figuring the Population Bomb*, 6, 14–21.

15. Bashford, *Global Population*, 5.

16. J. Victor Koschmann, "Introduction to Total War and 'Modernization,'" in *Total War and "Modernization*," eds. Yasushi Yamanouchi, J. Victor Koschmann, and Ryūichi Narita (Ithaca: Cornell University East Asia Program, 2001), xi.

17. Masao Maruyama, "Nationalism in Japan: Its Theoretical Background and Prospects," in *Thought and Behavior in Modern Japanese Politics* (London: Oxford University Press, 1969). This article was originally published in the Japanese magazine *Chūō kōron* in 1951. Meanwhile, J. Victor Koschmann also points out Maruyama's view of Japan's "incomplete project of modernity" in contrast to the universalized conception of Western modernity. J. Victor Koschmann, "Maruyama Masao and the Incomplete Project of Modernity," in *Postmodernism and Japan*, eds. Masao Miyoshi and H. D. Harootunian (Durham: Duke University Press, 1989), 123–141.

18. Carol Gluck explains the discursive rupture between the wartime and the postwar period as one of the main characteristics of postwar Japan that presented itself as a new beginning through a binary narrative of "feudalistic/fascist" versus "democratic." Carol Gluck, "The 'End' of the Postwar: Japan at the Turn of the Millennium," *Public Culture* 10, no. 1 (1997): 1–23.

19. Naoki Sakai sharply points out that the binary historico-geopolitical pairing (i.e., modern–premodern and the West–non-West) has served as a discursive scheme according to which Japan presented itself as a particular unity (i.e., nation) as opposed to the universal, putative entity of the West. Naoki Sakai, "Modernity and Its Critique: The Problem of Universalism and Particularism," in *Postmodernism and Japan*, 93–122.

20. Although both biopolitics and governmentality are mainly discussed vis-à-vis the European historical context in Foucault's discussions of both notions, there has been a body of research that draws on Foucault's frameworks to examine forms of power targeting population in Asian contexts and to engage with a broader conversation of modernity without essentializing a region in a culturalist manner. Examples of those works include Mark Driscoll, *Absolute Erotic, Absolute Grotesque: The Living, Dead, and Undead in Japan's Imperialism, 1895–1945* (Durham: Duke University Press, 2010); Greenhalgh and Winckler, *Governing China's Population*; Stephen Legg and Deana Heath, eds. *South Asian Governmentalities: Michel Foucault and the Question of Postcolonial Orderings* (Cambridge, UK: Cambridge University Press, 2018); Takeda, *The Political Economy of Reproduction in Japan*.

21. Michel Foucault, *Society Must Be Defended: Lectures at the Collège de France, 1975–1976* (New York: Picador, 2003), 245.

22. Ibid., 243.

23. Ibid., 246.

24. Foucault's discussions on governmentality are mainly found in Michel Foucault, "Governmentality," in *The Foucault Effect: Studies in Governmentality: With Two Lectures by and an Interview with Michel Foucault*, eds. Graham Burchell, Colin Gordon, and Peter Miller (Chicago: University of Chicago Press, 1991), 87–104; Michel Foucault, *Security, Territory, Population: Lectures at the Collège de France: 1977–1978* (Basingstoke: Palgrave Macmillan, 2009); Michel Foucault, *The Birth of Biopolitics: Lectures at the Collège de France, 1978–1979* (New York: Palgrave Macmillan, 2011).

25. Foucault, *Security, Territory, Population*, 115.

26. Foucault, "Governmentality," 102.

27. Mitchell Dean, *The Signature of Power Sovereignty, Governmentality and Biopolitics* (Los Angeles: Sage, 2013), 39–41.

28. Foucault, "Governmentality," 103.

29. In a similar vein, Susan Greenhalgh and Edwin A. Winckler argue against the culturalist objection about the use of Foucault's ideas in Chinese historical contexts and highlight the usefulness of Foucault's governmentality as an "entry point" into an investigation of modern power relations embedded in China under PRC rule. Greenhalgh and Winckler, *Governing China's Population*, 31–33.

30. There is a rich body of literature that attempts a postcolonial reading of biopolitics by discussing the interplay between biopolitical rationalities and colonialism/imperialism and the dyad of racial inclusion and exclusion justified by colonial biopolitics. Such work includes Sarah A. Radcliffe, *Dilemmas of Difference: Indigenous Women and the Limits of Postcolonial Development Policy* (Durham: Duke University Press, 2015); Annmaria M. Shimabuku, *Alegal: Biopolitics and the Unintelligibility of Okinawan Life* (New York: Fordham University Press, 2018); Ann Laura Stoler, *Race and the Education of Desire: Foucault's History of Sexuality and the Colonial Order of Things* (Durham: Duke University Press, 1995).

Chapter 1

1. International Birth Control Conference, *Report of the Fifth International Neo-Malthusian and Birth Control Conference, Kingsway Hall, London, July 11th to 14th, 1922* (London: W. Heinemann, 1922).

2. For the history of the conference, see Margaret Sanger, "Introduction to Proceedings of the Sixth International Neo-Malthusian and Birth Control Conference," *Speeches and Writings of Margaret Sanger, 1911–1959*, accessed September 18, 2022, https://m-sanger.org/items/show/1276.

3. International Birth Control Conference, *Report of the Fifth International Neo-Malthusian and Birth Control Conference*, 75.

4. Alison Bashford, *Global Population: History, Geopolitics, and Life on Earth* (New York: Columbia University Press, 2014), 56.

5. The Malthusian League (1877–1927) was a British organization that coined the term "neo-Malthusianism" to refer to a campaign for checks on population growth by means of birth control. The league was founded during the trial of Annie Besant and Charles Bradlaugh, two British secularists, for publishing Charles Knowlton's book describing contraceptive methods. Neo-Malthusianists who were involved in the league contributed to reconfiguring Malthus's theory of population from a humanitarian perspective to advocate preventive checks on population growth and ultimately to address poverty through birth control methods. On the history of the Malthusian League, see Bashford, *Global Population*, 39–43; F. D'Arcy, "The Malthusian League and the Resistance to Birth Control Propaganda in Late Victorian Britain," *Population Studies* 31, no. 3 (1977): 429–448; Rosanna Ledbetter, *A History of the Malthusian League, 1877–1927* (Columbus: Ohio State University Press, 1976). For the spread of neo-Malthusian movements across Europe and the United States between the late nineteenth century and the early twentieth, see Robert Jütte, *Contraception: A History*, trans. Vicky Russell (Cambridge, UK: Polity Press, 2008), 106–156.

6. Bashford, *Global Population*, 57.

7. International Birth Control Conference, *Report of the Fifth International Neo-Malthusian and Birth Control Conference*, 1.

8. Marx's criticism of Malthus's approach to population is addressed in his article "Critique of the Gotha Program" (1891) where he stated that

> if [the Malthusian] theory is correct, then again I *cannot* abolish the law even if I abolish wage labor a hundred times over, because the law then governs not only the system of wage labor but every social system. . . . [T]he economists have been proving for fifty years and more that socialism cannot abolish poverty, *which has its basis in nature*, but can only make it *general*, distribute it simultaneously over the whole surface of society!

Karl Marx, "Critique of the Gotha Program," in *The Marx-Engels Reader*, ed. Robert Tucker (New York: Norton, 1978), 534–535; italics in original. This letter was written in 1875 and later published in *New Zeit* in 1891.

9. Karl Marx, *Capital: A Critique of Political Economy*, vol. 1, trans. Ben Fowkes (Harmondsworth: Penguin Books, 1976), 792–793.

10. For more on leftists' criticism of Malthusian population theory, see John M. Sherwood, "Engels, Marx, Malthus, and the Machine," *American Historical Review* 90, no. 4 (1985): 837–865; William Petersen, "Marxism and the Population

Question: Theory and Practice," *Population and Development Review* 14 (1988): 77–101.

11. August Bebel, *Woman and Socialism*, trans. Meta Stern Lilienthal (New York: Socialist Literature Co., 1910), 484. I discuss Bebel's influence on Yamakawa Kikue, Japanese socialist feminist, in Chapter 2.

12. Vladimir Lenin, "The Working Class and Neo-Malthusianism," Marxists Internet Archive, originally published 1913, accessed October 13, 2022, https://www.marxists.org/archive/lenin/works/1913/jun/29.htm.

13. Yoshimi Takeuchi, *What Is Modernity?: Writings of Takeuchi Yoshimi*, trans. Richard Calichman (New York: Columbia University Press, 2005), 54.

14. For the wartime economic boom and the rise in grain price in the post–World War I period, see Andrew Gordon, *A Modern History of Japan: From Tokugawa Times to the Present* (New York: Oxford University Press, 2009), 139–144; Takafusa Nakamura, *Economic Growth in Prewar Japan* (New Haven: Yale University Press, 1983), 144–156; Kozo Yamamura, "The Japanese Economy, 1911–1930: Concentration, Conflicts, and Crises," in *Japan in Crisis: Essays on Taishō Democracy*, eds. Gail Lee Bernstein, Bernard S. Silberman, and Harry D. Harootunian (Princeton: Princeton University Press, 1974), 299–328.

15. For the history of the rice riots of 1918, see Andrew Gordon, *Labor and Imperial Democracy in Prewar Japan* (Berkeley: University of California Press, 1991), 60–61; Mikiso Hane, *Peasants, Rebels, Women, and Outcastes: The Underside of Modern Japan* (Lanham: Rowman & Littlefield, 2003), 160–161.

16. Kenji Mori, "The Development of the Modern Koseki," in *Japan's Household Registration System and Citizenship: Koseki, Identification and Documentation*, eds. David Chapman and Karl Jakob Krogness (London: Routledge, 2014), 59–60.

17. On Sugi Kōji's role in the modernization of population statistics in Japan, see Akira Hayami, "Koji Sugi and the Emergence of Modern Population Statistics in Japan: The Influence of German Statistics," in *Population, Family and Society in Pre-Modern Japan: Population, Family and Society in Pre-Modern Japan* (Boston: Brill, 2010), 369–376.

18. Nagayama Sadanori, "Nihon no kanchō tōkei no hatten to gendai" [The development of the official statistics in Japan], *Nihon tōkei gakkaishi* 16, no. 1 (1986): 102.

19. Kawasaki Shigeru, "Nihon no tōkeigaku no rekishiteki hatten ni okeru kōteki tōkei no yakuwari" [Roles of official statistics in the historical development of statistics in Japan], *Nihon tōkei gakkaishi* 49, no. 2 (2020): 170–171.

20. Nihon hōrei sakuin [Index to the Japanese laws and regulations in force], "Dai 16 kai teikoku gikai shūgiin kokusei chōsa ni kansuru hōritsuan iinkai daiichigō meiji 35 nen 2 gatsu 24 nichi" [The House of Representatives at the 16th Imperial Diet, the Committee on the Proposal for the National Census Bill, no. 1, February 24, 1902], accessed February 17, 2022, https://teikokugikai-i.ndl.go.jp/simple/detailPDF?minId=001611002X00119020224&page=1.

21. Michel Foucault, "Governmentality," in *The Foucault Effect: Studies in Governmentality: With Two Lectures by and an Interview with Michel Foucault*, eds. Graham Burchell, Colin Gordon, and Peter Miller (Chicago: University of Chicago Press, 1991), 114.

22. Ibid., 99.

23. Nagayama, "Nihon no kanchō tōkei no hatten to gendai," 104.

24. Yoshiro Matsuda, "Formation of the Census System in Japan: 1871–1945—Development of the Statistical System in Japan Proper and Her Colonies," *Hitotsubashi Journal of Economics* 21, no. 2 (1981): 55; for the classification of Han-Taiwanese and Indigenous populations facilitated by the colonial government of Taiwan and its impact on the birth of Indigeneity, see Paul D. Barclay, *Outcasts of Empire: Japan's Rule on Taiwan's "Savage Border," 1874–1945* (Oakland: University of California Press, 2018).

25. Ann Laura Stoler, *Race and the Education of Desire: Foucault's History of Sexuality and the Colonial Order of Things* (Durham: Duke University Press, 1995), 15.

26. The data of national census conducted since 1920 is archived online. See the website for e-Stat, "Kokusei chōsa," e-Stat, https://www.e-stat.go.jp/SG1/estat/GL02100104.do?tocd=00200521.

27. Ishimoto Keikichi, "*Waga jinkō mondai to sanji chōsetsu ron*" [An essay on population problem and birth control], in *Sei to seishoku no jinken mondai shiryō shūsei* [Collection of documents on sexual and reproductive rights, hereinafter *SSJ*], vol. 2, eds. Ogino Miho, Matsubara Yōko, and Saitō Hikaru (Tokyo: Fuji shuppan, 2000), 161; translation is mine. Originally published 1922 by Nihon sanji chōsetsu kenkyūkai [Japanese Society for the Study of Birth Control].

28. Francis Galton, *Inquiries into Human Faculty and Its Development* (London: Macmillan, 1883), 24–25.

29. Unno Yukinori, *Nihon jinshu kaizōron* [On reforming the Japanese race] (Tokyo: Fuzanbō, 1910); on the parallel between Galton and Unno in terms of their advocacy for both positive and negative eugenics, see Honda Sōshi, *Kindai nihon no yūseigaku: "tasha" zō no seiritsu o megutte* [Eugenics in modern Japan: on the formation of images of "others"] (Tokyo: Akashi shoten, 2022), 19–36.

30. On Yamanouchi Shigeo's eugenics movement, see Sumiko Otsubo, "Between Two Worlds: Yamanouchi Shigeo and Eugenics in Early Twentieth-Century Japan," *Annals of Science* 62, no. 2 (2005): 205–231.

31. On Nagai Hisomu's eugenics movement during the interwar period, see Fujino Yutaka, *Nihon fashizumu to yūsei shisō* [Fascism and eugenic ideas in Japan] (Kyoto-shi: Kamogawa shuppan, 1998), 52–77. I discuss Nagai's integral role in establishing wartime population policies in detail in Chapter 4.

32. Ujihara Sukezō, "Minzoku eisei gaku" [The study of race hygiene], in *SSJ*, vol. 16 (2000), 1–23. Originally published 1914 by Nankōdō.

33. Ibid., 30.

34. Saitō Itsuki, "Yūshu-ron kenkyū" [The study of eugenics], *Shakai to Kyūsai* 3, no. 1 (1919): 7–20.

35. Ibid., 9.

36. Ibid., 14–15; translation is mine.

37. Takano Iwasaburō, "Jinkō zōka no keizaiteki kansatsu" [Economic views on the population growth], *Kokka gakkai zasshi* 32, no. 7 (1918): 41–42; translation is mine.

38. Takano Iwasaburō, "Ryō ka shitsu ka" [Quantity or quality], *Kokka gakkai zasshi* 32, no. 11 (1918): 145.

39. Francis Galton, "Eugenics: Its Definition, Scope, and Aims," *American Journal of Sociology* 10, no. 1 (1904): 3.

40. Fredric Jameson, *Archaeologies of the Future: The Desire Called Utopia and Other Science Fictions* (London: Verso, 2005), 12.

41. For Kaizō's lecture series, see Christopher T. Keaveney, *The Cultural Evolution of Postwar Japan: The Intellectual Contributions of Kaizō's Yamamoto Sanehiko* (New York: Palgrave Macmillan, 2013), 65–86.

42. The Home Ministry of Japan (Naimu-shō) initially declined to issue Sanger a visa on the grounds that foreigners who might disturb the peace and corrupt public morals were forbidden from entering the country. However, Hanihara Masanao, the vice minister of the Foreign Office who happened to be on the same vessel as Sanger on her way to Japan, was persuaded; the Home Ministry gave conditional approval for her entry and allowed her to offer public lectures on issues other than contraception. For the details of Sanger's visit to Japan, there are some contemporary accounts in the *Birth Control Review* as follows: "Margaret Sanger in Japan," *Birth Control Review* (May 1922), and "Margaret Sanger in Japan," *Birth Control Review* (June 1922).

43. "Mrs. Sanger Is Given Permit to Deliver Address," *Japan Times* (March 14, 1922).

44. Yamamoto Senji, "Sanji chōsetsu, ketsuron, sono igō" [Birth control, an epilogue, and afterwards], in *Yamamoto Senji zenshū* [Yamamoto Senji collection], vol. 3, eds. Sasaki Toshiji and Odagiri Akinori (Tokyo: Chōbunsha, 1979), 592. Originally published in the newspaper *Taiyō* in 1926. The "Black Ships" reference originated with the arrival of American black ships led by Commodore Matthew Perry in Tokyo Bay in 1853. Perry's arrival, demanding that Japan open trade with the United States, marks what Alexis Dudden calls the "moment of shock and awe," which forced Japanese leaders to transform the country into a modern, Western-modeled nation-state. Alexis Dudden, "Matthew Perry in Japan, 1852–1854," in *East Asia in the World: Twelve Events That Shaped the Modern International Order*, eds. Stephan Haggard and David C. Kang (Cambridge, UK: Cambridge University Press, 2020), 196.

45. It should be noted that not all the founding members of Chōsetsukai supported the neo-Malthusian view of population. For example, Yamakawa Kikue criticized the neo-Malthusian account of poverty and claimed that poverty was caused by the unfair distribution of wealth under capitalism. In this light, Chōsetsukai embedded disunity among activists with differing political positions. In Chapter 2, I will discuss in more detail the different views of the two feminist members of Chōsetsukai, Yamakawa and Ishimoto.

46. The first issue of *Shōkazoku* was published on May 13, 1922. Chōsetsukai then ceased the publication of its journal following the disbanding of the group. *Shōkazoku* was reprinted in *SSJ*, vol. 14 (2003), 1–4. The booklets published by Chōsetsukai include Ishimoto Shizue, "Sanji seigen ron o sho hōmen yori kansatsu shite" [A general observation of the arguments for birth control] (October 1922), in *SSJ*, vol. 2, 80–85; Ishimoto, "Waga jinkō mondai to sanji chōsetsu ron," 160–169; Matsumura Shōnen, "Seibutsu gaku jō yori mita sanji chōsetsu ron" [Birth control from a biological perspective] (1923), in *SSJ*, vol. 2, 174–201.

47. Nihon sanji chōsetsu kenkyūkai, "Sanji chōsetsu kenkyūkai shui-sho" [A prospectus for sanji chōsetsu kenkyūkai], in *SSJ*, vol. 2, 201. Originally published July 1922; translation is mine.

48. Ibid.

49. Abe Isoo and Majima Kan, *Sanji seigen no riron to jissai* [The theory and reality of birth control] (Tokyo: Bungaku gakkai shuppan-bu, 1925), 8.

50. Ibid., 23–24.

51. Michel Foucault, "Technologies of the Self," in *Technologies of the Self: A Seminar with Michel Foucault*, eds. Luther H. Martin, Huck Gutman, and Patrick H. Hutton (Amherst: University of Massachusetts Press, 1988), 18.

52. Abe Isoo, *Seikatsu mondai kara mita sanji chōsetsu* [Birth control from the perspective of living problems], (Tokyo: Tōkyōdō, 1931), 125.

53. Ibid., 133–134.

54. Abe's account of capitalism resonates with other contemporary socialists who approached to the problems accompanying rapid industrialization during the 1920–30s through social reforms. For instance, Kawakami Hajime, a leading advocate of Marxism during this period, initially deemed Marxism a science for redistributing limited amounts of wealth. Kawakami promoted the ethical aspects of Marxist thought as a solution to social problems, without denouncing the capitalist economy itself. However, Kawakami's earlier position of advocating moral reforms was altered later, and he became an advocate of radical Marxism. Consequently, Kawakami disagreed with Abe's promotion of birth control and urged a fundamental transformation of the capitalist system. Gail Lee Bernstein, "Kawakami Hajime: A Japanese Marxist in Search of the Way," in *Japan in Crisis: Essays on Taishō Democracy*, eds. Gail Lee Bernstein, Bernard S. Silberman, and Harry D. Harootunian (Princeton: Princeton University Press, 1974), 88–89; Masako Gavin, "Poverty and Its Possible Cures: Abe Isoo and Kawakami Hajime," *East Asia* 24, no. 1 (2007): 28–31.

55. Ishimoto, "Sanji seigen ron o sho hōmen yori kansatsu shi te," 81.

56. Matsumura Shōnen, "Seibutsu gaku jō yori mita sanji chōsetsu ron," 179.

57. Ibid., 183; translation is mine.

58. Abe and Majima, *Sanji seigen no riron to jissai*, 57–58.

59. Abe Isoo, "Jinkō mondai kara mitaru sanji seigen" [Considering birth control on the grounds of population problem], *Kakusei* 26, no. 8 (1936): 1–4.

60. Abe published *Sterilization for Human Betterment* (New York: Macmillan, 1929) under the title *Funin kekkon to ningen kaizō* [Sterile marriages and human betterment] (Tokyo: Shunyōdō, 1930). Abe's favorable comments on eugenic sterilization in light of Gosney's movement in California can be found in various articles including Abe Isoo, "Sanji seigen no yūseigakuteki kenkai" [Birth control on eugenic grounds], *Sanji chōsetsu hyōron* 4, no. 6 (1931): 2–5; "Jinkō mondai no ryōteki hōmen to shitsuteki hōmen" [The quantitative and qualitative dimensions of population problem], *Jinkō mondai* 2, no. 4 (1938): 48–60.

61. Sabine Frühstück, *Colonizing Sex: Sexology and Social Control in Modern Japan* (Berkeley: University of California Press, 2003), 147–148.

62. For Abe's shifting view on overpopulation, see Frühstück, *Colonizing Sex*, 147–148; Abe Tsunehisa, "Abe Isoo to fujin mondai" [Abe Isoo and women's issues], in *Abe Isoo no kenkyū* [The study of Abe Isoo], ed. Nakamura Naoyoshi (Tokyo: Waseda daigaku shakai kagaku kenkyūjo, 1990), 178; Hayashi Yōko, "Abe Isoo ni okeru 'heiwa' ron to danshu-ron: dansei-sei no mondai no kakawari o kijikuni" [On the notion of "peace" and sterilization in Abe Isoo: concerning the problem of manliness], *Jenda shi gaku* 5 (2009): 35–49.

63. For feminist discussions and the state policies around motherhood protection and their effects of re-gendering motherhood, see later chapters, especially Chapters 2, 3, and 5.

64. Hiratsuka Raichō, "Shakai kaizō ni taisuru fujin no shimei" [Women's mission concerning social reform], quoted in Chizuko Ueno, *Nationalism and Gender* (Melbourne: Trans Pacific Press, 2004), 45. Originally published 1920.

65. Hiratsuka Raichō, "Hinin no kahi o ronzu" [Arguing about the pros or cons of contraception], quoted in Ueno, *Nationalism and Gender*, 45. Originally published 1917.

66. Ueno, *Nationalism and Gender*, 30–32; Michiko Suzuki, *Becoming Modern Women: Love and Female Identity in Prewar Japanese Literature and Culture* (Stanford: Stanford University Press, 2010), 110–113.

67. On the Japanese feminists' complicity with the wartime regime and their underlying logic to the legitimation of gender roles, see Barbara Molony, "From 'Mothers of Humanity' to 'Assisting the Emperor': Gendered Belonging in the Wartime Rhetoric of Japanese Feminist Ichikawa Fusae," *Pacific Historical Review* 80, no. 1 (2011): 1–27; Ryuichi Narita, "Women's Total War: Gender and Wartime Mobilization in the Japanese Empire, 1931–1945," in *The Palgrave Handbook of Mass Dictatorship*, eds. Paul Corner and Jie-Hyun Lim (London: Palgrave Macmillan, 2016), 337–349.

68. A critical observation on the superficial association of eugenics with authoritarian fascist regimes has been made by historians who contextualized eugenics in relation to political, social, and scientific discourse. Representative examples include Daniel J. Kelves, *In the Name of Eugenics: Genetics and the Uses of Human Heredity* (New York: Knopf, 1985); Diane B. Paul, "Eugenics and the Left," *Journal of the History of Ideas* 45, no. 4 (1984): 567–590; Nancy Leys Stepan, *The Hour of Eugenics: Race, Gender, and Nation in Latin America* (Ithaca: Cornell University Press, 1996).

69. Foucault, "Governmentality," 102. In Chapters 3 and 4, I will delve into the governmentalization of the Japanese state with more detail.

70. There were mainly two laws concerning administrative control of the press during the prewar period: the Publication Law (Shuppan hō) of 1893 and the Newspaper Law (Shinbunshi hō) of 1909. The former was targeted at general publication including books, pamphlets, and leaflets whereas the latter covered general newspapers and periodical publication. In the rise of radical thought and publications peddling radical socialism since the late 1910s, liberal government and bureaucrats of the Home Ministry utilized the censorship laws primarily to suppress so-called dangerous thought (*kiken shisō*). Although neither censorship laws stipulated an obvious definition of dangerous thought, the arbitrary standard of the violation of public order (*annei chitsujo*) and morals and manners (*fūzoku*) legitimized the oppression of radical political thought and obscenity. The intensified control of the press during the Taishō period typifies the duplicity of Taishō Democracy in terms of the governmental regulation of radical ideas under the veneer of liberalism. For the evolving mechanism of censorship in Japan during the Taishō period, see Gregory James Kasza, *The State and the Mass Media in Japan, 1918–1945* (Berkeley: University of California Press, 1988), 28–53; Richard H. Mitchell, *Censorship in Imperial Japan* (Princeton: Princeton University Press, 1983), 172–253; Max M. Ward, *Thought Crime: Ideology and State Power in Interwar Japan* (Durham: Duke University Press, 2019), 21–48.

71. Yamamoto Senji, "Seiteki inpeishugi no tameni okiru heigai no ichirei" [An example of harmful effects of sexual obscurantism], in *Yamamoto Senji zenshū*, vol. 3, 99–113. Originally published in *Nihon to Nihonjin* in September 1922.

72. Yamamoto Senji, "Jinsei seibutsugaku shōin" [The introduction of the biology of human life], in *Yamamoto Senji zenshū*, vol. 1, 59–60.

73. Euthenics refers to the practice and science of improving human environ-

ments as a way to maximize human well-being. In her 1910 book, Ellen S. Richards, one of the first female American chemist and a pioneer of home economics, defined euthenics as "hygiene for the present generation" as opposed to eugenics, by which she meant "hygiene for the future generation." In the same vein, Yamamoto translated euthenics as *gense kaizengaku* (literally, the study of improving the present life) to distinguish it from the biological approach to life improvement. Richards, *Euthenics, the Science of Controllable Environment: A Plea for Better Living Conditions as a First Step Toward Higher Human Efficiency* (Boston: Whitcomb & Barrows, 1910), Project Gutenberg, http://www.gutenberg.org/ebooks/31508; Senji, "Jinsei seibutsugaku shōin," 60.

74. Yamamoto Senji, "Sanga joshi Kazoku seigen hō hihan" (1922) [The critique of Ms. Sanger's "Family Limitation"], in *Yamamoto Senji zenshū*, vol. 3, 26.

75. Ibid., 58–61.

76. Ibid., 61; translation is mine.

77. Ibid., 56.

78. Sasaki Toshiji, *Yamamoto Senji*, vol. 1 (Kyoto: Chōbunsha, 1974), 303.

79. Yamamoto Senji, "A Personal Letter to Margaret Sanger" (April 1923). In this letter, Yamamoto gave a detailed update on the process of the birth control group organization and the ongoing situation of the birth control campaigns. The letter is reprinted in *Yamamoto Senji zenshū*, vol. 7, 145–155.

80. Ibid., 146.

81. In addition, several public lectures led by Yamamoto continued between February and April 1923. Under the pretext of sex education, Yamamoto gave lectures on the use of contraceptive devices mainly to schoolteachers and college students in Matsue, Tottori, Kyoto, and Kochi. Ibid., 151–152.

82. *The Osaka Asahi Shinbun*, the former *Asahi Shinbun*, was one of the major newspapers in Kansai region and known as its left-leaning opinions. *The Shinbun* published articles on the ongoing birth control movement in Kansai region including "Sanji seigen no jissai undō: Kansai no rōdō kumiai ni jukushita kiun, ko no shussan wo osoreru hisanna jijitsu" [The actual movement of birth control: the time is ripe for the Kansai Labor Union, a miserable fact about people who fear giving birth] (January 5, 1923); "Rōdō dantai no sanji seigen: jissai mondai ni totsunyu senden kōen ni dai ippo wo" [Labor Union's birth control movement: diving into actual issues with a first step to a promotion lecture] (January 7, 1923); and "Shasetsu: sanji seigen no jissai undō" [Editorial: the actual birth control movement] (January 10, 1923).

83. "Shasetsu: Sanji seigen no senden" [Editorial: the promotion of birth control], *Osaka Mainichi Shinbun* (March 13, 1923).

84. Later, Yamamoto recalled that the *Osaka Mainichi Shinbun*'s attacks on birth control proved "an efficient advertisement" for the group. Yamamoto, "A Personal Letter to Margaret Sanger," 146.

85. Noda Kimiko, *Sanji seigen kenkyū* [The study of birth control] (Osaka: Sanji Seigen Kenkyūkai, 1923).

86. Ibid., 205.

87. Marx, *Capital*, 793.

88. Noda, *Sanji seigen kenkyū*, 31.

89. Ibid., 16.; translation is mine.

90. Yamamoto Senji also mentioned the importance of birth control in the class movement. He criticized the messianic stance of some labor activists in their pursuit

of the revolution while neglecting immediate problems encountered by the proletariat, figuratively noting that "what suffering proletarians really need is a bird in the hand than two in the bush." Yamamoto Senji, "Sanji chōsetsu hyōron kara sei to shakai e (I)" [From the *Birth Control Review* to *Sex and Society* (I)], *Sei to shakai*, no. 9 (1925): 13.

91. The hostility among Marxists and leftists towards birth control came to the fore when the "Proposal for the Promotion of Birth Control" (Sanji seigen shōrei-an) was not approved in the Fourth General Meeting of the Japan Farmers Union in February 1925. In the following month, Sōdōmei rejected the proposal for incorporating the birth control movement into the federation's organizational goal. These instances indicate the prevailing antipathy among the leftist organizations towards birth control on the ground of ideological antagonism and negligence of reproductive labour. Interestingly, Kutsumi Fusako from Seigenkai was one of Sōdōmei's delegates who objected to the proposal on the basis that Sōdomei fought economic battles for the proletariat whereas birth control was "simply a means of self-defense." Kutsumi Fusako, "Naniyueni wareware wa hantaishitaka: Sōdōmei taikai ni teishutsu sareshi BC an" [Why did we object to the proposal for BC campaign submitted to the National Meeting of Sōdōmei?] *Sanji chōsetsu hyōron*, no. 4 (1925): 53.

92. *Sanji chōsetsu hyōron* was published between February 1925 and May 1926, a total of fourteen issues. The chief editor was Yamamoto, and contributing writers included Yamamoto himself, Yasuda Tokutarō, Abe Isoo, Suzuki Bunji (the president of Sōdōmei), Kaji Tokijirō (a medical doctor who ran People's Hospital [Heimin byōin] in Tokyo), Katō Tokiya (a medical doctor who ran People's Hospital in Osaka), Majima Kan (a commissioned medical doctor of Tokyo Municipal Social Affairs Bureau), and Unno Yukinori. The magazine was retitled *Sei to shakai* (Sex and society) from the ninth issue released in October 1925. Entire issues were reprinted by Fuji shuppan in 1983.

93. Kanda Ryūichi (Birth Control Research Society in Osaka), "Osaka no sanji seigen undō" [Birth control movement in Osaka], *Sanji chōsetsu hyōron*, no. 1 (February 1925): 26–27.

94. Diane B. Paul, *Controlling Human Heredity: 1865 to the Present* (Amherst: Humanity Books, 1998), 3.

95. Koike Shirō, "Jidai ni genwaku sare taru marusasu" [Malthus, blinded by his time], *Sei to shakai*, no. 14 (May 1926): 24. It is noted that "jinrui kairyō gaku" (the study of the betterment of the human race) or "jinshu kaizō ron" (the theory of the renovation of the race) were initially used to refer to eugenics. Yuehtsen Juliette Chung, *Struggle for National Survival: Eugenics in Sino-Japanese Contexts, 1896–1945* (New York: Routledge, 2002), 14.

96. Since launching the CBC, Stopes repeatedly emphasized differences between neo-Malthusianism and the constructive birth control movement despite her membership of the Malthusian League, a British birth control advocacy organization founded in 1877. According to the CBC's manifesto, the primary goal of the group was "to bring home to all the fundamental nature of the reforms involved in conscious and constructive control of conception and the illumination of sex life as a basis of racial progress." Stressing the benefits of birth control exclusively on eugenic grounds, Stopes made explicit the difference between her goal and that of the Malthusian League by arguing that the former was "to spread a knowledge of the law of population" instead of merely restricting fertility. Marie Stopes, "Differences

Between the Malthusian League and the CBC: What Are They?," *Birth Control News* (July 1922): 4.

97. Yamamoto Senji, "Kensetsu teki sanji chōsetsu to wa donna mono ka: eikoku no sanji chōsetsu no kinjō (II)" [What is constructive birth control: current situations of the British birth control movement (II)], *Sanji chōsetsu hyōron*, no. 2 (March 1925): 12–16.

98. Havelock Ellis, *Sex in Relation to Society*, vol. 6 of *Studies in the Psychology of Sex* (Philadelphia: F. A. Davis, 1927), Project Gutenberg, https://www.gutenberg.org/files/13615/13615-h/13615-h.htm. Chapter 7 of the book, "The Science of Procreation," was translated and serially published in *Hyōron* (no. 7– no. 13). Ellis's other essays—including "The Objects of Marriage" (1920), "Children and Parents" (1922), "The Love-Rights of Women" (1918), and "The Play-Function of Sex" (1921)—were translated and published in different issues of *Hyōron*.

99. Koike, "Jidai ni genwaku sare taru marusasu," 24; Yamamoto Senji, "Sanji chōsetsu wa tenri ni somuku ka" [Does birth control go against the law of nature?], *Sei to shakai*, no. 13 (March 1926): 18–23.

100. In 1926, three different political parties were founded after the Universal (Male) Suffrage Act (Futsū senkyo hō), whose purpose was to extend male suffrage to male citizens (over the age of 25). These parties include the Social Democratic Party (Shakai Minshūtō, right wing), the Japan Labor-Farmer Party (Nihon Rōdō Nōmintō, centrist), and the Labor-Farmer Party (Rōdō Nōmintō, leftist). For the 1925 labor split, see Stephen S. Large, *Organized Workers and Socialist Politics in Interwar Japan* (Cambridge, UK: Cambridge University Press, 1981), 51–71.

101. It should be noted that the enactment of the Universal Suffrage Act of 1925 reveals the maleness of universality as the act excluded women from voting rights. On the issues of the Universal (Male) Suffrage Act from a feminist perspective, see Vera C. Mackie, *Feminism in Modern Japan: Citizenship, Embodiment, and Sexuality* (Cambridge, UK: Cambridge University Press, 2003), 58–65.

102. Toshiji, *Yamamoto Senji*, vol. 2, 121–382.

103. Ibid., 340–359.

104. Sheldon M. Garon, *The State and Labor in Modern Japan* (Berkeley: University of California Press, 1987), 152–156.

105. Ibid., 150.

106. Musansha Sanji Seigen Dōmei, "Musansha sanji seigen dōmei sengen: Kōryō kiyaku" [Manifesto of the Proletariat Birth Control League: codes and rules], in *Nihon josei undō shiryō shūsei* [Collection of documents related to women's movements in Japan], vol. 7, ed. Suzuki Yūko (Tokyo: Fuji shuppan, 1995), 686–688. Originally published June 6, 1931.

107. Kurahara Korehito, a socialist critic who led the All-Japan Proletarian Arts League (Zen Nihon Musansha Geijitsu Renmei, or NAPF) in 1928 and then the KOP movement since 1931, began to use "circles" (*ban*) first in Japan. Referencing *Proletkult,* Kurahara used *ban* to denote support organs for spreading cultural or scientific activities, or class aesthetics under the supervision of the central proletarian organization. Simon Andrew Avenell, *Making Japanese Citizens: Civil Society and the Mythology of the Shimin in Postwar Japan* (Berkeley: University of California Press, 2010), 44–46.

108. The Manchurian Incident, also known as the Mukden Incident, was allegedly initiated by the Japanese Kwantung Army. The initial battle between the Japanese and Chinese forces eventually led to Japan's invasion of Manchuria and

Inner Mongolia and to the establishment of Manchukuo. In Chapter 3 I will discuss in detail the impact of the foundation of Manchukuo in 1932 on population discourse. For the importance of the Manchurian Incident in the history of the Fifteen Years' War, see Shunsuke Tsurumi, *An Intellectual History of Wartime Japan, 1931–1945* (London: KPI, 1986), 33–41.

109. Sandra Wilson, *The Manchurian Crisis and Japanese Society* (London: Routledge, 2002), 105–109.

110. Proletarian writer Matsuda Tokiko (1905–2004) wrote a novel titled *Josei-sen* (The line of women) in 1936, in which she depicted the leading member of the Pro-BC birth control movement, Yamamoto Kotoko (1903–1935). Matsuda Tokiko, *Josei-sen* (Tokyo: Akebi shobō, 1995).

Chapter 2

1. Chizuko Ueno, *The Modern Family in Japan: Its Rise and Fall* (Melbourne: Trans Pacific Press, 2009), 84.

2. Barbara Molony, "Equality Versus Difference: The Japanese Debate over 'Motherhood Protection,' 1915–50," in *Japanese Women Working*, ed. Janet Hunter (New York: Routledge, 1993), 126.

3. Yosano Akiko, "Josei no tettei shita dokuritsu" [Women's complete independence], in *Shiryō bosei hogo ronsō* [Documents on the motherhood protection debate], ed. Kōuchi Nobuko (Tokyo: Domesu shuppan, 1984), 85–86. Originally published in *Fujin kōron* March 1918.

4. Olive Schreiner authored *Woman and Labor* (London: T. F. Unwin, 1911) to criticize women's domesticity as "sex parasitism" and advocate women's economic independence. For more on Yosano's response to Schreiner's feminist thoughts, see Laurel Rasplica Rodd, "Yosano Akiko and the Taisho Debate over the 'New Woman,'" in *Recreating Japanese Women, 1600–1945*, ed. Gail Lee Bernstein (Berkeley: University of California Press, 1991), 175–198. Meanwhile, Ellen Key's maternal feminism inspired early Japanese feminists including Hiratsuka who herself translated Key's work *Love and Marriage* (New York and London: G. P. Putnam's Sons, 1911) in 1913. On Hiratsuka's favorable reception of Key's thoughts, see Dina Lowy, "Love and Marriage: Ellen Key and Hiratsuka Raichō Explore Alternatives," *Women's Studies* 33, no. 4 (2004): 361–380; Jan Bardsley, "The New Woman of Japan and the Intimate Bonds of Translation," *Review of Japanese Culture and Society* 20 (2008): 206–225.

5. Hiratsuka Raichō, "Bosei hogo no shuchō wa iraishugi ka" [Is it an argument for motherhood protection parasitism?], in *Shiryō bosei hogo ronsō*, 86–91. Originally published in *Fujin kōron* (May 1918).

6. Yamada Waka, "Bosei hogo mondai: Yosano si to Hirano si no shoron ni tsuite" [The issue of motherhood protection: on the views of Mmes. Yosano and Hirano], in *Shiryō bosei hogo ronsō*, 147–160. Originally published in *Taiyō* (September 1918). The term "matricentric feminism" is from Andrea O'Reilly's *Matricentric Feminism: Theory, Activism, and Practice* (Bradford, ON: Demeter Press, 2016). O'Reilly deliberately focuses on matricentric feminism to cast light on mothers, the heretofore marginalized category of woman. I adopted this term from an opposite angle, namely, to highlight the overrepresentation of motherhood in prewar feminism in Japan.

7. Yamakawa Kikue, "Fujin wo uragiru fujinron wo hyōsu" [Comments on the

"women" discourse that betrays women], in *Shiryō bosei hogo ronsō*, 117–131. Originally published in *Shin Nihon* (August 1918).

8. For wartime feminism and its cooperation with the state, see Sheldon Garon, "Women's Groups and the Japanese State: Contending Approaches to Political Integration, 1890–1945," *Journal of Japanese Studies* 19, no. 1 (1993): 5–41; Barbara Molony, "From 'Mothers of Humanity' to 'Assisting the Emperor': Gendered Belonging in the Wartime Rhetoric of Japanese Feminist Ichikawa Fusae," *Pacific Historical Review* 80, no. 1 (2011): 1–27; Sumiko Otsubo, "Feminist Maternal Eugenics in Wartime Japan," *U.S.–Japan Women's Journal* 17 (1999): 39–76. The feminist discourse on motherhood during the wartime period will be further examined in later chapters, especially Chapters 4 and 5.

9. For the right to self-determination advocated by Ūman Ribu, or Japanese women's liberation movement in the 1970s, see Setsu Shigematsu, *Scream from the Shadows: The Women's Liberation Movement in Japan* (Minneapolis: University of Minnesota Press, 2012), 65–102.

10. For the discourse of motherhood in prewar and wartime Japan, see Molony, "Equality Versus Difference," 123–148; "From 'Mothers of Humanity' to 'Assisting the Emperor,'" 1–27; Naoko Tomie, "The Political Process of Establishing the Mother-Child Protection Law in Prewar Japan," *Social Science Japan Journal* 8, no. 2 (2005): 239–251; Kathleen S. Uno, *Passages to Modernity: Motherhood, Childhood, and Social Reform in Early Twentieth Century Japan* (Honolulu: University of Hawaii Press, 1999).

11. Ōhara Shakai Mondai Kenkyūsho, *Nihon rōdō nenkan* [Labor yearbook of Japan] (Tokyo: Rōdō junpōsha, 1922), 335–345.

12. Yoshiro Matsuda, "Formation of the Census System in Japan: 1871–1945—Development of the Statistical System in Japan Proper and Her Colonies," *Hitotsubashi Journal of Economics* 21, no. 2 (1981): 56.

13. Ōhara Shakai Mondai Kenkyūsho, *Nihon rōdō nenkan*, 344.

14. Ibid., 344–345.

15. Linda Gordon, "Voluntary Motherhood: The Beginnings of Feminist Birth Control Ideas in the United States," *Feminist Studies* 1, no. 3/4 (1973): 16–17.

16. For feminists' advocacy for reproductive control and eugenics under the slogan of voluntary motherhood, see Susanne Klausen and Alison Bashford, "Fertility Control: Eugenics, Neo-Malthusianism, and Feminism," in *The Oxford Handbook of the History of Eugenics*, eds. Alison Bashford and Philippa Levine (New York: Oxford University Press, 2010), 108–109.

17. Marouf Arif Hasian, *The Rhetoric of Eugenics in Anglo-American Thought* (Athens: University of Georgia Press, 1996), 77–88.

18. David M. Kennedy, *Birth Control in America: The Career of Margaret Sanger* (New Haven: Yale University Press, 1970), 22–23.

19. There were a series of minor changes in the subtitle first to "Dedicated to the Cause of Voluntary Motherhood" in the issue of April 1918 and then to "Dedicated to Voluntary Motherhood" in the issue of April 1919. After the American Birth Control League (ABCL) was formed in November 1921, the *Birth Control Review* became the official organ of the ABCL. The modification of subtitle in the issue of January 1922 concerns this organizational change.

20. Margaret Sanger, *Woman and the New Race* (New York: Brentano, 1920), 226.

21. Ibid.

22. Sanger, *Woman and the New Race*, 5; Yamakawa translated most parts of the first chapter, "Woman's Error and Her Debt," including the quote above into Japanese in her article "Tasan shugi no noroi" [The curse of pronatalism], in *Josei no hangyaku* [Women's rebel], ed. Suzuki Yūko (Tokyo: Iwanami shoten, 2011), 198–205. Originally published in *Taikan* (1920).

23. Ishimoto Shizue, "Shin-marusasu shugi" (Tokyo: Nihon panfuretto hakkōsho, 1921).

24. Ibid., 1. In Ishimoto's pamphlet, she used "voluntary parenthood" as the English equivalent for *jishuteki bosei*, but I conjecture that "parenthood" is a misprint for motherhood. The historical context of the American birth control movement buttresses this conjecture. Sanger advocated for voluntary motherhood whereas another American feminist Mary Ware Dennett put forward the concept of "voluntary parenthood" through her organization called the Voluntary Parenthood League. In the early 1920s, Sanger and Dennett were rivals due to their advocacy of different strategies for the birth control movement. Considering Ishimoto's close connection with Sanger, "voluntary motherhood" appears to be correct. As for the relationship between Sanger and Dennett, see Patricia Walsh Coates, *Margaret Sanger and the Origin of the Birth Control Movement, 1910–1930: The Concept of Women's Sexual Autonomy* (Lewiston: Edwin Mellen Press, 2008), 188–189.

25. Gilles Deleuze and Félix Guattari, *A Thousand Plateaus: Capitalism and Schizophrenia* (Minneapolis: University of Minnesota Press, 1987), 62.

26. Article 5 of the Public Peace Police Law had prevented women from attending political meetings or joining political organizations. The amendment of Article 5 marked a watershed for Japan's feminist movement. Notably, it led to the formation of women's organizations and the diversification of feminist strategies. Mackie, *Feminism in Modern Japan*, 58–60; Barbara Molony, "Women's Rights, Feminism, and Suffragism in Japan, 1870–1925," *Pacific Historical Review* 69, no. 4 (2000): 654–655.

27. Asha Nadkarni, *Eugenic Feminism: Reproductive Nationalism in the United States and India* (Minneapolis: University of Minnesota Press, 2014), 7.

28. Ishimoto Shidzué (Shizue), *Facing Two Ways: The Story of My Life* (New York: Farrar & Rinehart, 1935), 164.

29. Agnes Smedley, "The Awakening of Japan," *Birth Control Review* 4, no. 2 (February 1920): 6–8.

30. Helen M. Hopper, *A New Woman of Japan: A Political Biography of Katō Shidzue* (Boulder: Westview Press, 1996), 11.

31. Aiko Takeuchi-Demirci, *Contraceptive Diplomacy: Reproductive Politics and Imperial Ambitions in the United States and Japan* (Stanford: Stanford University Press, 2018), 11.

32. Hopper, *A New Woman of Japan*, 20; Elise K. Tipton, "Ishimoto Shizue: The Margaret Sanger of Japan," *Women's History Review* 6, no. 3 (1997): 343.

33. Ishimoto, "Shin-marusasu shugi," i–ii.

34. Ibid., 6.

35. Ibid., 6–8.

36. Ibid., 9.

37. Ibid., 10. For a social discourse of "cultural living" in the context of post-WWI in Japan, see Harry D. Harootunian, *Overcome by Modernity: History, Cul-*

ture, and Community in Interwar Japan (Princeton: Princeton University Press, 2011), 15.
38. Ishimoto, "Shin-marusasu shugi," 10.
39. Ibid., 13.
40. The detailed history of *Chōsetsukai* is covered in Chapter 1 of this book.
41. Ishimoto Shizue, "Fujin kaihō to sanji chōsetsu" [Women's liberation and birth control], in *SSJ*, vol. 14, 3; translation is mine. Originally published in *Shōkazoku* (May 1922).
42. Ishimoto Shizue, "Sanji seigen ron o sho hōmen yori kansatsu shite" [A general observation of the arguments for birth control] (October 1922), in *SSJ*, vol. 2, 1.
43. Ibid., 2–8.
44. Michel Foucault, *Society Must Be Defended: Lectures at the Collège de France, 1975–1976* (New York: Picador, 200), 255.
45. Ogawa Ryūshiro, *Ninshin chōsetsu no jitsuchishiki* [Actual knowledge of birth control] (Tokyo: Nihon ninshin chōsetsu sōdansho, 1924), 47–54.
46. Hopper, *A New Woman of Japan*, 36–37.
47. Ishimoto Shizue and Keikichi had been separated since 1931 when the baron left for Manchuria. It was not until 1944 that they were legally divorced due to the legal challenge of divorce under the Imperial Household Law. In the same year her divorce was granted, Ishimoto married Katō Kanjū, a leading labor activist and the chair of the Proletarian Party. Hopper, *A New Woman of Japan*, 44–48.
48. Ogino Miho, *"Kazoku keikaku" e no michi: kindai nihon no seishoku o meguru seiji* [The road to family planning politics over reproduction in modern Japan] (Tokyo: Iwanami shoten, 2008), 55.
49. Ōta Tenrei, *Nihon sanji chōsetsu hyakunenshi* [The hundred-year history of Japan's birth control] (Tokyo: Shuppan kagaku sōgō kenkyūjo, 1976), 143–144.
50. Ibid., 145; Ogino, *"Kazoku keikaku" e no michi*, 57.
51. Nihon sanji chōsetsu fujin dōmei, "Sechigarai yononaka ni" [In a world full of difficulties], in *SSJ*, vol. 7 (2001), 130. Originally published February 1934.
52. Ishimoto Shizue, "Sanji chōsetsu no kokoroe" [The knowledge of birth control], in *SSJ*, vol. 7, 291. Originally published September 1936.
53. Nihon sanji chōsetsu fujin dōmei, "Sechigarai yononaka ni," 130.
54. Ibid.; translation is mine.
55. For Yamakawa's feminist activism in prewar and postwar Japan, see Yamakawa Kikue seitan hyakunen o kinensuru kai [The Society to Commemorate the 100th Anniversary of Yamakawa Kikue's Birth], *Gendai feminizumu to Yamakawa Kikue: renzoku kōza "Yamakawa Kikue to gendai" no kiroku* [Modern feminism and Yamakawa Kikue: lecture series on the records of "Yamakawa Kikue and modernity"] (Tokyo: Yamato shobō, 1990); Elyssa Faison, "Women's Rights as Proletarian Rights: Yamakawa Kikue, Suffrage, and the 'Dawn of Liberation,'" in *Rethinking Japanese Feminisms*, eds. James Welker, Ayako Kano, and Julia C. Bullock (Honolulu: University of Hawaii Press, 2018), 15–33; Ayala Klemperer-Markham and Ofra Goldstein-Gidoni, "Socialist Egalitarian Feminism in Early Postwar Japan: Yamakawa Kikue and the 'Democratization of Japan,'" *U.S.–Japan Women's Journal* 42 (2012): 3–30.
56. Yamakawa authored several articles on the birth control issue during the period between 1920 and 1921, which included Yamakawa, "Tasan shugi no noroi," *Taikan*,

no. 10 (1920); "Josei no hangyaku: seishin teki oyobi busshitsu teki hōmen yori mitaru sanji seigen mondai" [Women's rebel: birth control problem in light of spiritual and material aspects], *Kaihō*, no. 1 (1921); "Sanji seigen mondai" [The problem of birth control], *Onna no sekai*, no. 1 (1921); "Sanji chōsetsu ron to shakai shugi" [The discussion of birth control and socialism], *Shakai shugi kenkyū*, no. 6 (1921). The abovementioned articles were reprinted in a collected volume of Yamakawa's writings titled *Josei no hangyaku*, vol. 2 of *Yamakawa Kikue shū* [The complete works of Yamakawa Kikue], ed. Suzuki Yūko (Tokyo: Iwanami shoten, 2011).

57. Yamakawa, "Sanji chōsetsu ron to shakai shugi," 283.

58. For Yamakawa's biography, I consulted the following books: Mikiso Hane, *Reflections on the Way to the Gallows: Rebel Women in Prewar Japan* (Berkeley: University of California Press, 1988); Yamakawa Kikue, *Women of the Mito Domain: Recollections of Samurai Family Life* (Tokyo: University of Tokyo Press, 1992); Suzuki Yūko, *Wasurerareta shishōka Yamakawa Kikue: feminizumu to senjika no teikō* [Forgotten theorist Yamakawa Kikue: feminism and resistance during the wartime period] (Tokyo: Nashi no ki, 2022).

59. Mitsutoshi Azuma, "Labor Legislation in Japan," *Annals of the Hitotsubashi Academy* 1, no. 2 (1951): 183–184. As for the gender implications of the Factory Law, see Elyssa Faison, *Managing Women: Disciplining Labor in Modern Japan* (Berkeley: University of California Press, 2007), 22–26.

60. For the spread of mass circulation magazines in the Taishō period, see Sarah Frederick, *Turning Pages: Reading and Writing Women's Magazines in Interwar Japan* (Honolulu: University of Hawaii Press, 2006), 1–25.

61. Yamakawa Kikue seitan hyakunen o kinensuru kai, *Gendai feminizumu to Yamakawa Kikue*, 217.

62. Mackie, *Feminism in Modern Japan*, 79.

63. Ibid., 81–84; Yamakawa Kikue Seitan Hyakunen o Kinensuru Kai, *Gendai feminizumu to Yamakawa Kikue*, 218–219. Yamakawa's "Thesis on Women's Division," drafted originally in 1925, is reprinted in *Yamakawa Kikue shū*, vol. 4 of *Musan kaikyū no fujin undō* [The proletarian women's movement] (Tokyo: Iwanami shoten, 2011), 102–112.

64. For the transition of Sanger's thoughts from radical socialism to neo-Malthusian, middle-class-based reformism due to state repression, and personal struggle from poor health and financial issues, see Coates, *Margaret Sanger and the Origin of the Birth Control Movement, 1910–1930*, 181–212; Joan M. Jensen, "The Evolution of Margaret Sanger's 'Family Limitation' Pamphlet, 1914–1921," *Signs* 6, no. 3, spring (1981): 548–567.

65. Yamakawa, "Sanji chōsetsu ron to shakai shugi," 284.

66. Ibid., 286.

67. Abe Isoo's *Seikatsu mondai kara mita sanji chōsetsu* [Birth control from a livelihood perspective] (Tokyo: Tokyodō, 1931) typifies neo-Malthusianist accounts of population whereas Kawakami's *Jinkō mondai hihan* [Critiques of the population problem] (Tokyo: Sōbunkaku, 1927) gives a glimpse into socialist accounts on the population issues. For the detailed analysis of the debate between neo-Malthusianism and socialism, see Chapter 1 in this book.

68. Yamakawa, "Sanji chōsetsu ron to shakai shugi," 284–286.

69. Yamakawa, "Tasan shugi no noroi," 201.

70. Richard J. Wiltgen, "Marx's and Engels's Conception of Malthus: The Heritage of a Critique," *Organization & Environment* 11, no. 4 (1998): 451–452.

71. In her 1921 article "Sanji chōsetsu ron to shakai shugi," Yamakawa introduces prominent European leftist socialists' writings including Marx's *Capital: A Critique of Political Economy*, vol. 1 (1867), Bebel's *Woman and Socialism* (1879), and Kropotkin's *Fields, Factories and Workshops: Or Industry Combined with Agriculture and Brain Work with Manual Work* (1899). It should be noted that Yamakawa's brief reference on Marx's critique of Malthus might be misleading because the crucial point Marx made in his analysis of overpopulation was not the optimism of human evolution, but the nature of relative surplus population as a necessary condition for the capitalist mode of production. For Marx's concept of relative surplus population, see Marx, *Capital*, 781–870.

72. August Bebel, *Woman and Socialism* (New York: Socialist Literature Co., 1910). The Japanese translation of the quote is included in Yamakwa's "Sanji chōsetsu ron to shakai shugi," 281–282.

73. Yamakwa "Sanji chōsetsu ron to shakai shugi," 282.

74. Marx, *Capital*, 793. On Marx's notion of despotism of capitals and its impact on the population debate in interwar Japan, see Chapter 1.

75. Sanger, *Woman and the New Race*, 145–150.

76. Yamakwa "Sanji chōsetsu ron to shakai shugi," 282–283.

77. Ibid., 284.

78. Ibid.

79. Sakai Toshihiko (1871–1933), a prominent socialist intellectual, was one of the few male socialists who attended to the gendered division of labor within the socioeconomic structure. He advocated women's reproductive autonomy while criticizing both neo-Malthusianism and pronatalism for serving for the bourgeois class. For Sakai's argument for the women's rights to abortion, see Sakai Toshihiko, "Umu jiyū to uma nu jiyū" [The freedom of giving birth and not giving birth], in *Shiryō sei to ai o meguru ronsō* [Sources on debates about sex and love], ed. Orii Miyako (Tokyo: Domesu shuppan, 1991), 185–188. Originally published in *Sekaijin* in 1916. Also, for Japanese socialist debates on sexuality, see Ishikawa Shoji, "Shakai shugisha ni okeru 'sei' to seiji: nihon no 1920–30 nendai o chūshin toshite" [The gender role of women in the Japanese socialist movement during the 1920s and 30s], *Nenpō seiji gaku* 54 (2003): 161–177.

80. Yamakawa "Sanji chōsetsu ron to shakai shugi," 285.

81. Yamakawa, "Tasan shugi no noroi," 202.

82. Yamakawa and Ishikawa debated through articles published in *Onna no sekai* (Women's world). The articles include (in chronological order): Ishikawa, "Shakai shugi sha kara mita fujin kyūsai: ippuippu seido wa shizen de jiyū de junketsu de aru" [A socialist view on the relief of women: monogamy as nature, freedom, and purity], *Onna no sekai* (February 1921); Yamakawa, "Ishikawa Sanshirō to hininron" [Ishikawa Sanshirō and a discussion of contraception], *Onna no sekai* (March 1921); Ishikawa, "Hininron ni tsuite: Yamakawa kikue joshi ni mōsu" [On contraception: a message to madam Yamakawa], *Onna no sekai* (April 1921); and Yamakawa, "Hinin zehi nitsuite futatabi Ishikawa Sanshirō ni atau" [A follow-up message to Mr. Ishikawa on the pros and cons of contraception], *Onna no sekai* (June 1921).

83. Ishikawa, "Shakai shugi sha kara mita fujin kyūsai," 34.

84. Yamakawa, "Ishikawa Sanshirō to hininron," 244.

85. Eve Kosofsky Sedgwick, "Sexualism and the Citizen of the World: Wycherley, Sterne, and Male Homosocial Desire," *Critical Inquiry* 11, no. 2 (1984): 227.

86. Yamakawa, "Ishikawa Sanshirō to hininron," 246–247; translation is mine.

87. Shibahara Urako (1877–1955) played a key role in the two birth control consultation centers in Osaka until she was arrested for performing abortions in June 1933. Frühstück, *Colonizing Sex*, 163.

88. Ibid.

89. For Yamakawa's wartime writing focused on women's history as exemplified in *Women of the Mito Domain (Buke no josei*, 1943), see E. Patricia Tsurumi, "The Accidental Historian, Yamakawa Kikue," *Gender & History* 8, no. 2 (1996): 258–276.

Chapter 3

1. The demographic phenomena reconstituted into a form of scientific knowledge includes fertility, mortality, nuptiality, migration, productivity, labor and social affairs, and employment. As noted, I deliberately choose to use the term "population science" rather than "demography" to avoid the reductive characterization of a gamut of academic fields and professionals participating in the production of knowledge on the patterns, projections, and governance of populations. Demography as an academic discipline was yet to be established in the prewar period in Japan; moreover, the trajectory of the development of population research shows its inherently interdisciplinary nature, mobilizing knowledge across social science disciplines and bridging science and policies. The process of the making of population science in Japan parallels the historical trajectory of demography in the United States. The creation of the Population Association of America in 1931, the nation's first institution for scientific research on demographic phenomena and policies, was an interdisciplinary effort facilitated by sociologists, economists, statisticians, and so forth, who shared Malthusian and racialist visions. On the development of U.S. demography, see Susan Greenhalgh, "The Social Construction of Population Science: An Intellectual, Institutional, and Political History of Twentieth-Century Demography," *Comparative Studies in Society and History* 38, no. 1 (1996): 26–66; Dennis Hodgson, "The Ideological Origins of the Population Association of America," *Population and Development Review* 17, no. 1 (1991): 1–34.

2. Michel Foucault, "Governmentality," in *The Foucault Effect: Studies in Governmentality: With Two Lectures by and an Interview with Michel Foucault*, eds. Graham Burchell, Colin Gordon, and Peter Miller (Chicago: University of Chicago Press, 1991), 102.

3. I borrowed "co-production" from Sheila Jasanoff who suggests using this notion as an analytic tool for cross cutting the epistemological divide between science and politics or between knowledge and society, and for investigating how scientific orderings and social orderings inform and constitute each other. Sheila Jasanoff, "The Idiom of Co-Production," in *States of Knowledge: The Co-Production of Science and Social Order*, ed. Sheila Jasanoff (London: Routledge, 2004), 1–12.

4. Greenhalgh's *Just One Child: Science and Policy in Deng's China* takes a similar approach—the use of the "co-production" framework in an analysis of population science—in examining the making of population science and its impact on the shaping of China's one-child policy. Susan Greenhalgh, *Just One Child: Science and Policy in Deng's China* (Berkeley: University of California Press, 2008).

5. M. G. E. Kelly calls this imperialist dimension of the biopolitical governance of life a "biopolitical imperialism." With this notion, Kelly emphasizes how thana-

topolitics inevitably operates at the limit of biopolitical regulation in the current era of neo-liberalism and globalization. M. G. E. Kelly, "International Biopolitics: Foucault, Globalisation and Imperialism," *Theoria (Pietermaritzburg)* 57, no. 123 (2010): 1–26.

6. Alison Bashford, *Global Population: History, Geopolitics, and Life on Earth* (New York: Columbia University Press, 2014), 49–50.

7. Suzuki Bunji (1885–1946), leftist activist and founder of a labor organization called the Yūaikai (Friendly Society), is another pro–birth control activist, but his rationale for advocating birth control was in line with neo-Malthusianism. Suzuki's view of overpopulation is articulated in his 1926 article "Jinkō mondai" [Population problem] in *Keizaiōrai* [Economic correspondence] in which Suzuki reiterated the neo-Malthusian concerns about overpopulation as a root cause of various social issues. Given his continued involvement in the birth control movement through engaging in Chōsetsukai, *Seigenkai*'s magazine *Sanji seigen hyōron*, and Chūō Sanji chōsetsu sōdansho (central birth control counseling clinics) throughout the 1920s, Suzuki's motivation appears to concern utilizing birth control as a reformist tool of the labor movement without necessarily subverting the capitalist social structure. For Suzuki's social reformism, see Stephen S. Large, "The Japanese Labor Movement, 1912–1919: Suzuki Bunji and the Yūaikai," *Journal of Asian Studies* 29, no. 3 (1970): 559–579. For Marxist economist Kawakami Hajime's critique of Suzuki's account of overpopulation for his failure to understand capitalist social relations, see Kawakami Hajime, *Jinkō mondai hihan* [Critique of the population problem] (Tokyo: Sōbunkaku, 1927), 43–50.

8. Sidney Xu Lu, *The Making of Japanese Settler Colonialism: Malthusianism and Trans-Pacific Migration, 1868–1961* (Cambridge, UK, and New York: Cambridge University Press, 2019), 189–190.

9. Takata Yasuma, "Umeyo fueyo" [Be fruitful and multiply], *Keizaiōrai* 1, no. 5 (1926), 15–16.

10. This article, originally published in his own journal *Shakai mondai kenkyū*, no. 74 (August 1926), was reprinted in a book titled *Jinkō mondai hihan*, 51–64.

11. Kawakami, *Jinkō mondai hihan*, 38.

12. Takata maintained a keen interest in the totalizing concept of ethnic nation (*minzoku*) on which he conducted sociological research beginning in the 1930s. During wartime, Takata was appointed as the first director of the Minzoku kenkyūsho (Ethnic Research Institute), founded in 1943, a government-sponsored research center that aimed to promote ethnographic and anthropological research on various ethnicities within the Japanese empire. For Takata's ethnonationalism embedded in his sociological work, see Kevin M. Doak, "Building National Identity Through Ethnicity: Ethnology in Wartime Japan and After," *Journal of Japanese Studies* 27, no. 1 (2001): 1–39.

13. Minami Ryōzaburō, *Jinkōron hattenshi: Nihon ni okeru jyūnenkan no sō gyōseki* [The history of the development of population theories: all the achievements made in Japan in the last decade] (Tokyo: Sanseidō, 1936): 1–29; Nakanishi Yasuyuki, "Takada Yasuma no jinkō riron to shakaigaku" [Takata Yasuma 's theory of population and sociology], *Keizai-ronsō* 140, no. 5–6 (1987): 62–63.

14. "Jinkō shokuryō mondai chōsa kenkyūkai kansei" [Administration law regarding the Population and Food Problems Investigation Committee], *Kanpō gogai* (July 7, 1927): 1.

15. Jinkō mondai kenkyūkai [The Society for Population Problem Studies], *Jinkō*

mondai kenkyūkai 50-nen ryakushi [A fifty-year history of the Society for Population Problem Studies] (Tokyo: Jinkō mondai kenkyūkai, 1983), 3–8.

16. Nagai Tōru, *Nihon jinkōron* [The study of the Japanese population] (Tokyo: Ganshōdō shoten, 1929), 64–65; translation is mine.

17. Nagai Tōru, "Kajō jinkō no shitsugyō to no kankei o ronjite jinkō mondai no honshitsu ni oyobu" [Towards the essence of the population problem by discussing the relation between overpopulation and unemployment], *Jinkō mondai* 1, no. 3 (1936): 37–41.

18. Nagai, *Nihon jinkōron*, 19.

19. In many articles, Nagai traced the trajectory of population theories, beginning from Malthus's theory of population and food to Darwin's theory of evolution to Marx's study of capitalism. For this stream of intellectual history, Nagai noted that theories of the law of population had moved from economics to biology, then to social Darwinism, and finally to socialism. His emphasis on social science and sociology, therefore, reveals his effort to keep a critical distance from the existing theories and to reframe the law of population. Nagai Tōru, "Sekai no jinkō-ron yori nihon no jinkō-ron e (I)" [From the global theory of population to the Japanese theory of population (I)], *Taiyō* 34, no. 1 (1928): 2–10.

20. Nagai, *Nihon jinkōron*, 32.

21. For Nagai's drafts and the official reports of the Department of Population, see Jinkō shokuryō mondai chōsakai, *Jinkō shokuryō mondai chōsakai jinkō-bu tōshin setsumei* [Annotations on the reports of the Department of Population by the Population and Food Problems Investigation Committee] (Tokyo: Jinkō shokuryō mondai chōsakai, 1930).

22. Ibid., 1–3.

23. Ibid., 57.

24. Ibid., 57–58; translation is mine.

25. Foucault, "Governmentality," 100.

26. Jinkō shokuryō mondai chōsakai, *Jinkō shokuryō mondai chōsakai jinkō-bu tōshin setsumei*, 57.

27. Ibid., 39–40.

28. Tiana Norgren, *Abortion Before Birth Control: The Politics of Reproduction in Postwar Japan* (Princeton: Princeton University Press, 2001), 28–29.

29. The IUSIPP was reorganized as the International Union for the Scientific Study of Population in 1947 and has continued its international activities since then in conjunction with the United Nations. "Interim Report of the Proceedings of the First General Assembly of the International Union for the Scientific Investigation of Population Problems," *Journal of the American Statistical Association* 23, no. 163 (1928): 306–317; Matthew Connelly, *Fatal Misconception: The Struggle to Control World Population* (Cambridge, MA: Belknap Press, 2008), 70–74.

30. "Interim Report of the Proceedings of the First General Assembly of the IUSIPP," 308.

31. Ibid.

32. For Nitobe Inazō's biographical information, see John F. Howes, ed., *Nitobe Inazo: Japan's Bridge Across the Pacific* (London: Routledge, 2021); Teruhiko Nagao, *Nitobe Inazo: From Bushido to the League of Nations* (Sapporo: Graduate School of Letters, Hokkaido University, 2006). As for Nitobe's thoughts and political careers as an internationalist, the following work provides a critical look into his nationalist and/or regionalist stance paradoxically embedded in his advocacy of

international order. Thomas W. Burkman, "Nitobe Inazō: From World Order to Regional Order," in *Culture and Identity: Japanese Intellectuals During the Interwar Years*, ed. J. Thomas Rimer (Princeton: Princeton University Press, 2014), 191–216; George M. Oshiro, "Nitobe Inazō and Japanese Nationalism," in *Japanese Cultural Nationalism: At Home and in the Asia-Pacific*, ed. Roy Starrs (Kent: Global Oriental, 2004), 61–79.

33. Nitobe Inazō, "Nitobe Ianzō iin ikensho" [Nitobe Inazō's statement of opinion], in *Jinkō mondai kenkyūkai 50-nen ryakushi*, 8. Originally published 1929.

34. Nagai Tōru (drafter), "Jinkō mondai ni kansuru jōsetsu chōsa kikan setchi ni kansuru kengian" [A recommendation to establish a permanent investigating organization about population problems], in *Jinkō mondai kenkyūkai 50-nen ryakushi*, 20.

35. Nagai Tōru, "Wagakuni ni okeru jinkō mondai ni kansuru chōsa kenkyū kikan no raireki ni tsuite" [History of the Organization for Research and Study in Japan Concerning Population Problems], *Jinkō mondai kenkyūsho nenpō* 5 (1960): 1.

36. Ueda Teijirō, *Nihon jinkō seisaku* [Japan's population policies] (Tokyo: Chikura shobō, 1937), 61–62.

37. Ueda Teijirō, *Shin jiyū shugi* [Neo-liberalism] (Tokyo: Dōbunkan, 1927), 140–151.

38. Nasu Shiroshi, *Jinkō shokuryō mondai* [Problems of population and food] (Tokyo: Nihon Hyōron-sha, 1927), 97–163.

39. Lu, *The Making of Japanese Settler Colonialism*, 178.

40. Since 1925, the Japanese government subsidized Latin American emigration via the migration business company, Kaigai kōgyō kabushiki gaisha (Overseas Enterprise Co., Ltd.). From the 1920s until the late-1930s, approximately 180,000 Japanese migrated to Latin American countries among which Brazil was the most favored destination. For Japanese migration to Latin America, see Toake Endoh, *Exporting Japan: Politics of Emigration Toward Latin America* (Urbana and Chicago: University of Illinois Press, 2009), 59–79.

41. Chōsen sōtokufu [Government-General of Korea], *Jinkō mondai ni kansuru hōsaku no sankōan* [Reference for solutions to population problems] (Keijō: Chōsen sōtokufu, 1927).

42. Jinkō shokuryō mondai chōsakai, *Jinkō-bu tōshin setsumei*, 23–25.

43. Chōsen sōtokufu, *Jinkō mondai ni kansuru hōsaku*, 5–6.

44. Nagai, *Nihon jinkōron*, 196–197.

45. Colonial administrations were also aware of the practical difficulty of promoting Japanese colonial migration. For example, the Government-General of Korea reported in 1927 that the barriers to Japanese migration to Korea included various issues: a lack of understanding about Korea's local situation; the Japanese people's preference to stay in Japan proper; different standards of living between the metropole and colonial Korea; insufficient infrastructure in Korea in terms of police, hygiene, education, transportation, and entertainment; and Korea's poor productivity. Chōsen sōtokufu, *Jinkō mondai ni kansuru hōsaku*, 8–9.

46. Jinkō shokuryō mondai chōsakai, *Jinkō-bu tōshin setsumei*, 23–24; translation is mine.

47. Robert Young, *Empire, Colony, Postcolony* (Chichester, West Sussex: John Wiley, 2015), 31.

48. Nitobe Inazō and Yanaihara Tadao, *Nitobe Hakase shokumin seisaku kōgi*

oyobi ronbunshū [Collections of lectures and dissertations by Dr. Nitobe on Colonial Policies] (Tokyo: Iwanami shoten, 1943), 172.

49. Nitobe made this remark at the IPR Conference in 1929, which indicates his view of internationalism as a harmonious, coordinated regime consisting of different nations. "Opening Address at the Kyoto Conference of the Institute of Pacific Relations (Given on October 28, 1929)," in *The Works of Inazō Nitobe*, vol. 4 (Tokyo: University of Tokyo Press, 1972), 352–359; His theory of colonization can be found in Nitobe Inazō, "Nihon no shokumin" [Japan's colonization], in *Nitobe Inazō zenshū* [The complete works of Nitobe Inazō], vol. 21 (Tokyo: Kyōbunkan, 1986), 483–493.

50. "Nitobe Says Japan for Co-Operation—Head of Japanese Delegation to Kyoto Conference Tells Nation's Will to Aid," *The Trans-Pacific* (November 7, 1929): 9.

51. For imperialism and colonialism embedded in Nitobe's internationalist aspirations, see Thomas W. Burkman, *Japan and the League of Nations: Empire and World Order, 1914–1938* (Honolulu: University of Hawaii Press, 2008), 142–164; Alexis Dudden, "Japanese Colonial Control in International Terms," *Japanese Studies* 25 no. 1 (2005): 1–20; Kitaoka Shinichi, "Nitobe Inazō ni okeru teikoku shugi to kokusai shugi" [Nitobe Inazō's imperialism and internationalism], in *Iwanami kōza kindai nihon to shokuminchi 4: tōgō to shihai no ronri* [Iwanami lecture: modern Japan and its colonies 4: logics of integration and rule], eds. Ōe Shinobu, Asada Kyōji, and Mitani Taichirō (Tokyo: Iwanami shoten, 1993), 179–203.

52. Nitobe and Yanaihara, *Nitobe Hakase shokumin seisaku kōgi oyobi ronbunshū*, 11–13; Nitobe Inazō, "Shokumin no shūkyoku mokuteki" [The ultimate goal of colonization], in *Nitobe Hakase shokumin seisaku kōgi oyobi ronbunshū*, 382–401. Originally published in *Hōgaku kyōkai zasshi* 31, no. 12 (1913).

53. "Japan's Soul Is in Its Food Problems—Professor Nasu Says Food and Population Questions Are Very Deep," *The Trans-Pacific* (November 21, 1929): 11.

54. Nitobe, "Nihon no shokumin," 483.

55. As for Nitobe's plan to promote the sugar industry in Taiwan, Ryū Fumihiko notes that colonial industrialization played a crucial role in the economic policies of the Japanese empire, particularly in terms of the colonial division of labor between Japan proper as the core and its colonies as periphery. While I agree with Ryū's point, my analysis also sheds light on the importance of population policies in shaping the economic plans of the Empire. Ryū Fumihiko, "Nitobe Inazō no Taiwan tōgyō seisaku to shokumin shisō no tenkai" [The development of Nitobe Inazō's Taiwan sugar industry policy and his colonial thoughts], *Ajia bunka kenkyū* 14 (2007): 73.

56. Jinkō shokuryō mondai chōsakai, *jinkō-bu tōshin setsumei*, 83–84.

57. Yanaihara's thoughts on population problems in both national and international contexts—and possible solutions including emigration, colonization, and social, technological, economic improvement—are found in his book *Jinkō mondai* [Population problems] (Tokyo: Iwanami Shoten, 1928). Also, for scholarly research on Yanaihara's thoughts on emigration and colonization, see Murakami Katsuhiko, "Yanaihara Tadaō ni okeru shokuminron to shokumin seisaku" [Yanaihara Tadaō's theory on colonialism and colonial policy], in *Iwanami kōza kindai nihon to shokuminchi*, vol. 4, 205–237; Pak Yangsin, "Sikmin chŏngch'aekhak ŭi sinchip'yŏng kwa manchu munche insik—Yanaihara Tadao lŭl chungsimŭlo" [The new horizons

of colonial policy studies and recognition of Manchurian problems—focusing on Yanaihara Tadao's arguments], *Manjuyŏn'gu* 21 (2016): 157–188; Susan C. Townsend, *Yanaihara Tadao and Japanese Colonial Policy: Redeeming Empire* (Richmond: Curzon, 2000), 70–98.

58. The slogan "Manchuria as Japan's lifeline" was used by politicians and militarists who supported Japanese expansion into Manchuria. Matsuoka Yōsuke (1880–1946), a diplomat known for his speech condemning the League of Nations and announcing Japan's withdrawal in 1933, is credited as the first person to use the term "lifeline." This slogan was used to propagate a utopian image of Manchuria, as well as the importance of its territory for Japan's national defense and economic development. Pak, "Sikmin chŏngch'aekhak ŭi sinchip'yŏng," 171; Townsend, *Yanaihara Tadao and Japanese Colonial Policy*, 177–178.

59. Nitobe, "The Manchurian Question and Sino-Japanese Relations (xi.21 .1932)," in *The Works of Inazō Nitobe*, vol. 4, 231–232; emphasis added.

60. It is worth noting that some works discuss the distinctive characteristics of Japan's settler colonialism in Taiwan and Korea in terms of Japanese (or Okinawan in the case of Taiwan) migration to the colonies primarily in their own economic interests, as well as their negotiation between colonial administrations and colonial subjects, and between imperial embodiment and colonial liminality. See Hiroko Matsuda, *Liminality of the Japanese Empire: Border Crossings from Okinawa to Colonial Taiwan* (Honolulu: University of Hawaii Press), 2018; Jun Uchida, *Brokers of Empire: Japanese Settler Colonialism in Korea, 1876–1945* (Cambridge, MA: Harvard University Asia Center, 2011).

61. Marius B. Jansen, *The Making of Modern Japan* (Cambridge, MA: Belknap Press, 2000), 590–592.

62. Penelope Francks, *Rural Economic Development in Japan: From the Nineteenth Century to the Pacific War* (London: Routledge, 2006), 209–217; Thomas R. H. Havens, *Farm and Nation in Modern Japan: Agrarian Nationalism, 1870–1940* (Princeton: Princeton University Press, 1974), 135–141.

63. A total of twenty-four issues of *Population Problem* were published between February 1935 and March 1944. For the brief history of the PPRS, see Jinkō mondai kenkyūkai, *Jinkō mondai kenkyūkai 50-nen ryakushi*, 25–39.

64. Jinkō mondai kenkyūkai, *Jinkō mondai kōenshū* [A collection of lectures on population problems], vol. 1 (Tokyo: Jinkō mondai kenkyūkai, 1934), 5.

65. Jinkō mondai kenkyūkai, *Jinkō mondai kenkyūkai 50-nen ryakushi*, 34–35.

66. Inoue Masaji, *Ijyū to kaitaku* [Migration and development], vol. 1 (Tokyo: Nihon shokumin tsūshin-sha, 1930), 360–362.

67. For the emergence of agrarianism in modern Japan, see Havens, *Farm and Nation in Modern Japan*, 3–14.

68. Shiroshi Nasu, *Aspects of Japanese Agriculture: A Preliminary Survey* (New York: International Secretariat, Institute of Pacific Relations, 1941), 107–119. This book is a revised edition of *Land Utilization in Japan* (Tokyo: Institute of Pacific Relations, 1929).

69. For Katō Kanji's popular agrarianism, see Thomas R. H. Havens, "Katō Kanji (1884–1965) and the Spirit of Agriculture in Modern Japan," *Monumenta Nipponica* 25, no. 3/4 (1970): 249–266. The phrase "agricultural colonization" is from Katō Kanji, *Nihon nōson kyōiku* [Japanese farm education] (Tokyo: Tōyō tosho, 1936), 197.

70. For Katō Kanji and the Katō group, see Asada Kyōji, "Manshū nōgyō imin seisaku no ritsuan katei" [The process of planning the policy of peasant emigration to Manchuria], in *Nihon teikokushugika no Manshū imin* [emigration to Manchuria under Japanese imperialism], ed. Manshu iminshi kenkyukai (Tokyo: Ryūkei shosha, 1976), 24–29; Im Sŏngmo, "Manchu nongŏpimin chŏngch'aek ŭl tullŏssan kwantongkun, chosŏn ch'ongtokpu ŭi taelip kwa kŭ kwikyŏl" [The conflict between the Kwantung Army and the Korean Government General over the agricultural emigration policy to Manchuria and its consequence], *Ilbonyŏksayŏn'gu* 29 (2009): 139–141; Louise Young, *Japan's Total Empire: Manchuria and the Culture of Wartime Imperialism* (Berkeley: University of California Press, 1998), 318–322.

71. Asada, "Manshū nōgyō imin seisaku no ritsuan katei," 7–8.

72. Ibid., 25–28.

73. Manshūkoku Tsūshinsha, *Manshū kaitaku nenkan* [The yearbook of Manchuria colonization] (Tokyo: Howa shuppan, 1986), 129. Originally published 1944.

74. For the "One Million Households to Manchuria Plan," see ibid., 44–50.

75. Jinkō mondai kenkyūkai, "Ishokumin shinkō hōsaku ni kansuru kengi" [A policy proposal for the promotion of emigration and settlement], *Jinkō mondai* 1 no. 4 (1936): 16–24.

76. In the proposal for the promotion of emigration and settlement, the PPRS notes that private sectors must take a leading role in promoting the campaign for emigration and settlement while the government should play a subsidiary role, such as regulating the emigration campaign and protecting Japanese settlers. However, this statement contradicts the basic premise of this proposal, namely, "establishing comprehensive national policies on migration and settlement inside and outside Japan proper." This self-contradiction reflects PPRS wariness of international opinion, given its loaded comment that "the government should avoid being misunderstood as directly planning and managing the migration campaign." Ibid., 17–20.

77. Young, *Japan's Total Empire*, 330. Echoing Young's argument, my analysis of overpopulation attends to its discursive dimensions—that is, the social process in which the overpopulation theme emerged as a form of rational knowledge, instead of overpopulation as an established fact.

78. Jinkō mondai kenkyūkai, "Manshū imin ni kansuru kengi" [A proposal for the emigration to Manchuria], *Jinkō mondai* 1 no. 4 (1936): 25–26; translation is mine.

79. In the first and the second national meetings of the PPRS, held in November 1937 and October 1938, its members discussed the need for a national institute that would integrate population policies. *Jinkō mondai kenkyūkai 50-nen ryakushi*, 56–57; Jinkō mondai kenkyūkai, *Dai ni kai jinkō mondai zenkoku kyōgikai hokoku-sho* [A report from the second national meeting of National Institute of Population Problems] (Tokyo: Jinkō mondai kenkyūkai, 1939), 42–43.

80. This wartime discourse of homogenizing the population in the name of the Yamato race was led by Tachi Minoru and Koya Yoshio, both the leading members of the National Institute of Population Problems. For the transition in population policy during wartime and the roles of the National Institute of Population Problems, see Takaoka, *Sōryokusen taisei to fukushi kokka*, 169–197.

81. Yamanouchi Yasushi, "Total-War and System Integration: A Methodological Introduction," in *Total War and "Modernization,"* eds. Narita Ryūichi, Yamanouchi Yasushi, and J. Victor Koschmann (Ithaca: East Asia Program, Cornell University, 1998), 3–4.

Chapter 4

1. Drawing on the notion of total war, I emphasize the systematic mobilization and rationalization of an entire society to support war efforts. Yamanouchi Yasushi, "Total-War and System Integration: A Methodological Introduction," in *Total War and "Modernization,"* eds. Narita Ryūichi, Yamanouchi Yasushi, and J. Victor Koschmann (Ithaca: East Asia Program, Cornell University, 1998), 3–4.

2. Naikaku [Cabinet of Japan], Kokka sōdōin hō [National mobilization law], original script signed by the emperor, 1938 Law No. 55, 1, accessed July 20, 2021, https://www.digital.archives.go.jp/das/image/F0000000000000035654.

3. The national conservative movement during the Weimar period is often called "conservative revolution" or "new nationalism," which refers to a set of reactionary or conservative thoughts appearing in the aftermath of World War I to oppose democracy and liberalism while upholding military values and cultural nationalism. Ernst Jünger is one of the most significant new nationalists in the years of the Weimar Republic, who pursued ways in which "military values and structures" would be carried forward into "peacetime society." Despite the similarity between Jünger's conservative nationalism and the Nazis' national socialism, Jünger's relations to the Nazi Party remain ambiguous. Roger Woods, *The Conservative Revolution in the Weimar Republic* (Houndmills, Basingstoke, Hampshire: Macmillan, 1996), 7–28.

4. J. Victor Koschmann, "Introduction to Total War and 'Modernization,'" in *Total War and "Modernization,"* xi–xii.

5. For a critical approach to Japanese fascism and its modern (instead of antimodern) characteristics, see Yamanouchi, "Total-War and System Integration," 1–39; Harry D. Harootunian, *Overcome by Modernity: History, Culture, and Community in Interwar Japan* (Princeton: Princeton University Press, 2011); Alan Tansman, *The Aesthetics of Japanese Fascism* (Berkeley: University of California Press, 2009); Alan Tansman, ed., *The Culture of Japanese Fascism* (Durham: Duke University Press, 2009).

6. Achille Mbembe, *Necropolitics* (Durham: Duke University Press, 2019), 66.

7. Ibid.

8. The Marco Polo Bridge (Lugouqiao) Incident refers to a military clash between troops from the Imperial Japanese Army and the Republic of China's National Revolutionary Army. This incident, which transpired just south of Peking (Beijing), marks the beginning of the second Sino-Japanese war. Yang Tianshi, "Chiang Kai-shek and the Battles of Shanghai and Nanjing," in *The Battle for China: Essays on the Military History of the Sino-Japanese War of 1937–1945*, eds. Mark Peattie, Edward Drea, and Hans van de Ven (Redwood City: Stanford University Press, 2010), 143–145.

9. Richard Morris Titmuss, *Problems of Social Policy* (London: H. M. Stationery Office, 1950). Asa Briggs also considers World War II as one of the crucial, although not the sole, factors in the development of the welfare state. Briggs underlines that World War II contributed to the emergence of universal schemes with regard to welfare policies in wartime Britain that aimed to boost national unity and a sense of equality among its citizens. Asa Briggs, "The Welfare State in Historical Perspective," *European Journal of Sociology* 2, no. 2 (1961): 225–227.

10. Aly's account implies that German National Socialism was built on the support of its citizens who were the primary beneficiaries of Nazi's social policies and at least passive accessories to the systemic atrocities against Jews. Götz Aly, *Hitler's*

Beneficiaries: Plunder, Race War, and the Nazi Welfare State (New York: Metropolitan, 2007).

11. Gregory J. Kasza, "War and Welfare Policy in Japan," *Journal of Asian Studies* 61, no. 2 (2002): 417–435.

12. Kōsei-shō 20-nenshi henshū i'inkai [Editorial board for the twenty years of the Ministry of Health and Welfare], *Kosei-shō 20-nenshi* [The twenty years of the Ministry of Health and Welfare] (Tokyo: Kōsei mondai kenkyūkai, 1960), 94–96.

13. Kasza, "War and Welfare," 422–423; Takaoka Hiroyuki, *Sōryokusen taisei to fukushi kokka: senjiki Nihon no shakai kaikaku kōsō* [Total war system and the welfare state: Japan's wartime plan for social reform] (Tokyo: Iwanami shoten, 2011), 44–70.

14. Koizumi Chikahiko, *Gunjin eisei* [Military hygiene] (Tokyo: Kinbara shōten, 1927), 2.

15. Ibid.; Koizumi Chikahiko, "Hoken kokusaku no konpon mondai" [The fundamental problem of national health policies], *Nihon sangyo eisei kyōkai kaiho* 15, no. 11 (1938): 827–828.

16. "Eisei-shō setsuritsu mondai no keii" [The details of issues about the establishment of the Hygiene Ministry], *Gunidan zasshi* 279 (August 1936): 1151.

17. Koizumi, "Hoken kokusaku no konpon mondai," 827–828.

18. Kōsei-shō 20-nenshi henshū i'inkai, *Kōseishō 20-nenshi*, 94–95.

19. The February 26 Incident, a coup d'état attempted by young Imperial Japanese Army officers in 1936, eventually contributed to the cleansing of the rebel faction within the Japanese Army and the military takeover of the Japanese government. It should be noted, however, that the rise of militarism was by no means a smooth transition but was accompanied by a backlash from the civilian government. The growing tension over the control of the government between military and civilian leaders is exemplified by the so-called Hara-kiri mondō, a dispute between Army Minister Terauchi Hisaichi and Seiyūkai Diet member Hamada Kunimatsu over the Army's interference in politics and the potential growth of fascism in January 1937. This dispute immediately resulted in the resignation of Hirota Kōki's entire cabinet. On the February 26 Incident, see Ben-Ami Shillony, *Revolt in Japan: The Young Officers and the February 26, 1936 Incident* (Princeton: Princeton University Press, 1973).

20. Kōsei-shō 20-nenshi henshū i'inkai, *kōseishō 20-nenshi*, 96–97.

21. "Hoken shakai-shō (kashō) setchi yōkō" [A proposal to establish the (tentatively named) Ministry of Public Health and Social Affairs], in *Kokka sōdōinshi* [The history of state total mobilization] (Fujisawa-shi: Kokka sōdōinshi kankōkai, 1975), 697–698. Originally published July 9, 1937.

22. "Hoken shakai-shō (kashō) setchi no riyū" [The reasons for establishing the (tentatively named) Ministry of Public Health and Social Affairs], in *Kokka sōdōinshi*, 700. Originally published July 1937.

23. Ibid.; translation is mine.

24. Ibid.

25. Jinkō shokuryō mondai chōsakai, *Jinkō shokuryō mondai chōsakai jinkō-bu tōshin setsumei* [Annotations on the reports of the Department of Population by the Population and Food Problems Investigation Committee] (Tokyo: Jinkō shokuryō mondai chōsakai, 1930), 1–3.

26. "Hon kyōkai de Kiyoura (Kiyoura Keigo) kaichō na o motte tōkyoku ni shakai-shō shinsetsu nami jidō-kyoku tokkyo kata yōbō o gushin" [The CASW

submitted comments under the name of President Mr. Kiyoura to the government to demand the establishment of the Ministry of Social Affairs and the Children's Bureau], *Shakai jigyō ihō* (July 1937): 3.

27. Ibid., 5.

28. Kōsei-shō 20-nenshi henshū i'inkai, *Kōseishō 20-nenshi*, 104–106.

29. Ibid., 106. For the shifting terminology of welfare in Japan in the prewar years, see Toshimitsu Shinkawa and Yuki Tsuji, "Conceptual Development of Welfare and Social Policy in Japan," in *Analysing Social Policy Concepts and Language: Comparative and Transnational Perspectives*, ed. Daniel Béland (Bristol: Policy Press, 2014), 197–200.

30. "Chokurei dai 7 gō kōsei-shō kansei" [Imperial Ordinance no. 7: the enactment of Kōsei-Shō], National Archives of Japan Digital Archive, originally published January 10, 1938, accessed July 25, 2021, https://www.digital.archives.go.jp/DAS/meta/Detail_F0000000000000035693.

31. Naikaku, Kokumin kenkō hoken hō: hōritsu dai 60-gō [Law no. 60: national health insurance], National Archives of Japan Digital Archive, originally published March 31, 1938, accessed October 31, 2021, https://www.digital.archives.go.jp/DAS/meta/Detail_F0000000000000035659.

32. Kōsei-shō, *Isei hachijūnenshi* [The eighty-year history of the healthcare system] (Tokyo: Insatsukyoku chōyōkai, 1955), 831; Yoneyuki Sugita, "Japan's Epoch-Making Health-Insurance Reforms, 1937–1945," *Japan Forum* 25, no. 1 (March 2013): 124–130.

33. Chŏng Ilyŏng, "Ilche sikminchiki chosŏn kanisaengmyŏngpohŏm ŭl t'onghae pon 'kongkong' ŭi kimansŏng" [The deception of "publicness" through the simplified life insurance in the Japanese colonial period], *Yŏksahakyŏn'gu* 75 (2019): 179–214.

34. Tseng Yaofen, "Nippon tōchi jidai no Taiwanjin no seiho kanyū nikansuru kenkyū" [A study of why Taiwan people purchased life insurance under Japanese colonial rule: political incentive or economic incentive?], *Hokengaku Zasshi* 601 (2008): 187–206.

35. Briggs, "The Welfare State in Historical Perspective," 221.

36. In colonial Taiwan, the National Physical Fitness Law (Kokumin tairyoku hō) was promulgated in 1942 while the Campaign for Healthy People (Kenmin undō) began in the same year in colonial Korea. Fujino Yutaka explains that the implementation of public health policies in colonial Taiwan and Korea was deeply related to the enforcement of conscription in these colonial territories to resolve the shortage of wartime labor. Fujino, *Nihon fashizumu to yūsei shisō*, 358–365.

37. Takashi Fujitani, *Race for Empire: Koreans as Japanese and Japanese as Americans During World War II* (Berkeley: University of California Press, 2013), 25.

38. "Shasetsu: rōmu dōin to jinkō mondai" [Editorial: the forced labor mobilization and population problems], *Tokyo Asahi Shinbun* (July 5, 1939).

39. Ibid.

40. "Jinkō mondai kenkyūsho ni oite tadachini chōsa kenkyū ni chakusu beki shuyō chōsa kenkyū jikō" [Prioritized list of the research projects of the IPP], *SPP* 1, no. 1 (April 1940): 70–71; translation is mine.

41. Okazaki Ayanori, "Shussanryoku chōsa kekka no gaisetsu" [An outline of the fertility survey results], *SPP* 1, no. 7 (October 1940): 2.

42. Ibid., 1–3.

43. Ibid., 15.

44. Michel Foucault, "Governmentality," in *The Foucault Effect: Studies in Governmentality: With Two Lectures by and an Interview with Michel Foucault*, eds. Graham Burchell, Colin Gordon, and Peter Miller (Chicago: University of Chicago Press, 1991), 100.
45. Ibid., 99–100.
46. For Alfred Ploetz and his role in the development of Rassenhygiene, see Eric J. Engstrom, "Fashioning Racial Selves: Reflexive Practices in the Society for Racial Hygiene," *Culture, Medicine and Psychiatry* 35, no. 4 (2011): 546–562; Sheila Faith Weiss, "The Race Hygiene Movement in Germany," *Osiris* (Bruges) 3, no. 3 (1987): 193–236.
47. Stefan Kühl, *For the Betterment of the Race: The Rise and Fall of the International Movement for Eugenics and Racial Hygiene* (New York: Palgrave Macmillan, 2013), 123.
48. Yokoyama Takashi, *Nihon ga yūseishakai ni narumade: kagaku keimō, medhia, seishoku no seiji* [The history of eugenic society in Japan: scientific enlightenment, media, and politics of reproduction] (Tokyo: Keiso shobo, 2015), 153–183.
49. Minzoku eisei kenkyūkai, *Minzoku eisei shiryō* [Sources on race hygiene] (Tokyo: Shizu-sha, 1938), 1–2.
50. Hiroshima Kiyoshi, "Gendai nihon jinkō seisaku-shi shōron (2): kokumin yūsei hō ni okeru jinkō no shitsu seisaku to ryō seisaku" [An essay on the history of population policies in modern Japan (2): policies on the quality and quantity of population according to the National Eugenic Law], *SPP*, no. 160 (1981): 62.
51. Minzoku eisei kenkyūkai, *Minzoku eisei shiryō*, 4–5.
52. Ibid., 5–6; translation is mine.
53. Ibid., 4–5.
54. "Kokumin yūsei hō no kōfu" [The promulgation of the National Eugenic Law], *SPP* 1, no. 2 (May 1940): 71.
55. For the sterilization law in Nazi Germany and the American influence on its enforcement, see Stefan Kühl, *The Nazi Connection: Eugenics, American Racism, and German National Socialism* (New York: Oxford University Press, 2002). Also, on sterilization laws in twenty-seven states in America, see Mark A. Largent, *Breeding Contempt: The History of Coerced Sterilization in the United States* (New Brunswick: Rutgers University Press, 2007).
56. William R. LaFleur, Gernot Böhme, and Susumu Shimazono, eds., *Dark Medicine: Rationalizing Unethical Medical Research* (Bloomington: Indiana University Press, 2007), 225.
57. Arita Hachirō, "The International Situation and Japan's Position" (June 29, 1940), in *Sources of Japanese Tradition*, vol. 2, comp. Arthur E. Tiedemann (New York: Columbia University Press, 2008), 622.
58. Ibid.
59. "Kokudo keikaku settei yōkō" [Outline for the establishment of National Land Planning], *SPP* 1, no. 7 (October 1940): 112–114. For further analysis of wartime national land planning, see Aaron Stephen Moore, *Constructing East Asia: Technology, Ideology, and Empire in Japan's Wartime Era, 1931–1945* (Stanford: Stanford University Press, 2013), 135–148.
60. "Kokudo keikaku settei yōkō," 113.
61. Ibid., 114.
62. Ibid., 113. National Land Planning divided the "comprehensive population

distribution plan" into four parts including deployment in urban areas, functional distributions, regional distributions, and migration.

63. Jinkō mondai kenkyūkai, *Jinkō mondai shiryō dai 43 shū no 1: jinkō, minzoku, kokudo* [Documents on population problems 43 (1): population, ethnic nation, land] (Tokyo: Jinkō mondai kenkyūkai, 1942).

64. Ibid., 8–11.

65. Ibid., 8.

66. "Jinkō seisaku kakuritsu yōkō no kettei" [The endorsement of the Guidelines for Establishing Population Policy], *SPP* 2, no. 2 (February 1941): 55.

67. Ibid.; translation is mine.

68. "The state of emergency . . . [that has become] the rule" is originally drawn from Walter Benjamin's "Theses on the Philosophy of History." Adding to Benjamin's understanding of the state of exception, Agamben highlights that "[the state of exception] not only appears increasingly as a technique of government rather than an exceptional measure, but it also lets its own nature as the constitutive paradigm of the juridical order come to light." Walter Benjamin, "Theses on the Philosophy of History," in *Illuminations* (New York: Harcourt, Brace & World, 1968), 257; Giorgio Agamben, *State of Exception* (Chicago: University of Chicago Press, 2005), 7.

69. Ibid., 86.

70. "Kōsei-shō kansei chū kaisei to jinkō-kyoku no sōsetsu" [Revision of parts of the organization of MHW and the establishment of the Population Bureau], *SPP* 2, no. 8 (August 1941): 44–47.

71. Ifukube Toshiko, *Kekkon no zenshin* [The progress of marriage] (Tokyo: Shin taishū sha, 1943), 149.

72. Sumiko Otsubo, "Feminist Maternal Eugenics in Wartime Japan," *U.S.-Japan Women's Journal* 17 (1999): 43–51.

73. "Atarashii kekkon jyūsoku" [Ten new rules for marriage], *Chūgai shōgyō shinpō* (October 4, 1939), accessed October 11, 2022, https://hdl.handle.net/20.500.14094/0100239919.

74. "Kekkon sōdan ni okeru kenkō mondai ni kansuru shidō shishin," *SPP* 2, no. 9 (September 1941): 60–61.

75. Ibid., 52

76. "Kenmin undō jisshi yōkō" [The outlines for the campaign for healthy people], *SPP* 3, no. 4 (April 1942): 52.

77. Ibid., 51.

78. Paul H. Kratoska, *Asian Labor in the Wartime Japanese Empire: Unknown Histories* (Armonk: Sharpe, 2005), 11.

79. "Kōsei-shō bunka kitei no kaisei" [Revision of the codes of the MHW subdivision], *SPP* 4, nos. 10–12 (October–December 1943): 60–62.

Chapter 5

1. Carol Gluck, *Japan's Modern Myths: Ideology in the Late Meiji Period* (Princeton: Princeton University Press, 1985), 187–189.

2. Yoshiko Miyake, "Doubling Expectations: Motherhood and Women's Factory Work Under State Management in Japan in the 1930s and 1940s," In *Recreating Japanese Women, 1600–1945*, ed. Gail Lee Bernstein (Berkeley: University of California Press, 1991), 269.

3. As noted in Chapter 2, for instance, Ishimoto was arrested in 1937 for her engagement with radical political activities and birth control campaign, and she was eventually banned from participating in any public activities throughout the wartime years. Sabine Frühstück, *Colonizing Sex: Sexology and Social Control in Modern Japan* (Berkeley: University of California Press, 2003), 163.

4. As for the interactions between feminists and the state in wartime Japan (including the co-optation of feminism by the state) to seek for the eugenic protection of mothers, see Miyake, "Doubling Expectations," 267–295; Sumiko Otsubo, "Feminist Maternal Eugenics in Wartime Japan," *U.S.–Japan Women's Journal* 17 (1999): 39–76; Sumiko Otsubo, "Engendering Eugenics: Feminists and Marriage Restriction Legislation in the 1920s," in *Gendering Modern Japanese History*, eds. Barbara Molony and Kathleen Uno (Cambridge, MA: Harvard University Asia Center, 2005), 225–256; Chizuko Ueno, *Nationalism and Gender* (Melbourne: Trans Pacific Press, 2004), 43–51.

5. Ueno, *Nationalism and Gender*, 49.

6. "Bosei hogo hō seitei sokushin fujin renmei kiyaku" [The rules of the League for the Promotion of the Legal Protection of Motherhood], in *Nihon fujin mondai shiryō shūsei* [Collected documents on Japanese women's issues] vol. 2, ed. Ichikawa Fusae (Tokyo: Domesu shuppan, 1977), 477–478; Vera C. Mackie, *Feminism in Modern Japan: Citizenship, Embodiment, and Sexuality* (Cambridge, UK: Cambridge University Press, 2003), 104–105.

7. "Bosei hogo hō seitei sokushin fujin renmei dai ikkai zenkoku i'inkai" [The first national committee of the League for the Promotion of the Legal Protection of Motherhood], in *Nihon fujin mondai shiryō shūsei*, vol. 2, 486–487; Sheldon M. Garon, *Molding Japanese Minds: The State in Everyday Life* (Princeton: Princeton University Press, 1997), 142.

8. "Bosei hogo hō" [The mother-child protection law], in *Nihon fujin mondai shiryō shūsei*, vol. 2, 488–489.

9. Ibid., 492.

10. I adopted "fertile womb battalion" as the English translation of *kodakara butai* from Jennifer Robertson's "Blood Talks: Eugenic Modernity and the Creation of New Japanese," *History and Anthropology* 13, no. 3 (2002): 199. Robertson illuminates eugenic rationalities underlying the wartime state's pronatalist policy that glorified women's fertility and healthy bodies of children. Echoing her analysis of the importance of corporeality in eugenic discourse, I borrow Robertson's translation to highlight instrumentalized women's corporeality for the sake of population growth.

11. "Kōsei-shō no yūryō tashi katei hyōshō nami futai chōsa" [The MHW's commendation for families with many healthy children and additional investigation], *SPP* 1, no. 3 (June 1940): 73–74.

12. As to the similarity between Germany's *Mutterkreuz* and Japan's National Commendation for Families with Many Healthy Children, see Frühstück, *Colonizing Sex*, 167; for the implementation of *Mutterkreuz* in 1938 to honor German mothers who conceived and raised at least four children, see Anson Rabinbach and Sander L. Gilman, *The Third Reich Sourcebook* (Berkeley: University of California Press, 2019), 307.

13. "Kosei-shō shakaikyoku no yūryō tashi katei hyōshō ni kansuru futai chōsa no happyō" [The investigation results regarding the Social Affairs Bureau (MHW)'s

commendation for families with multiple superior children], *SPP* 1, no. 9 (December 1940): 66–69.

14. Akagawa Manabu collected the titles of news articles on the national commendation for the "fertile womb battalion" covered in two local newspapers. The collected news titles give us a glimpse into the conventional usage of the notion of a fertile womb battalion to refer to families with many children in local newspapers during the wartime. Akagawa Manabu, "Shinbun ni arawareta 'umeyo fuyaseyo': Shinano Mainichi Shinbun to Tokyo Asahi Shinbun niokeru jinkō seisaku" [Umeyo, Fuyaseyo in newspaper: pronatalist policy during World War II reported by Sinano Mainichi Shinbun and Tokyo Asahi Shinbun], *Jinbun kagaku ronshū* 38 (2004): 133–148.

15. Tsuchiya Hidemaro, "Onna bakaride jyūichinin kyōdai, nakayoshi kodakarabbutai hōmon" [Eleven siblings, all female: a visit to a fertile womb battalion with strong bonds], *Fujokai* 62, no. 6 (1940): 226; Tanaka Mitsuko, "Nihon ichi no kodakara butai, jyūroku no shiroto-ke, Nagasaki" [The best fertile womb battalion in Japan, the Shiroto family with sixteen children from Nagasaki], *Gahō yakushin no nihon* 5, no. 12 (1940).

16. The Patriotic Association for Japanese Literature was founded in 1942, and more than 3,000 Japanese writers and intellectuals including the president Tokutomi Sohō were members of the association. On the Patriotic Association for Japanese Literature, see Ben-Ami Shillony, *Politics and Culture in Wartime Japan* (Oxford: Clarendon Press, 1981), 116–117.

17. Tatsuno Kyūshi, "Nihon ichi kodakara butaichō" [The commander of Japan's best fertile womb battalion], in *Nihon no haha*, ed. Nihon bungaku hōkokukai [Patriotic Association for Japanese Literature] (Tokyo: Shunyōdō Shoten, 1943), 42.

18. Ruth A. Miller, *The Limits of Bodily Integrity: Abortion, Adultery, and Rape Legislation in Comparative Perspective* (Aldershot: Ashgate, 2007), 12.

19. Examples of the media coverage on various fertile womb battalions are as follows: Tsuchiya,"Onna bakaride jyūichinin kyōdai, nakayoshi kodakarabbutai hōmon," 220–227; Aikawa Yuri, "Kōa no kodakara jyūsannin, Furusawabutai wo tou" [Asia's precious thirteen children: a visit to Furukawa's battalion], *Fujokai* 62, no. 6 (1940): 228–233; "Kodakara ikka no sōryoku atsumete" [Pull everyone together from the fertile womb battalion], *Shashin shūhō*, no. 298 (November 1943): 16–17.

20. "Kenmin undō jisshi yōkō" [The outlines for the campaign for healthy people], *SPP* 3, no. 4 (April 1942): 60; translation is mine.

21. "Ninsanpu techō kitei no seitei" [The establishment of the Handbook for the Expectant Mother's ordinance], *SPP* 3, no. 8 (August 1942): 32–34.

22. Ibid.

23. Ogino Miho points out the surveillance function of the handbook by arguing that the policy was designed to identify all pregnant women. Ogino Miho, "From Natalism to Family Planning: Population Policy in Wartime and the Post-War Period," in *Gender, Nation and State in Modern Japan*, eds. Andrea Germer, Vera C. Mackie, and Ulrike Wohr; trans. Leonie Stickland (London: Routledge, 2014), 201–202.

24. "Ninsanpu techō kitei no seitei," 33.

25. According to the MHW's investigation, as of 1939, the number of villages

without medical doctors was 2,676 across the nation, and its number showed an upward trend. To resolve the shortage issue and improve the nationwide healthcare assistance, the MHW founded a state-sponsored group called Nihon iryōdan (Japan Medical Organization) in 1942. "Kōsei-shō eiseikyoku no zenkoku muison chōsa" [A national investigation of villages without medical doctors by the Hygiene Bureau, the Ministry of Health and Welfare], *SPP* 1, no. 2 (May 1940): 74–75; "Nihon iryōdan setsuritsu i'inkai no seiritsu" [The establishment of the committee members for the Japan Medical Organization], *SPP* 3, no. 5 (May 1942): 42–43.

26. "Ninsanpu techō kitei no seitei," 33.

27. "Nihon bosei hogokai no setsuritsu" [The foundation of the Society for the Protection of Mothers], *SPP* 3, no. 5 (May 1942): 43–44.

28. On the Sanikukai and its affiliated maternity hospital, see Sally A. Hastings, *Neighborhood and Nation in Tōkyō, 1905–1937* (Pittsburgh: University of Pittsburgh Press, 1995), 54–55.

29. "Nihon bosei hogokai no setsuritsu," 44.

30. "Ninpu-kun" [The maxim for expecting mothers], in *Bosei no hogo* [The protection of mothers], ed. Taisei yokusankai [Imperial Rule Assistance Association] (Tokyo: Kokumin tosho kankōkai, 1944), 42–43; translation is mine.

31. For the roles of the Greater Japan Women's Association in promoting the idea of patriotic mothers on the home front, see Ryoko Okamura, "Making Patriotic Mothers: Images of Motherhood and the Role of Government-Sponsored Women's Organizations in Japan's Home Front," *U.S.-Japan Women's Journal* 55–56 (2019): 55–79; Sandra Wilson, "Family or State?: Nation, War, and Gender in Japan, 1937–45," *Critical Asian Studies* 38, no. 2 (2006): 209–238.

32. Dai Nihon Fujinkai [Greater Japan Women's Association], *Dai nihon fujinkai gaikyō* [A general outlook of the Greater Japan Women's Association] (1943), 1–3, 20, accessed October 28, 2022, https://www.ndl.go.jp/modern/img_r/087/087-001r.html.

33. Wilson, "Family or State?," 215.

34. "Dai nihon fujinkai kōryō gaisetsu" [Annotated code of the Greater Japan Women's Association], *Nihon Fujin* 1, no. 3 (1943): 80.

35. Dai Nihon Fujinkai, *Dai nihon fujinkai gaikyō*, 4.

36. In principle, each supervisor appointed by Nippu for overseeing maternal and children health held a dual title *kenmin shunin* (public health supervisor) and *bosei hodō i'in* (maternal assistance committee). Dai Nihon Fujinkai Nagoya-shi shibu [Nagoya city branch of the Greater Japan Women's Association], *Kenmin shunin (bosei hodō i'in) no katsudō ni tsuite* [On activities of public health supervisors] (Nagoya: Jidō shinbunsha, 1944), 1.

37. Ibid., 1–6.

38. Fujitani, *Race for Empire*, 44–45. In colonial Taiwan, the volunteer army system was introduced in 1942 while the conscription system was implemented in 1945. On the politicization of medicine and the changing discourse of health and reproduction in the wake of the war in colonial Taiwan, see Ming-cheng Miriam Lo, *Doctors Within Borders Profession, Ethnicity, and Modernity in Colonial Taiwan* (Berkeley: University of California Press, 2002), 109–117.

39. Ishida Sentarō, "Kōsei kyoku no tanjō ni saishite" [On the occasion of the birth of the Bureau of Health and Welfare], *Chōsen*, no. 320 (1942): 22–24, quoted in An T'ae-yun, *Singmin chŏngch'i-wa mosŏng* [Colonial politics and motherhood] (P'aju: Han'guk haksul chŏngbo, 2006), 127.

40. An, *Singmin chŏngch'i-wa mosŏng*, 126–137; Sonja M. Kim, *Imperatives of Care: Women and Medicine in Colonial Korea* (Honolulu: University of Hawaii Press, 2019), 135–136.

41. Eunjung Kim, *Curative Violence: Rehabilitating Disability, Gender, and Sexuality in Modern Korea* (Durham: Duke University Press, 2016), 59.

42. An, *Singmin chŏngch'i-wa mosŏng*, 162.

43. Giorgio Agamben, *Means Without End: Notes on Politics* (Minneapolis: University of Minnesota Press, 2000), preface.

44. On the theoretical and methodological reflections of intersectionality, see Devon W. Carbado et al., "Intersectionality: Mapping the Movements of a Theory," *Du Bois Review* 10, no. 2 (2013): 303–312; Sumi Cho, Kimberlé Williams Crenshaw, and Leslie McCall, "Toward a Field of Intersectionality Studies: Theory, Applications, and Praxis: Intersectionality: Theorizing Power, Empowering Theory," *Signs: Journal of Women in Culture and Society* 38, no. 4 (2013): 785–810; Patricia Hill Collins, *Intersectionality as Critical Social Theory* (Durham: Duke University Press, 2019); Kimberlé Williams Crenshaw, "Mapping the Margins: Intersectionality, Identity Politics, and Violence Against Women of Color," *Stanford Law Review* 43, no. 6 (1991): 1241–1299.

45. Kimberlé Williams Crenshaw, "Demarginalizing the Intersection of Race and Sex: A Black Feminist Critique of Antidiscrimination Doctrine, Feminist Theory and Antiracist Politics," *University of Chicago Legal Forum* 1989, no. 1 (1989): 139–167.

46. Crenshaw, "Mapping the Margins," 1242.

47. According to Yoshiaki Yoshimi, the first comfort station was constructed in Shanghai in March 1932 by the Imperial Japanese Navy. The operation of comfort stations in China was followed by Japan's military expansion into North China since 1932. This earlier history of comfort stations provides a convincing rationale for scholars to estimate the number of comfort women up to 400,000 as Peipei Qiu et al. point out. While I agree with the need to expand the timeline of the history of Japan's military sexual slavery to grasp the evolution of colonial sexual violence institutionalized throughout the Asia-Pacific War (1931–1945), this chapter strategically focuses on the period between 1937 and 1945 to clarify what the military sexual slavery system represents as to the instrumentalization of the female body and sexuality under the biopolitical regime. As for the history of the mobilization of comfort women during the Pacific War, see Peipei Qiu, Zhiliang Su, and Lifei Chen, *Chinese Comfort Women: Testimonies from Imperial Japan's Sex Slaves* (Oxford: Oxford University Press, 2014); Chunghee Sarah Soh, *The Comfort Women: Sexual Violence and Postcolonial Memory in Korea and Japan* (Chicago: University of Chicago Press, 2008); Yoshiaki Yoshimi, *Comfort Women: Sexual Slavery in the Japanese Military During World War II* (New York: Columbia University Press, 2000).

48. The nature of comfort stations has been variously categorized by scholars. For example, Yoshiaki Yoshimi distinguishes comfort stations according to who operated them, namely military-run, civilian-run, and military-designated facilities. Meanwhile, Chunghee Sarah Soh breaks down the types of comfort stations into three categories, that is, concessionary, paramilitary, and criminal to clarify different levels of commercial orientation and that of military control over the comfort stations. Yoshimi, *Comfort Women*, 88–90; Soh, *The Comfort Women*, 117–118.

49. Yoshimi, *Comfort Women*, 94–96.
50. Qiu et al., *Chinese Comfort Women*, 38.
51. There are some official documents that verify the institutional regulation and management of Japanese prostitutes who sailed to China to serve as comfort women. The authorities that were in charge of enforcing pertinent regulations included the Ministry of Home Affairs, the Ministry of Army, local governments, and local police. The documents that confirm the state's institutional effort to mobilize and deploy Japanese prostitutes include "Shanghai hakengun nairikugun ianjo ni okeru shakufu boshū ni kansuru ken" [On the recruitment of barmaids for comfort stations for the military in the Expeditionary Army in Shanghai] (January 19, 1938); "Shina tokō fujyo no toriatsukai ni kansuru ken" [On the treatment of women traveling to China] (February 18, 1938); both materials are collected in ref. A05032040800, National Archives of Japan Digital Archive, Japan Center for Asian Historical Records (hereinafter *JACAR*), Tokyo, accessed October 17, 2022, https://www.digital.archives.go.jp/das/image/M0000000000001675555.
52. For the history of sex work preceding the wartime mobilization of Japanese comfort women, see Caroline Norma, *The Japanese Comfort Women and Sexual Slavery During the China and Pacific Wars* (London: Bloomsbury Academic, 2016), 66–78.
53. Yoshimi, *Comfort Women*, 65–68; Qiu et al., *Chinese Comfort Women*, 21–34.
54. For the role of the Ministry of Army, see Yoshimi, *Comfort Women*, 58–61. Also, the following document gives an indication of the relationship between the Ministry of Army and Expeditionary Forces in China in implementing the military sexual slavery system. Rikugun-shō [Ministry of Army], "Gun ianjo jyūgyōfu nado boshū ni kansuru ken" [On the recruitment of female workers for military comfort stations] (March 4, 1938), *JACAR*, ref. C04120263400, accessed January 16, 2022, https://www.jacar.archives.go.jp/das/image-j/C04120263400.
55. The documents that verify the military authorities' enforcement of the use of condoms in comfort stations are as follows: Rikugun-shō, "Fukukan kaidō jisshi no ken tsūchō" [Notifications on the meeting of adjutants] (September 1942), *JACAR*, ref. C04123834600, accessed January 16, 2022, https://www.jacar.archives.go.jp/das/image-j/C04123834600; Gunsei kanbu Bizaya shibu Iroiro shutchōjō [Iloilo Office, Visaya Branch, Military Administration Department], "Ianjo kitei sōhu no ken" [On the sending of the comfort station regulations] (November 22, 1942), in *Seifu chōsa: "jūgun ianfu" kankei shiryō shūsei* [Collection of materials relating to the wartime comfort women issue: government of Japan survey], vol. 3 (Tokyo: Ryūkei shosha, 1997), 187–193; Mandarei chūtonchi shireibu [Mandalay garrison headquarters], "Chūtonchi ianjo kitei" [Regulations of garrison comfort stations] (May 26, 1943), in *Seifu chōsa: "jūgun ianfu,"* vol. 4 (1997), 281–293.
56. The Women's International Tribunal on Japanese Military Sexual Slavery of 2000 was organized by non-governmental women's organizations across Asia to correct the failure of the Tokyo War Crimes Trial (1946–1948) to hold military leaders accountable for the Japanese military sexual slavery system and to revisit the sexual slavery system from the perspectives of human rights and shared experiences of military sexual crimes transnationally. For the implications of the Women's Tribunal, see Christine M. Chinkin, "Women's International Tribunal on Japanese Military Sexual Slavery," *American Journal of International Law* 95, no. 2 (2001): 335–341.

57. "Transcript of Oral Judgment delivered on 4 December 200l by the Judges of the Women's International War Crimes Tribunal on Japan's Military Sexual Slavery" (December 4, 2001), accessed January 16, 2022, http://www.iccwomen.org/wigjdraft1/Archives/oldWCGJ/tokyo/summary.html.

58. Ibid.

59. Ibid.

60. The Japanese military forces' documents that verify the enforcement of medical examination of comfort women included Takamori butai [Takamori unit], "Takamori butai tokushu ian gyōmu kitei" [Rules on special comfort services in Takamori unit] (October 11–21, 1940), *JACAR*, ref. C13070262500, accessed January 17, 2022, https://www.jacar.archives.go.jp/das/meta/C13070262500; Dai jyūgō shidan gun'ibu [Medical department, 15th division], "Eisei gyōmu yōhō" [Bulletin on hygiene management] (January/February 1943), in *Seifu chōsa: "jūgun ianfu,"* vol. 3, 213–225; Allied Translator and Interpreter Section, "Research Report no. 120" (November 15, 1945), ref. AUS043_57_00C0411, Record Group 554, Archives of Korean History, National Archives and Records Administration, Gyeonggi-do, South Korea, accessed January 17, 2022, http://archive.history.go.kr/id/AUS043_57_00C0411.

61. Allied Translator and Interpreter Section, "Research Report no. 120," 9–17.

62. Ibid., 10.

63. Ibid.

64. Ibid., 10–11.

Epilogue

1. For extensive research on the final stage of the Asia-Pacific War and Japan's defeat, see Marc Gallicchio, *Unconditional: The Japanese Surrender in World War II* (New York: Oxford University Press, 2020).

2. Minoru Tachi, *Population Trend and Economic Growth in Japan*, National Institute of Population and Society Security Research, reprint of the paper presented to the Round Table on Economic Development with Special Reference to East Asia of International Economic Association (April 1960), 9, accessed February 21, 2022, https://www.ipss.go.jp/history/EnglishPamphletSeries/pdf/J000008733.pdf.

3. Ibid., 11.

4. Tatsuo Honda, "Population Problems in Postwar Japan: Now Facing Their Transitional Difficulties," vol. 1, National Institute of Population and Social Security Research (January 1957), 19, accessed February 21, 2022, https://www.ipss.go.jp/history/EnglishPamphletSeries/pdf/J000008723.pdf.

5. Institute of Population Problems (IPP), *Annual Reports of the Institute of Population Problems* (Tokyo: Ministry of Health and Welfare, 1960), 1–5.

6. On the impact of American population science and policies on the family planning program in postwar Japan, see Aya Homei, "The Science of Population and Birth Control in Post-War Japan," in *Science, Technology, and Medicine in the Modern Japanese Empire*, eds. Philip C. Brown and David G. Wittner (London: Routledge, 2016), 227–243.

7. Japan International Cooperation Agency (JICA), "Nihon no jinkō keiken" [Demographic experiences in Japan] (2003), accessed October 18, 2022, https://www.jica.go.jp/jica-ri/IFIC_and_JBICI-Studies/jica-ri/publication/archives/jica/field/pdf/2003_08e.pdf.

8. Sugita Naho, *Jinkō, kazoku, seimei to shakai seisaku* [Population, family, life and social policy] (Kyoto-shi: Hōritsu bunkasha, 2010), 216–219.

9. Aiko Takeuchi-Demirci, *Contraceptive Diplomacy: Reproductive Politics and Imperial Ambitions in the United States and Japan* (Stanford: Stanford University Press, 2018), 183–188.

10. Tiana Norgren, *Abortion Before Birth Control: The Politics of Reproduction in Postwar Japan* (Princeton: Princeton University Press, 2001), 66.

11. Fujino Yutaka, *Sengo minshushugi ga unda yūsei shiso—yūsei hogo hō no shiteki kenshō* [Eugenics ideas born out of postwar democracy: a historical investigation of the Eugenic National Law] (Tokyo: Rikka shuppan, 2021), 38–44.

12. Institute of Population Problems (IPP), *Eugenic Protection Law in Japan* (Tokyo: Ministry of Health and Welfare, 1960), 3–5.

13. Ibid., 11.

14. Mainichi shinbun shuzaihan [Mainichi news team], *Kyōsei funin—kyū-yūsei hogo hō wo tou* [Forced sterilization: an inquiry into the former Eugenic Protection Law] (Tokyo: Mainichi shinbun shuppan, 2019), 10.

BIBLIOGRAPHY

Works are organized into sections: collections, works in English, works in Japanese, and works in Korean. They are alphabetized by the style of their language, and Asian author names are ordered by the standard order of Asian names (surname first followed by given name).

Collected Works
Jinkō mondai kenkyū. Collected in Kokuritsu shakai hoshō jinkō mondai kenkyūsho. April 1940–. Abbreviated *SPP.* https://www.ipss.go.jp/syoushika/bunken/sakuin/jinko/jsakuin1.htm.
Ogino Miho, Matsubara Yōko, and Hikaru Saitō, eds. *Sei to seishoku no jinken mondai shiryō shūsei.* 35 vols. Tokyo: Fuji shuppan, 2000–2003. Abbreviated *SSJ.*
Sanji chōsetsu hyōron / Sei to shakai. Kyoto: Sanji chōsetsu hyōronsha, February 1925–May 1926. Reprinted. Tokyo: Fuji shuppan, 1983.
Sasaki Toshiji, and Akinori Odagiri, eds. *Yamamoto Senji zenshū.* 7 vols. Tokyo: Chōbunsha, 1979.
Suzuki Yūko. *Yamakawa Kikue shū.* 7 vols. Tokyo: Iwanami shoten, 2011.

Digital Archives
American Birth Control League. *The Birth Control Review.* Hathi Trust Digital Library, n.d. https://catalog.hathitrust.org/Record/000675880.
Archives of Korean History, National Archives and Records Administration, Gyeonggi-do, South Korea. http://archive.history.go.kr.
National Archives of Japan Digital Archive, Japan Center for Asian Historical Records. Tokyo. Abbreviated *JACAR.* https://www.jacar.go.jp/english/.
Project Gutenberg. https://www.gutenberg.org.

Sources by Language
ENGLISH
Agamben, Giorgio. *Means Without End: Notes on Politics.* Minneapolis: University of Minnesota Press, 2000.
———. *State of Exception.* Chicago: University of Chicago Press, 2005.
Allied Translator and Interpreter Section. "Research Report No. 120" (November 15, 1945). Archives of Korean History, National Archives and Records Adminis-

tration. Accessed January 17, 2022. http://archive.history.go.kr/id/AUS043_57_00C0411.
Aly, Götz. *Hitler's Beneficiaries: Plunder, Race War, and the Nazi Welfare State*. New York: Metropolitan, 2007.
Arita, Hachirō. "The International Situation and Japan's Position" (June 29, 1940). In *Sources of Japanese Tradition*, edited by Arthur E. Tiedemann. New York: Columbia University Press, 2008.
August, Bebel. *Women and Socialism*. New York: Socialist Literature Co., 1879.
Avenell, Simon Andrew. *Making Japanese Citizens: Civil Society and the Mythology of the Shimin in Postwar Japan*. Berkeley: University of California Press, 2010.
Azuma, Mitsutoshi. "Labor Legislation in Japan." *Annals of the Hitotsubashi Academy* 1, no. 2 (1951): 181–195.
Barclay, Paul D. *Outcasts of Empire: Japan's Rule on Taiwan's "Savage Border," 1874–1945*. Oakland: University of California Press, 2018.
Bardsley, Jan. "The New Woman of Japan and the Intimate Bonds of Translation." *Review of Japanese Culture and Society* 20 (2008): 206–225.
Bashford, Alison. *Global Population: History, Geopolitics, and Life on Earth*. New York: Columbia University Press, 2014.
Bebel, August. *Woman and Socialism*. Translated by Meta Stern Lilienthal. New York: Socialist Literature Co., 1910.
Benjamin, Walter. *Illuminations*. New York: Harcourt, Brace & World, 1968.
Bernstein, Gail Lee. "Kawakami Hajime: A Japanese Marxist in Search of the Way." In *Japan in Crisis: Essays on Taisho Democracy*, edited by Harry D. Harootunian, Bernard S. Silberman, and Gail Lee Bernstein, 86–109. Princeton: Princeton University Press, 1974.
Briggs, Asa. "The Welfare State in Historical Perspective." *European Journal of Sociology* 2, no. 2 (1961): 221–258.
Burkman, Thomas W. *Japan and the League of Nations: Empire and World Order, 1914–1938*. Honolulu: University of Hawaii Press, 2008.
———. "Nitobe Inazō: From World Order to Regional Order." In *Culture and Identity: Japanese Intellectuals During the Interwar Years*, edited by J. Thomas Rimer, 191–216. Princeton: Princeton University Press, 2014.
Carbado, Devon W., Kimberlé Williams Crenshaw, Vickie M. Mays, and Barbara Tomlinson. "Intersectionality: Mapping the Movements of a Theory." *Du Bois Review* 10, no. 2 (2013): 303–312.
Chinkin, Christine M. "Women's International Tribunal on Japanese Military Sexual Slavery." *American Journal of International Law* 95, no. 2 (2001): 335–341.
Cho, Sumi, Kimberlé Williams Crenshaw, and Leslie McCall. "Toward a Field of Intersectionality Studies: Theory, Applications, and Praxis: Intersectionality: Theorizing Power, Empowering Theory." *Signs: Journal of Women in Culture and Society* 38, no. 4 (2013): 785–810.
Chodorow, Nancy. *The Reproduction of Mothering: Psychoanalysis and the Sociology of Gender*. Berkeley: University of California Press, 1978.
Chung, Yuehtsen Juliette. *Struggle for National Survival: Eugenics in Sino-Japanese Contexts, 1896–1945*. New York: Routledge, 2002.
Coates, Patricia Walsh. *Margaret Sanger and the Origin of the Birth Control Movement, 1910–1930: The Concept of Women's Sexual Autonomy*. Lewiston: Edwin Mellen Press, 2008.

Connelly, Matthew. *Fatal Misconception: The Struggle to Control World Population*. Cambridge, MA: Belknap Press, 2008.

———. "Seeing Beyond the State: The Population Control Movement and the Problem of Sovereignty." *Past & Present* 193 (2006): 197–233.

Crenshaw, Kimberlé Williams. "Demarginalizing the Intersection of Race and Sex: A Black Feminist Critique of Antidiscrimination Doctrine, Feminist Theory and Antiracist Politics." *University of Chicago Legal Forum* 1989, no. 1 (1989): 139–167.

———. "Mapping the Margins: Intersectionality, Identity Politics, and Violence Against Women of Color." *Stanford Law Review* 43, no. 6 (1991): 1241–1299.

Curtis, Bruce. *The Politics of Population: State Formation, Statistics, and the Census of Canada, 1840–1875*. Toronto: University of Toronto Press, 2001.

D'Arcy, F. "The Malthusian League and the Resistance to Birth Control Propaganda in Late Victorian Britain." *Population Studies* 31, no. 3 (1977): 429–448.

Dean, Mitchell. *The Signature of Power Sovereignty, Governmentality and Biopolitics*. Los Angeles: Sage, 2013.

Deleuze, Gilles, and Félix Guattari. *A Thousand Plateaus: Capitalism and Schizophrenia*. Minneapolis: University of Minnesota Press, 1987.

Doak, Kevin M. "Building National Identity Through Ethnicity: Ethnology in Wartime Japan and After." *Journal of Japanese Studies* 27, no. 1 (2001): 1–39.

Driscoll, Mark. *Absolute Erotic, Absolute Grotesque: The Living, Dead, and Undead in Japan's Imperialism, 1895–1945*. Durham: Duke University Press, 2010.

Dudden, Alexis. "Japanese Colonial Control in International Terms." *Japanese Studies* 25, no. 1 (2005): 1–20.

———. "Matthew Perry in Japan, 1852–1854." In *East Asia in the World: Twelve Events That Shaped the Modern International Order*, edited by Stephan Haggard and David C. Kang, 188–205. Cambridge, UK: Cambridge University Press, 2020.

Ellis, Havelock. *Sex in Relation to Society*, vol. 6 of *Studies in the Psychology of Sex*. Philadelphia: F. A. Davis Co., 1927. Reprinted in Project Gutenberg (2004). https://www.gutenberg.org/files/13615/13615-h/13615-h.htm.

Endoh, Toake. *Exporting Japan: Politics of Emigration Toward Latin America*. Urbana: University of Illinois Press, 2009.

Engstrom, Eric J. "Fashioning Racial Selves: Reflexive Practices in the Society for Racial Hygiene." *Medicine and Psychiatry* 35, no. 4 (2011): 546–562.

Faison, Elyssa. *Managing Women: Disciplining Labor in Modern Japan*. Berkeley: University of California Press, 2007.

———. "Women's Rights as Proletarian Rights: Yamakawa Kikue, Suffrage, and the 'Dawn of Liberation.'" In *Rethinking Japanese Feminisms*, edited by James Welker, Ayako Kano, and Julia C. Bullock, 15–33. Honolulu: University of Hawaii Press, 2018.

Foucault, Michel. *The Birth of Biopolitics: Lectures at the Collège de France, 1978–1979*. New York: Palgrave Macmillan, 2011.

———. *Discourse and Truth: The Problematization of Parrhesia* (six lectures given by Michel Foucault at the University of California, Berkeley, October–November 1983). Edited by Joseph Pearson. http://foucault.info/documents/parrhesia/index.html.

———. "Governmentality." In *The Foucault Effect: Studies in Governmentality: With Two Lectures by and an Interview with Michel Foucault*, edited by Graham

Burchell, Colin Gordon, and Peter Miller, 87–104. Chicago: University of Chicago Press, 1991.
———. *Security, Territory, Population: Lectures at the Collège de France: 1977–1978.* Basingstoke: Palgrave Macmillan, 2009.
———. *Society Must Be Defended: Lectures at the Collège de France, 1975–1976.* New York: Picador, 2003.
———. "Technologies of the Self." In *Technologies of the Self: A Seminar with Michel Foucault,* edited by Luther H. Martin, Huck Gutman, and Patrick H. Hutton. Amherst: University of Massachusetts Press, 1988.
Francks, Penelope. *Rural Economic Development in Japan: From the Nineteenth Century to the Pacific War.* London: Routledge, 2006.
Frederick, Sarah. *Turning Pages: Reading and Writing Women's Magazines in Interwar Japan.* Honolulu: University of Hawaii Press, 2006.
Frühstück, Sabine. *Colonizing Sex: Sexology and Social Control in Modern Japan.* Berkeley: University of California Press, 2003.
Fujitani, Takashi. *Race for Empire: Koreans as Japanese and Japanese as Americans During World War II.* Berkeley: University of California Press, 2013.
Gallicchio, Marc. *Unconditional: The Japanese Surrender in World War II.* New York: Oxford University Press, 2020.
Galton, Francis. "Eugenics: Its Definition, Scope, and Aims." *American Journal of Sociology* 10, no. 1 (1904): 45–51.
———. *Inquiries into Human Faculty and Its Development.* London: Macmillan, 1883.
Garon, Sheldon M. *Molding Japanese Minds: The State in Everyday Life.* Princeton: Princeton University Press, 1997.
———. *The State and Labor in Modern Japan.* Berkeley: University of California Press, 1987.
———. "Women's Groups and the Japanese State: Contending Approaches to Political Integration, 1890–1945." *Journal of Japanese Studies* 19, no. 1 (1993): 5–41.
Gavin, Masako. "Poverty and Its Possible Cures: Abe Isoo and Kawakami Hajime." *East Asia* 24, no. 1 (2007): 23–43.
Gluck, Carol. "The 'End' of the Postwar: Japan at the Turn of the Millennium." *Public Culture* 10, no. 1 (1997): 1–23.
———. *Japan's Modern Myths: Ideology in the Late Meiji Period.* Princeton: Princeton University Press, 1985.
Gordon, Andrew. *Labor and Imperial Democracy in Prewar Japan.* Berkeley: University of California Press, 1991.
———. *A Modern History of Japan: From Tokugawa Times to the Present.* New York: Oxford University Press, 2009.
Gordon, Linda. "Voluntary Motherhood: The Beginnings of Feminist Birth Control Ideas in the United States." *Feminist Studies* 1, no. 3/4 (1973): 5–22.
Gosney, Ezra Seymour, and Paul B. Popenoe. *Sterilization for Human Betterment: A Summary of Results of 6,000 Operations in California, 1909–1929.* New York: Macmillan, 1929.
Greenhalgh, Susan. *Just One Child: Science and Policy in Deng's China.* Berkeley: University of California Press, 2008.
———. "The Social Construction of Population Science: An Intellectual, Institutional, and Political History of Twentieth-Century Demography." *Comparative Studies in Society and History* 38, no. 1 (1996): 26–66.

Greenhalgh, Susan, and Edwin A. Winckler, *Governing China's Population: From Leninist to Neoliberal Biopolitics*. Stanford: Stanford University Press, 2005.
Hane, Mikiso. *Peasants, Rebels, Women, and Outcastes: The Underside of Modern Japan*. Lanham: Rowman & Littlefield, 2003.
———. *Reflections on the Way to the Gallows: Rebel Women in Prewar Japan*. Berkeley: University of California Press, 1988.
Harootunian, Harry D. *Overcome by Modernity: History, Culture, and Community in Interwar Japan*. Princeton: Princeton University Press, 2011.
Hasian, Marouf Arif. *The Rhetoric of Eugenics in Anglo-American Thought*. Athens: University of Georgia Press, 1996.
Hastings, Sally A. *Neighborhood and Nation in Tōkyō, 1905–1937*. Pittsburgh: University of Pittsburgh Press, 1995.
Havens, Thomas R. H. *Farm and Nation in Modern Japan: Agrarian Nationalism, 1870–1940*. Princeton: Princeton University Press, 1974.
———. "Katō Kanji (1884–1965) and the Spirit of Agriculture in Modern Japan." *Monumenta Nipponica* 25, no. 3/4 (1970): 249–266.
Hayami, Akira. *Population, Family and Society in Pre-Modern Japan: Population, Family and Society in Pre-Modern Japan*. Boston: Brill, 2010.
Hodgson, Dennis. "The Ideological Origins of the Population Association of America." *Population and Development Review* 17, no. 1 (1991): 1–34.
Homei, Aya. "The Science of Population and Birth Control in Post-War Japan." In *Science, Technology, and Medicine in the Modern Japanese Empire*, edited by Philip C. Brown and David G. Wittner, 227–243. London: Routledge, 2016.
Homei, Aya, and Yōko Matsubara. "Critical Approaches to Reproduction and Population in Post-War Japan." *Japan Forum* 33, no. 3 (2021): 307–317.
Honda, Tatsuo. "Population Problems in Postwar Japan: Now Facing Their Transitional Difficulties." Vol. 1. National Institute of Population and Social Security Research, January 1957. https://www.ipss.go.jp/history/EnglishPamphletSeries/pdf/J000008723.pdf.
Hopper, Helen M. *A New Woman of Japan: A Political Biography of Katō Shidzue*. Boulder: Westview Press, 1996.
Hovhannisyan, Astghik. "Preventing the Birth of 'Inferior Offspring': Eugenic Sterilizations in Postwar Japan." *Japan Forum* 33, no. 3 (2021): 383–401.
Howes, John F., ed. *Nitobe Inazo: Japan's Bridge Across the Pacific*. London: Routledge, 2021.
Inazō, Nitobe. "Opening Address at the Kyoto Conference of the Institute of Pacific Relations" (October 28, 1929). In *The Works of Inazō Nitobe*, vol. 4, 352–359. Tokyo: University of Tokyo Press, 1972.
Institute of Population Problems (IPP). *Annual Reports of the Institute of Population Problems*. Tokyo: Ministry of Health and Welfare, 1960.
———. *Eugenic Protection Law in Japan*. Tokyo: Ministry of Health and Welfare, 1960.
"Interim Report of the Proceedings of the First General Assembly of the International Union for the Scientific Investigation of Population Problems." *Journal of the American Statistical Association* 23, no. 163 (1928): 306–317.
International Birth Control Conference. *Report of the Fifth International Neo-Malthusian and Birth Control Conference, Kingsway Hall, London, July 11th to 14th, 1922*. London: W. Heinemann, 1922.

Jameson, Fredric. *Archaeologies of the Future: The Desire Called Utopia and Other Science Fictions.* London: Verso, 2005.
Jansen, Marius B. *The Making of Modern Japan.* Cambridge, MA: Belknap Press, 2000.
"Japan's Soul Is in Its Food Problems—Professor Nasu Says Food and Population Questions Are Very Deep." *The Trans-Pacific* (November 21, 1929).
Jasanoff, Sheila. "The Idiom of Co-Production." In *States of Knowledge: The Co-Production of Science and Social Order,* edited by Sheila Jasanoff, 1–12. London: Routledge, 2004.
Jensen, Joan M. "The Evolution of Margaret Sanger's 'Family Limitation' Pamphlet, 1914–1921." *Signs* 6, no. 3 (1981): 548–567.
Jünger, Ernst. "Total Mobilization" (1930). In *The Heidegger Controversy: A Critical Reader,* 119–139, edited by Richard Wolin. Cambridge, MA: MIT Press, 1992.
Jütte, Robert. *Contraception: A History.* Translated by Vicky Russell. Cambridge, UK: Polity Press, 2008.
Kasza, Gregory J. *The State and the Mass Media in Japan, 1918–1945.* Berkeley: University of California Press, 1988.
———. "War and Welfare Policy in Japan." *Journal of Asian Studies* 61, no. 2 (2002): 417–435.
Keaveney, Christopher T. *The Cultural Evolution of Postwar Japan: The Intellectual Contributions of Kaizō's Yamamoto Sanehiko.* New York: Palgrave Macmillan, 2013.
Kelly, M. G. E. "International Biopolitics: Foucault, Globalisation and Imperialism." *Theoria (Pietermaritzburg)* 57, no. 123 (2010): 1–26.
Kelves, Daniel J. *In the Name of Eugenics: Genetics and the Uses of Human Heredity.* New York: Knopf, 1985.
Kennedy, David M. *Birth Control in America: The Career of Margaret Sanger.* New Haven: Yale University Press, 1970.
Key, Ellen. *Love and Marriage.* New York and London: G. P. Putnam's Sons, 1911.
Kim, Eunjung. *Curative Violence: Rehabilitating Disability, Gender, and Sexuality in Modern Korea.* Durham: Duke University Press, 2016.
Kim, Sonja M. *Imperatives of Care: Women and Medicine in Colonial Korea.* Honolulu: University of Hawaii Press, 2019.
Klausen, Susanne, and Alison Bashford. "Fertility Control: Eugenics, Neo-Malthusianism, and Feminism." In *The Oxford Handbook of the History of Eugenics,* edited by Alison Bashford and Philippa Levine, 98–115. New York: Oxford University Press, 2010.
Klemperer-Markham, Ayala, and Ofra Goldstein-Gidoni. "Socialist Egalitarian Feminism in Early Postwar Japan: Yamakawa Kikue and the 'Democratization of Japan.'" *U.S.–Japan Women's Journal* 42 (2012): 3–30.
Koschmann, J. Victor. "Introduction to Total War and 'Modernization.'" In *Total War and "Modernization,"* edited by Yasushi Yamanouchi, J. Victor Koschmann, and Ryūichi Narita, xi–xvi. Ithaca: Cornell University East Asia Program, 2001.
———. "Maruyama Masao and the Incomplete Project of Modernity." In *Postmodernism and Japan,* edited by Masao Miyoshi and H. D. Harootunian, 123–141. Durham: Duke University Press, 1989.
Kratoska, Paul H. *Asian Labor in the Wartime Japanese Empire: Unknown Histories.* Armonk: Sharpe, 2005.

Kropotkin, Petr Alekseevich. *Fields, Factories and Workshops: Or Industry Combined with Agriculture and Brain Work with Manual Work*. New York: G. P. Putnam's Sons, 1899.
Kühl, Stefan. *For the Betterment of the Race: The Rise and Fall of the International Movement for Eugenics and Racial Hygiene*. New York: Palgrave Macmillan, 2013.
——. *The Nazi Connection: Eugenics, American Racism, and German National Socialism*. New York: Oxford University Press, 2002.
LaFleur, William R., Gernot Böhme, and Susumu Shimazono, eds. *Dark Medicine: Rationalizing Unethical Medical Research*. Bloomington: Indiana University Press, 2007.
Large, Stephen S. "The Japanese Labor Movement, 1912–1919: Suzuki Bunji and the Yūaikai." *Journal of Asian Studies* 29, no. 3 (1970): 559–579.
——. *Organized Workers and Socialist Politics in Interwar Japan*. Cambridge, UK: Cambridge University Press, 1981.
Largent, Mark A. *Breeding Contempt: The History of Coerced Sterilization in the United States*. New Brunswick: Rutgers University Press, 2007.
Ledbetter, Rosanna. *A History of the Malthusian League, 1877–1927*. Columbus: Ohio State University Press, 1976.
Legg, Stephen, and Deana Heath, eds. *South Asian Governmentalities: Michel Foucault and the Question of Postcolonial Orderings*. Cambridge, UK: Cambridge University Press, 2018.
Lenin, Vladimir. "The Working Class and Neo-Malthusianism." Marxists Internet Archive. Accessed October 14, 2022. https://www.marxists.org/archive/lenin/works/1913/jun/29.htm.
Lo, Ming-cheng Miriam. *Doctors Within Borders Profession, Ethnicity, and Modernity in Colonial Taiwan*. Berkeley: University of California Press, 2002.
Lowy, Dina. "Love and Marriage: Ellen Key and Hiratsuka Raichō Explore Alternatives." *Women's Studies* 33, no. 4 (2004): 361–380.
Lu, Sidney Xu. *The Making of Japanese Settler Colonialism: Malthusianism and Trans-Pacific Migration, 1868–1961*. Cambridge, UK, and New York: Cambridge University Press, 2019.
Mackie, Vera C. *Feminism in Modern Japan: Citizenship, Embodiment, and Sexuality*. Cambridge, UK: Cambridge University Press, 2003.
"Margaret Sanger in Japan." *Birth Control Review* 6, no. 5 (May 1922): 77–78.
"Margaret Sanger in Japan." *Birth Control Review* 6, no. 6 (June 1922): 101–104.
Maruyama, Masao. "Nationalism in Japan: Its Theoretical Background and Prospects." In *Thought and Behavior in Modern Japanese Politics*. London: Oxford University Press, 1969.
Marx, Karl. *Capital: A Critique of Political Economy*. Vol. 1. Translated by Ben Fowkes. Harmondsworth: Penguin Books, 1976.
——. "Critique of the Gotha Program." In *The Marx-Engels Reader*, edited by Robert Tucker, 525–541. New York: Norton, 1978.
——. *The Eighteenth Brumaire of Louis Bonaparte*. New York: International Publishers, 1963. Originally published 1852.
Matsubara, Yōko. "The Enactment of Japan's Sterilization Laws in the 1940s: A Prelude to Postwar Eugenic Policy." *Historia Scientiarum* 8, no. 2 (1998): 187–201.
Matsuda, Hiroko. *Liminality of the Japanese Empire: Border Crossings from Okinawa to Colonial Taiwan*. Honolulu: University of Hawaii Press, 2018.

Matsuda, Yoshiro. "Formation of the Census System in Japan: 1871–1945—Development of the Statistical System in Japan Proper and Her Colonies." *Hitotsubashi Journal of Economics* 21, no. 2 (1981): 44–68.
Mbembe, Achille. *Necropolitics*. Durham: Duke University Press, 2019.
McCann, Carole R. *Figuring the Population Bomb: Gender and Demography in the Mid-Twentieth Century*. Seattle: University of Washington Press, 2017.
Miller, Ruth A. *The Limits of Bodily Integrity: Abortion, Adultery, and Rape Legislation in Comparative Perspective*. Aldershot: Ashgate, 2007.
Mitchell, Richard H. *Censorship in Imperial Japan*. Princeton: Princeton University Press, 1983.
Miyake, Yoshiko. "Doubling Expectations: Motherhood and Women's Factory Work Under State Management in Japan in the 1930s and 1940s." In *Recreating Japanese Women, 1600–1945*, edited by Gail Lee Bernstein, 267–295. Berkeley: University of California Press, 1991.
Molony, Barbara. "Equality Versus Difference: The Japanese Debate over 'Motherhood Protection,' 1915–50." In *Japanese Women Working*, edited by Janet Hunter, 133–158. New York: Routledge, 1993.
———. "From 'Mothers of Humanity' to 'Assisting the Emperor': Gendered Belonging in the Wartime Rhetoric of Japanese Feminist Ichikawa Fusae." *Pacific Historical Review* 80, no. 1 (2011): 1–27.
———. "Women's Rights, Feminism, and Suffragism in Japan, 1870–1925." *Pacific Historical Review* 69, no. 4 (2000): 639–661.
Moore, Aaron Stephen. *Constructing East Asia: Technology, Ideology, and Empire in Japan's Wartime Era, 1931–1945*. Stanford, California: Stanford University Press, 2013.
Mori, Kenji. "The Development of the Modern Koseki." In *Japan's Household Registration System and Citizenship: Koseki, Identification and Documentation*, edited by David Chapman and Karl Jakob Krogness, 59–74. London: Routledge, 2014.
"Mrs. Sanger Is Given Permit to Deliver Address." *Japan Times*, March 14, 1922.
Nadkarni, Asha. *Eugenic Feminism: Reproductive Nationalism in the United States and India*. Minneapolis: University of Minnesota Press, 2014.
Nagao, Teruhiko. *Nitobe Inazo: From Bushido to the League of Nations*. Sapporo: Graduate School of Letters, Hokkaido University, 2006.
Nakamura, Takafusa. *Economic Growth in Prewar Japan*. New Haven: Yale University Press, 1983.
Narita, Ryuichi. "Women's Total War: Gender and Wartime Mobilization in the Japanese Empire, 1931–1945." In *The Palgrave Handbook of Mass Dictatorship*, edited by Paul Corner and Jie-Hyun Lim, 337–349. London: Palgrave Macmillan, 2016.
Nasu, Shiroshi. *Aspects of Japanese Agriculture: A Preliminary Survey*. New York: International Secretariat, Institute of Pacific Relations, 1941.
Nitobe, Inazō. "The Manchurian Question and Sino-Japanese Relations" (September 21, 1932). In *The Works of Inazō Nitobe*, vol. 4, 221–233. Tokyo: University of Tokyo Press, 1972.
"Nitobe Says Japan for Co-Operation—Head of Japanese Delegation to Kyoto Conference Tells Nation's Will to Aid." *The Trans-Pacific* (November 7, 1929).
Norgren, Tiana. *Abortion Before Birth Control: The Politics of Reproduction in Postwar Japan*. Princeton: Princeton University Press, 2001.

Norma, Caroline. *The Japanese Comfort Women and Sexual Slavery During the China and Pacific Wars*. London: Bloomsbury Academic, 2016.
Ogino, Miho. "From Natalism to Family Planning: Population Policy in Wartime and the Post-War Period." In *Gender, Nation and State in Modern Japan*, edited by Andrea Germer, Vera C. Mackie, and Ulrike Wohr, translated by Leonie Stickland, 198–210. London: Routledge, 2014.
Okamura, Ryoko. "Making Patriotic Mothers: Images of Motherhood and the Role of Government-Sponsored Women's Organizations in Japan's Home Front." *U.S.–Japan Women's Journal* 55–56 (2019): 55–79.
O'Reilly, Andrea. *Matricentric Feminism: Theory, Activism, and Practice*. Bradford: Demeter Press, 2016.
Oshiro, George M. "Nitobe Inazō and Japanese Nationalism." In *Japanese Cultural Nationalism: At Home and in the Asia-Pacific*, edited by Roy Starrs, 61–79. Kent: Global Oriental, 2004.
Otsubo, Sumiko. "Between Two Worlds: Yamanouchi Shigeo and Eugenics in Early Twentieth-Century Japan." *Annals of Science* 62, no. 2 (2005): 205–231.
———. "Engendering Eugenics: Feminists and Marriage Restriction Legislation in the 1920s." edited by Barbara Molony and Kathleen S. Uno, 225–256. Cambridge, MA: Harvard University Asia Center, 2005.
———. "Feminist Maternal Eugenics in Wartime Japan." *U.S.–Japan Women's Journal* 17 (1999): 39–76.
Otsubo, Sumiko, and James R. Bartholomew. "Eugenics in Japan: Some Ironies of Modernity, 1883–1945." *Science in Context* 11, no. 3–4 (1998): 545–565.
Paul, Diane B. *Controlling Human Heredity: 1865 to the Present*. Amherst: Humanity Books, 1998.
———. "Eugenics and the Left," *Journal of the History of Ideas* 45, no. 4 (1984): 567–590.
Petersen, William. "Marxism and the Population Question: Theory and Practice." *Population and Development Review* 14 (1988): 77–101.
Qiu, Peipei, Zhiliang Su, and Lifei Chen. *Chinese Comfort Women: Testimonies from Imperial Japan's Sex Slaves*. Oxford: Oxford University Press, 2014.
Rabinbach, Anson, and Sander L. Gilman. *The Third Reich Sourcebook*. Berkeley: University of California Press, 2019.
Radcliffe, Sarah A. *Dilemmas of Difference: Indigenous Women and the Limits of Postcolonial Development Policy*. Durham: Duke University Press, 2015.
Richards, Ellen S. *Euthenics, the Science of Controllable Environment: A Plea for Better Living Conditions as a First Step Toward Higher Human Efficiency*. Boston: Whitcomb & Barrows, 1910. Reprinted in Project Gutenberg, http://www.gutenberg.org/ebooks/31508.
Robertson, Jennifer. "Blood Talks: Eugenic Modernity and the Creation of New Japanese." *History and Anthropology* 13, no. 3 (2002): 191–216.
Rodd, Laurel Rasplica. "Yosano Akiko and the Taisho Debate over the 'New Woman.'" In *Recreating Japanese Women, 1600–1945*, edited by Gail Lee Bernstein, 175–198. Berkeley: University of California Press, 1991.
Sakai, Naoki. "Modernity and Its Critique: The Problem of Universalism and Particularism." In *Postmodernism and Japan*, edited by Masao Miyoshi and H. D. Harootunian, 93–122. Durham: Duke University Press, 1989.
Sanger, Margaret. "Introduction to Proceedings of the Sixth International Neo-Malthusian and Birth Control Conference." Speeches and Writings of Margaret

Sanger, 1911–1959 Accessed September 18, 2022. https://m-sanger.org/items/show/1276.
———. *Woman and the New Race*. New York: Brentano, 1920.
Schreiner, Olive. *Woman and Labor*. London: T. F. Unwin, 1911.
Sedgwick, Eve Kosofsky. "Sexualism and the Citizen of the World: Wycherley, Sterne, and Male Homosocial Desire." *Critical Inquiry* 11, no. 2 (1984): 226–245.
Shapin, Steven, and Simon Schaffer. *Leviathan and the Air-Pump: Hobbes, Boyle, and the Experimental Life*. Princeton: Princeton University Press, 1985.
Sherwood, John M. "Engels, Marx, Malthus, and the Machine." *American Historical Review* 90, no. 4 (1985): 837–865.
Shidzué (Shizue), Ishimoto. *Facing Two Ways: The Story of My Life*. New York: Farrar & Rinehart, 1935.
Shigematsu, Setsu. *Scream from the Shadows: The Women's Liberation Movement in Japan*. Minneapolis: University of Minnesota Press, 2012.
Shillony, Ben-Ami. *Politics and Culture in Wartime Japan*. Oxford: Clarendon Press, 1981.
———. *Revolt in Japan: The Young Officers and the February 26, 1936 Incident*. Princeton: Princeton University Press, 1973.
Shimabuku, Annmaria M. *Alegal: Biopolitics and the Unintelligibility of Okinawan Life*. New York: Fordham University Press, 2018.
Shinkawa, Toshimitsu, and Yuki Tsuji. "Conceptual Development of Welfare and Social Policy in Japan." In *Analysing Social Policy Concepts and Language: Comparative and Transnational Perspectives*, edited by Daniel Béland, 193–210. Bristol: Policy Press, 2014.
Smedley, Agnes. "The Awakening of Japan." *Birth Control Review* 4, no. 2 (February 1920): 6–8.
Soh, Chunghee Sarah. *The Comfort Women: Sexual Violence and Postcolonial Memory in Korea and Japan*. Chicago: University of Chicago Press, 2008.
Stepan, Nancy Leys. *The Hour of Eugenics: Race, Gender, and Nation in Latin America*. Ithaca: Cornell University Press, 1996.
Stoler, Ann Laura. *Race and the Education of Desire: Foucault's History of Sexuality and the Colonial Order of Things*. Durham: Duke University Press, 1995.
Stopes, Marie. "Differences Between the Malthusian League and the C.B.C.: What Are They?" *Birth Control News* (July 1922): 4.
Sugita, Yoneyuki. "Japan's Epoch-Making Health-Insurance Reforms, 1937–1945." *Japan Forum* 25, no. 1 (2013): 112–133.
Suzuki, Michiko. *Becoming Modern Women: Love and Female Identity in Prewar Japanese Literature and Culture*. Stanford: Stanford University Press, 2010.
Tachi, Minoru. "Population Trend and Economic Growth in Japan." National Institute of Population and Society Security Research, April 1960. https://www.ipss.go.jp/history/EnglishPamphletSeries/pdf/J000008733.pdf.
Takeda, Hiroko. *The Political Economy of Reproduction in Japan: Between Nation-State and Everyday Life*. London: RoutledgeCurzon, 2005.
Takeuchi, Yoshimi. *What Is Modernity?: Writings of Takeuchi Yoshimi*. Translated by Richard Calichman. New York: Columbia University Press, 2005.
Takeuchi-Demirci, Aiko. *Contraceptive Diplomacy: Reproductive Politics and Imperial Ambitions in the United States and Japan*. Stanford: Stanford University Press, 2018.

Tansman, Alan. *The Aesthetics of Japanese Fascism*. Berkeley: University of California Press, 2009.
———, ed. *The Culture of Japanese Fascism*. Durham: Duke University Press, 2009.
Terazawa, Yuki. *Knowledge, Power, and Women's Reproductive Health in Japan, 1690–1945*. Cham: Palgrave Macmillan, 2018.
Tianshi, Yang. "Chiang Kai-shek and the Battles of Shanghai and Nanjing." In *The Battle for China: Essays on the Military History of the Sino-Japanese War of 1937–1945*, edited by Mark Peattie, Edward Drea, and Hans van de Ven, 143–158. Redwood City: Stanford University Press, 2010.
Tipton, Elise K. "Ishimoto Shizue: The Margaret Sanger of Japan." *Women's History Review* 6, no. 3 (1997): 337–355.
Titmuss, Richard Morris. *Problems of Social Policy*. London: H. M. Stationery Office, 1950.
Tomie, Naoko. "The Political Process of Establishing the Mother-Child Protection Law in Prewar Japan." *Social Science Japan Journal* 8, no. 2 (2005): 239–251.
Townsend, Susan C. *Yanaihara Tadao and Japanese Colonial Policy: Redeeming Empire*. Richmond: Curzon, 2000.
"Transcript of Oral Judgment Delivered on 4 December 200l by the Judges of the Women's International War Crimes Tribunal on Japan's Military Sexual Slavery (December 4, 2001)." Accessed January 16, 2022. http://www.iccwomen.org/wigjdraft1/Archives/oldWCGJ/tokyo/summary.html.
Tsurumi, E. Patricia. "The Accidental Historian, Yamakawa Kikue." *Gender & History* 8, no. 2 (1996): 258–276.
Tsurumi, Shunsuke. *An Intellectual History of Wartime Japan, 1931–1945*. London: KPI, 1986.
Uchida, Jun. *Brokers of Empire: Japanese Settler Colonialism in Korea, 1876–1945*. Cambridge, MA: Harvard University Asia Center, 2011.
Ueno, Chizuko. *Nationalism and Gender*. Melbourne: Trans Pacific Press, 2004.
———. *The Modern Family in Japan: Its Rise and Fall*. Melbourne: Trans Pacific Press, 2009.
Uno, Kathleen S. *Passages to Modernity: Motherhood, Childhood, and Social Reform in Early Twentieth Century Japan*. Honolulu: University of Hawaii Press, 1999.
Ward, Max M. *Thought Crime: Ideology and State Power in Interwar Japan*. Durham: Duke University Press, 2019.
Weiss, Sheila Faith. "The Race Hygiene Movement in Germany." *Osiris* (Bruges) 3, no. 3 (1987): 193–236.
Wilson, Sandra. "Family or State?: Nation, War, and Gender in Japan, 1937–45." *Critical Asian Studies* 38, no. 2 (2006): 209–238.
———. *The Manchurian Crisis and Japanese Society*. London: Routledge, 2002.
Wiltgen, Richard J. "Marx's and Engels's Conception of Malthus: The Heritage of a Critique." *Organization & Environment* 11, no. 4 (1998): 451–460.
Woods, Roger. *The Conservative Revolution in the Weimar Republic*. Houndmills, Basingstoke, Hampshire: Macmillan, 1996.
Yamakawa, Kikue. *Women of the Mito Domain: Recollections of Samurai Family Life*. Tokyo: University of Tokyo Press, 1992.
Yamamoto, Senji. "A Personal Letter to Margaret Sanger" (April 1923). In *Yamamoto Senji Zenshū*, vol. 7, 145–155, edited by Toshiji Sasaki and Akinori Odagiri. Tokyo: Chōbunsha, 1979.

Yamamura, Kozo. "The Japanese Economy, 1911–1930: Concentration, Conflicts, and Crises." In *Japan in Crisis: Essays on Taishō Democracy*, edited by Gail Lee Bernstein, Bernard S. Silberman, and Harry D. Harootunian, 299–328. Princeton: Princeton University Press, 1974.

Yasushi, Yamanouchi. "Total-War and System Integration: A Methodological Introduction." In *Total War and "Modernization,"* edited by Narita Ryūichi, Yamanouchi Yasushi, and J. Victor Koschmann, 1–39. Ithaca: East Asia Program, Cornell University, 1998.

Yoshimi, Yoshiaki. *Comfort Women: Sexual Slavery in the Japanese Military During World War II*. New York: Columbia University Press, 2000.

Young, Louise. *Japan's Total Empire: Manchuria and the Culture of Wartime Imperialism*. Berkeley: University of California Press, 1998.

Young, Robert. *Empire, Colony, Postcolony*. Chichester, West Sussex: John Wiley, 2015.

JAPANESE

Abe Isoo. *Funin kekkon to ningen kaizō*. Tokyo: Shunyōdō, 1930.

———. "Jinkō mondai kara mitaru sanji seigen." *Kakusei* 26, no. 8 (1936): 1–4.

———. "Jinkō mondai no ryōteki hōmen to shitsuteki hōmen." *Jinkō mondai* 2, no. 4 (1938): 48–60.

———. "Sanji seigen no yūseigakuteki kenkai." *Sanji chōsetsu hyōron* 4, no. 6 (1931): 2–5.

———. *Seikatsu mondai kara mita sanji chōsetsu*. Tokyo: Tokyodō, 1931.

Abe Isoo and Majima Kan. *Sanji seigen no riron to jissai*. Tokyo: Bungaku gakkai shuppan-bu, 1925.

Abe Tsunehisa. "'Abe Isoo to fujin mondai.'" In *Abe Isoo no kenkyū*, edited by Naoyoshi Nakamura, 151–183. Tokyo: Waseda daigaku shakai kagaku kenkyūjo, 1990.

Aikawa Yuri. "Kōa no kodakara jyūsannin, furusawabutai o tou." *Fujokai* 62, no. 6 (1940): 228–233.

Akagawa Manabu. "Shinbun ni arawareta 'umeyo fuyaseyo': Shinano Mainichi Shinbun to Tokyo Asahi Shinbun ni okeru jinkō seisaku." *Jinbun kagaku ronshū* 38 (2004): 133–148.

Asada Kyōji. "Manshū nōgyō imin seisaku no ritsuan katei." In *Nihon teikokushugika no Manshū imin*, edited by Manshu iminshi kenkyukai, 24–29. Tokyo: Ryūkei shosha, 1976.

"Atarashii kekkon jyūsoku." *Chūgai shōgyō shinpō* (October 4, 1939). Accessed October 11, 2022. https://hdl.handle.net/20.500.14094/0100239919.

"Bosei hogo hō" (1937). In *Nihon fujin mondai shiryō shūsei*. In *Nihon fujin mondai shiryō shūsei*, vol. 2, *Seiji*, 488–489. Tokyo: Domesu shuppan, 1977.

"Bosei hogo hō seitei sokushin fujin renmei dai ikkai zenkoku i'inkai." In *Nihon fujin mondai shiryō shūsei*, vol. 2, *Seiji*, 486–487. Tokyo: Domesu shuppan, 1977.

"Chokurei dai 7 gō kōsei-shō kansei" (1938). National Archives of Japan Digital Archive. Accessed July 25, 2021. https://www.digital.archives.go.jp/DAS/meta/Detail_F0000000000000035693.

Chōsen sōtokufu. *Jinkō mondai ni kansuru hōsaku no sankōan*. Keijō: Chōsen sōtokufu, 1927.

Dai jyūgō shidan gun'ibu. "Eisei gyōmu yōhō" (January/February 1943). In *Seifu*

chōsa: "jūgun ianfu" kankei shiryō shūsei, 213–225. Tokyo: Ryūkei shosha, 1997.
Dai nihon fujinkai. *Dai nihon fujinkai gaikyō* (1943). Accessed October 28, 2022. https://www.ndl.go.jp/modern/img_r/087/087-001r.html.
"Dai nihon fujinkai kōryō gaisetsu." *Nihon gujin* 1, no. 3 (1943): 80.
Dai nihon fujinkai Nagoya-shi shibu. *Kenmin shunin no katsudō ni tsuite*. Nagoya: Jidō shinbunsha, 1944.
"Eisei-shō setsuritsu mondai no keii." *Gunidan zasshi* 279 (August 1936): 1151.
Fujime Yuki. *Sei no rekishigaku: kōshō seido, dataizai taisei kara baishun bōshihō, yūsei hogo hō taisei e*. Tokyo: Fuji shuppan, 1997.
Fujino Yutaka. *Nihon fashizumu to yūsei shisō*. Kyoto-shi: Kamogawa shuppan, 1998.
———. *Sengo minshushugi ga unda yūsei shiso—yūsei hogo hō no shiteki kenshō*. Tokyo: Rikka shuppan, 2021.
"Funin chiryō tekiyō, chakushōzenkensa wa handan miokuri, taigaijyusei nado taishō e, Kōsei-shō," *Asahi Newspaper*, December 15, 2021. https://digital.asahi.com/articles/ASPDH56YLPDHUTFL006.html.
Gunsei kanbu Bizaya shibu Iroiro shutchōjō. "Ianjo kitei sōhu no ken" (November 22, 1942). In *Seifu chōsa: "jūgun ianfu" kankei shiryō shūsei*, 187–193. Tokyo: Ryūkei shosha, 1997.
Hayashi Yōko. "Abe Isoo ni okeru 'heiwa' ron to danshu-ron: dansei-sei no mondai no kakawari o kijikuni." *Jenda shi gaku*, no. 5 (2009): 35–49.
Hiratsuka Raichō. "Bosei hogo no shuchō wa iraishugi ka" (1918). In *Shiryō bosei hogo ronsō*, edited by Nobuko Kōuchi, 86–91. Tokyo: Domesu shuppan, 1984.
Hiroshima Kiyoshi. "Gendai nihon jinkō seisaku-shi shōron: jinkō shishitsu gainen o megutte, 1916–1930." *SPP*, no. 154 (1980): 46–61.
———. "Gendai nihon jinkō seisaku-shi shōron (2): kokumin yūsei hō ni okeru jinkō no shitsu seisaku to ryō seisaku." *SPP*, no. 160 (1981): 61–77.
"Hoken shakai-shō (kashō) setchi no riyū" (1937). In *Kokka sōdōinshi*, 700. Fujisawa-shi: Kokka sōdōinshi kankōkai, 1975.
"Hoken shakai-shō (kashō) setchi yōkō" (1937). In *Kokka sōdōinshi*, 697–698. Fujisawa-shi: Kokka sōdōinshi kankōkai, 1975.
"Hon kyōkai de Kiyoura (Kiyoura Keigo) kaichō na o motte tōkyoku ni shakai-shō shinsetsu nami jidō-kyoku tokkyo kata yōbō o gushin." *Shakai jigyō ihō* (July 1937): 3.
Honda Sōshi. *Kindai nihon no yūseigaku: "tasha" zō no seiritsu o megutte*. Tokyo: Akashi shoten, 2022.
Ichikawa Fusae, ed. *Nihon fujin mondai shiryō shūsei*. Vol. 2, *Seiji*. Tokyo: Domesu shuppan, 1977.
Ifukube Toshiko. *Kekkon no zenshin*. Tokyo: Shin Taishūsha, 1943.
Inoue Masaji. *Ijyū to kaitaku*. Vol. 1. Tokyo: Nihon Shokumin Tsūshinsha, 1930.
Ishikawa Sanshirō. "Hininron ni tsuite: Yamakawa Kikue joshi ni mōsu." *Onna no sekai* 7, no. 4 (1921): 17.
———. "Shakai shugi sha kara mita fujin kyūsai: ippuippu seido wa shizen de jiyū de junketsu de aru." *Onna no sekai* 7, no. 2 (1921): 32–37.
Ishikawa Shoji. "Shakai shugisha ni okeru 'sei' to seiji: nihon no 1920–30 nendai o chūshin toshite." *Nenpō seiji gaku* 54 (2003): 161–177.
Ishimoto Keikichi. "Waga jinkō mondai to sanji chōsetsu ron" (1922). In *SSJ*, vol. 2, 160–169.

Ishimoto Shizue. "Fujin kaihō to sanji chōsetsu" (1922). In *SSJ*, vol. 14, 3.
———. "Sanji chōsetsu no kokoroe" (1936). In *SSJ*, vol. 7, 290–292.
———. "Sanji seigen ron o sho hōmen yori kansatsu shite" (October 1922). In *SSJ*, vol. 2, 80–85.
———. "Shin-marusasu shugi." Tokyo: Nihon panfuretto hakkōsho, 1921.
Japan International Cooperation Agency. "Nihon no jinkō keiken." 2003. Accessed October 18, 2022. https://www.jica.go.jp/jica-ri/IFIC_and_JBICI-Studies/jica-ri/publication/archives/jica/field/pdf/2003_08e.pdf.
"Jinkō mondai kenkyūsho ni oite tadachini chōsa kenkyū ni chakusu beki shuyō chōsa kenkyū jikō." *SPP* 1, no. 1 (April 1940): 70–71.
Jinkō mondai kenkyūkai. *Dai ni kai jinkō mondai zenkoku kyōgikai hokoku-sho.* Tokyo: Jinkō mondai kenkyūkai, 1939.
———. "Ishokumin shinkō hōsaku ni kansuru kengi." *Jinkō mondai* 1, no. 4 (1936): 16–24.
———. *Jinkō mondai kenkyūkai 50-nen ryakushi.* Tokyo: Jinkō mondai kenkyūkai, 1983.
———. *Jinkō mondai kōenshū.* Vol. 1. Tokyo: Jinkō mondai kenkyūkai, 1934.
———. *Jinkō mondai shiryō dai 43 shū no. 1: jinkō, minzoku, kokudo.* Tokyo: Jinkō mondai kenkyūkai, 1942.
———. "Manshū imin ni kansuru kengi" *Jinkō mondai* 1, no. 4 (1936): 25–29.
"Jinkō seisaku kakuritsu yōkō no kettei." *SPP* 2, no. 2 (February 1941): 55–57.
"Jinkō shokuryō mondai chōsa kenkyūkai kansei." *Kanpō gogai* (July 7, 1927).
Jinkō shokuryō mondai chōsakai. *Jinkō shokuryō mondai chōsakai jinkō-bu tōshin setsumei.* Tokyo: Jinkō shokuryō mondai chōsakai, 1930.
Kanda Ryūichi. "Osaka no sanji seigen undō." *Sanji seigen hyōron*, no. 1 (1925): 26–27.
Katō Kanji. *Nihon nōson kyōiku.* Tokyo: Tōyō tosho, 1936.
Kawakami Hajime. *Jinkō mondai hihan.* Tokyo: Sōbunkaku, 1927.
Kawasaki Shigeru. "Nihon no tōkeigaku no rekishiteki hatten ni okeru kōteki tōkei no yakuwari." *Nihon tōkei gakkaishi* 49, no. 2 (2020): 161–186.
"Kekkon sōdan ni okeru kenkō mondai ni kansuru shidō shishin." *SPP* 2, no. 9 (September 1941): 59–61.
"Kenmin undō jisshi yōkō." *SPP* 3, no. 4 (April 1942): 51–64.
Kitaoka Shinichi. "Nitobe Inazō ni okeru teikoku shugi to kokusai shugi." In *Iwanami kōza kindai nihon to shokuminchi 4: tōgō to shihai no ronri*, edited by Shinobu Ōe, Kyōji Asada, and Taichirō Mitani, 179–203. Tokyo: Iwanami shoten, 1993.
"Kodakara ikka no sōryoku atsumete." *Shashin shūhō*, no. 298 (November 1943): 16–17.
Koike Shirō. "Jidai ni genwaku sare taru marusasu." *Sei to shakai*, no. 14 (1926): 18–24.
Koizumi Chikahiko. *Gunjin eisei.* Tokyo: Kinbara shōten, 1927.
———. "Hoken kokusaku no konpon mondai." *Nihon sangyo eisei kyōkai kaiho* 15, no. 11 (1938): 827–833.
"Kokudo keikaku settei yōkō." *SPP* 1, no. 7 (October 1940): 112–115.
"Kokumin yūsei hō no kōfu." *SPP* 1, no. 2 (May 1940): 70–72.
"Kokusei chōsa," e-Stat. Accessed October 28, 2022. https://www.e-stat.go.jp/stat-search/files?page=1&toukei=00200521&result_page=1.
Kōsei-shō. *Isei hachijūnenshi.* Tokyo: Insatsukyoku chōyōkai, 1955.

"Kōsei-shō bunka kitei no kaisei." *SPP* 4, nos. 10–12 (October–December 1943): 60–62.
"Kōsei-shō eiseikyoku no zenkoku muison chōsa." *SPP* 1, no. 2 (May 1940): 74–75.
"Kōsei-shō kansei chū kaisei to jinkō-kyoku no sōsetsu." *SPP* 2, no. 8 (August 1941): 44–47.
"Kōsei-shō no yūryō tashi katei hyōshō nami futai chōsa." *SPP* 1, no. 3 (June 1940): 73–74.
"Kosei-shō shakaikyoku no yūryō tashi katei hyōshō ni kansuru futai chōsa no happyō." *SPP* 1, no. 9 (December 1940): 66–69.
Kōsei-shō 20-nenshi henshū i'inkai. *Koseishō 20-nenshi*. Tokyo: Kōsei mondai kenkyūkai, 1960.
Kutsumi Fusako, "Naniyueni wareware wa hantaishitaka: sōdōmei taikai ni teishutsu sareshi BC an." *Sanji chōsetsu hyōron*, no. 4 (1925): 53.
Mainichi shinbun shuzaihan. *Kyōsei funin—kyū-yūsei hogo hō o tou*. Tokyo: Mainichi shinbun shuppan, 2019.
Mandarei chūtonchi shireibu. "Chūtonchi ianjo kitei" (May 26, 1943). In *Seifu chōsa: "jūgun ianfu" kankei shiryō shūsei*, 281–293. Tokyo: Ryūkei shosha, 1997.
Manshūkoku tsūshinsha. *Manshū kaitaku nenkan*. Tokyo: Howa shuppan, 1986.
Matsuda Tokiko. *Josei-sen*. Tokyo: Akebi shobō, 1995.
Matsumura Shōnen. "Seibutsu gaku jō yori mita sanji chōsetsu ron" (1923). In *SSJ*, vol. 2, 174–201.
Minami Ryōzaburō. *Jinkōron hattenshi: nihon ni okeru jyūnenkan no sō gyōseki*. Tokyo: Sanseidō, 1936.
Minzoku eisei kenkyūkai. *Minzoku eisei shiryō*. Tokyo: Shizu-sha, 1938.
Murakami Katsuhiko. "Yanaihara Tadaō ni okeru shokuminron to shokumin seisaku." In *Iwanami kōza kindai nihon to shokuminchi 4: tōgō to shihai no ronri*, edited by Shinobu Ōe, Kyōji Asada, and Taichirō Mitani, 205–237. Tokyo: Iwanami shoten, 1993.
Muramatsu Yōko. "Funin chiryō no hoken tekiyō kakudai ni muketa ugoki." NLI Research Institute. Accessed February 14, 2022. https://www.nli-research.co.jp/report/detail/id=67353?pno=2&site=nli.
Musansha sanji seigen dōmei. "Musansha sanji seigen dōmei sengen: kōryō kiyaku" (1931). In *Nihon josei undō shiryō shūsei*, edited by Yūko Suzuki, 686–688. Tokyo: Fuji shuppan, 1995.
Nagai Tōru. "Jinkō mondai ni kansuru jōsetsu chōsa kikan setchi ni kansuru kengi-an." In *Jinkō mondai kenkyūkai 50-nen ryakushi*. Tokyo: Jinkō mondai kenkyūkai, 1983.
———. "Kajō jinkō no shitsugyō to no kankei o ronjite jinkō mondai no honshitsu ni oyobu." *Jinkō mondai* 1, no. 3 (1936): 37–41.
———. *Nihon jinkōron*. Tokyo: Ganshōdō shoten, 1929.
———. "Sekai no jinkō-ron yori nihon no jinkō-ron e (I)." *Taiyō* 34, no. 1 (1928): 2–10.
———. "Wagakuni ni okeru jinkō mondai ni kansuru chōsa kenkyū kikan no raireki ni tsuite." *Jinkō mondai kenkyūsho nenpō* 5 (1960): 1–5.
Nagayama Sadanori. "Nihon no kanchō tōkei no hatten to gendai." *Nihon tōkei gakkaishi* 16, no. 1 (1986): 101–109.
Naikaku "Kokka sōdōin hō" (1938). Accessed July 20, 2021. https://www.digital.archives.go.jp/das/image/F0000000000000035654.

———. "Kokumin kenkō hoken hō: hōritsu dai 60-gō" (1938). National Archives of Japan Digital Archive. Accessed October 31, 2021. https://www.digital.archives.go.jp/DAS/meta/Detail_F0000000000000035659.
Nakanishi Yasuyuki. "Takada Yasuma no jinkō riron to shakaigaku." *Keizai ronsō* 140, no. 5–6 (1987): 59–78.
Nasu Shiroshi. *Jinkō shokuryō mondai*. Tokyo: Nhon hyōron-sha, 1927.
"Nihon bosei hogokai no setsuritsu." *SPP* 3, no. 5 (May 1942): 43–44.
Nihon hōrei sakuin. "Dai 16 kai teikoku gikai shūgiin kokusei chōsa ni kansuru hōritsuan i'inkai daiichigō Meiji 35 nen 2 gatsu 24 nichi." Accessed February 17, 2022. https://teikokugikai-i.ndl.go.jp/simple/detailPDF?minId=001611002X00119020224&page=1.
"Nihon iryōdan setsuritsu i'inkai no seiritsu." *SPP* 3, no. 5 (May 1942): 42–43.
Nihon sanji chōsetsu fujin dōmei. "Sechigarai yononaka ni" (1934). In *SSJ*, vol. 7, 130.
Nihon sanji chōsetsu kenkyūkai. "Sanji chōsetsu kenkyūkai shui-sho" (1922). In *SSJ*, vol. 2, 201.
———. "Shōkazoku" (1922). In *SSJ*, vol. 14, 1–4.
"Ninsanpu techō kitei no seitei." *SPP* 3, no. 8 (August 1942): 32–34.
Nitobe Inazō. "Nihon no shokumin." In *Nitobe Inazō zenshū*, vol. 21, 483–493. Tokyo: Kyōbunkan, 1986.
———. "Nitobe Ianzō i'in ikensho" (1929). In *Jinkō mondai kenkyūkai 50-nen ryakushi*, 8. Tokyo: Jinkō mondai kenkyūkai, 1983.
———. "Shokumin no shūkyoku mokuteki" (1913). In *Nitobe Hakase shokumin seisaku kōgi oyobi ronbunshū*, edited by Nitobe Inazō and Yanaihara Tadao, 382–401. Tokyo: Iwanami shoten, 1943.
———. "Shokumin no shūkyoku mokuteki." *Hōgaku kyōkai zasshi* 31, no. 12 (1913): 94–118.
Nitobe Inazō and Yanaihara Tadao. *Nitobe hakase shokumin seisaku kōgi oyobi ronbunshū*. Tokyo: Iwanami shoten, 1943.
Noda Kimiko. *Sanji seigen kenkyū*. Osaka: Sanji seigen kenkyūkai, 1923.
Ogawa Ryūshiro. *Ninshin chōsetsu no jitsuchishiki*. Tokyo: Nihon ninshin chōsetsu sōdansho, 1924.
Ogino Miho. *"Kazoku keikaku" e no michi: kindai nihon no seishoku o meguru seiji*. Tokyo: Iwanami shoten, 2008.
———. "Shigenka sareru shintai: senzen, senchū, sengo no jinkō seisaku o megutte." *Gakujutsu no dōkō* 13, no. 4 (2008): 21–26.
Ōhara shakai mondai kenkyūsho. *Nihon rōdō nenkan*. Tokyo: Rōdō junpōsha, 1922.
Okazaki Ayanori. "Shussanryoku chōsa kekka no gaisetsu." *SPP* 1, no. 7 (October 1940): 1–95.
Ōta Tenrei. *Nihon sanji chōsetsu hyakunenshi*. Tokyo: Shuppan kagaku sōgō kenkyūjo, 1976.
Rikugun-shō. "Fukukan kaidō jisshi no ken tsūchō" (September 1942). *JACAR*. Accessed January 16, 2022. https://www.jacar.archives.go.jp/das/image-j/C04123834600.
———. "Gun ianjo jyūgyōfu nado boshū ni kansuru ken" (March 4, 1938). *JACAR*. Accessed January 16, 2022. https://www.jacar.archives.go.jp/das/image-j/C04120263400.

"Rōdō dantai no sanji seigen: jissai mondai ni totsunyu senden kōen ni dai ippo o." *Osaka Asahi Shinbun*, January 7, 1923.
Ryū Fumihiko. "Nitobe Inazō no Taiwan tōgyō seisaku to shokumin shiso no tenkai." *Ajia bunka kenkyū*, no. 14 (2007): 63–75.
Saitō Itsuki. "Yūshu-ron kenkyū." *Shakai to kyūsai* 3, no. 1 (1919): 7–20.
Sakai Toshihiko. "Umu jiyū to umanu jiyū" (1916). In *Shiryō sei to ai o meguru ronsō*, edited by Miyako Orii, 185–188. Tokyo: Domesu shuppan, 1991.
"Sanji seigen no jissai undō: Kansai no rōdō kumiai ni jukushita jiun, ko no shussan o osoreru hisanna jijitsu." *Osaka Asahi Shinbun*, January 5, 1923.
Sasaki Toshiji. *Yamamoto Senji*. 2 vols. Kyoto: Chōbunsha, 1974.
"Shanghai hakengun nairikugun ianjo ni okeru shakufu boshū ni kansuru ken" (January 19, 1938). *JACAR*. Accessed October 17, 2022. https://www.digital.archives.go.jp/das/image/M0000000000001675555.
"Shasetsu: rōmu dōin to jinkō mondai." *Tokyo Asahi Shinbun* (July 5, 1939).
"Shasetsu: sanji seigen no jissai undō." *Osaka Asahi Shinbun* (January 10, 1923).
"Shasetsu: sanji seigen no senden." *Osaka Mainichi Shinbun* (March 13, 1923).
"Shina tokō fujyo no toriatsukai ni kansuru ken" (February 18, 1938). *JACAR*. Accessed October 17, 2022. https://www.digital.archives.go.jp/das/image/M0000000001675555.
Sugita Naho. *Jinkō, kazoku, seimei to shakai seisaku*. Kyoto-shi: Hōritsu bunkasha, 2010.
———. "Nihon ni okeru jinkō-shakai hoshōron no keifu." *SPP* 73, no. 4 (2017): 239–253.
———. *Yūsei yūkyo to shakai seisaku: jinkō mondai no nihonteki tenkai*. Kyoto-shi: Hōritsu bunkasha, 2013.
Suzuki Yūko. *Wasurerareta shishōka Yamakawa Kikue: feminizumu to senjika no teikō*. Tokyo: Nashi no ki, 2022.
Taisei yokusankai. "Ninpu-kun." In *Bosei no hogo*. Tokyo: Kokumin tosho kankōkai, 1944.
Takamori butai. "Takamori butai tokushu ian gyōmu kitei" (October 11–21, 1940). *JACAR*. Accessed January 17, 2022. https://www.jacar.archives.go.jp/das/meta/C13070262500.
Takano Iwasaburō. "Jinkō zōka no keizaiteki kansatsu." *Kokka gakkai zasshi* 32, no. 7 (1918): 38–47.
———. "Ryō ka shitsu ka." *Kokka gakkai zasshi* 32, no. 11 (1918): 144–145.
Takaoka Hiroyuki. *Sōryokusen taisei to fukushi kokka: senjiki nihon no shakai kaikaku kōsō*. Tokyo: Iwanami shoten, 2011.
Takata Yasuma. "Umeyo fueyo." *Keizaiōrai* 1, no. 5 (1926): 15–16.
Tanaka Mitsuko. "Nihon ichi no kodakara butai, jyūroku no Shiroto-ke, Nagasaki." *Gahō yakushin no nihon* 5, no. 12 (1940).
Tatsuno Kyūshi. "Nihon ichi kodakara butaichō." In *Nihon no haha*, edited by Nihon bungaku hōkokukai, 35–42. Tokyo: Shunyōdō shoten, 1943.
Tseng Yaofen. "Nippon tōchi jidai no Taiwanjin no seiho kanyū nikansuru kenkyū." *Hokengaku zasshi* 601 (2008): 187–206.
Tsuchiya Hidemaro. "Onna bakaride jyūichinin kyōdai, nakayoshi kodakara butai hōmon." *Fujokai* 62, no. 6 (1940): 220–227.
Ueda Teijirō. *Nihon jinkō seisaku*. Tokyo: Chikura shobō, 1937.
———. *Shin jiyū shugi*. Tokyo: Dōbunkan, 1927.

Ueno Chizuko. *Kafuchōsei to shihonsei: Marukusu shugi feminizumu no chihei*. Tokyo: Iwanami shoten, 1990.
Ujihara Sukezō. "Minzoku eisei gaku" (1914). In *SSJ*, vol. 16, 1–23.
Unno Yukinori. *Nihon jinshu kaizōron*. Tokyo: Fuzanbō, 1910.
Yamada Waka. "Bosei hogo mondai: Yosano si to Hirano si no shoron ni tsuite" (1918). In *Shiryō bosei hogo ronsō*, edited by Nobuko Kōuchi, 147–160. Tokyo: Domesu shuppan, 1984.
Yamakawa Kikue. "Fujin o uragiru fujinron o hyōsu" (1918). In *Shiryō bosei hogo ronsō*, edited by Nobuko Kōuchi, 117–131. Tokyo: Domesu shuppan, 1984.
———. "Fujinbu te-ze" (1925). In *Yamakawa Kikue shū*, vol. 4, *Musan kaikyū no fujin undō*, 102–112. Tokyo: Iwanami shoten, 2011.
———. "Hinin zehi nitsuite futatabi Ishikawa Sanshirō ni atau" (1921). In *Yamakawa Kikue shū*, vol. 2, *Josei no hangyaku*, 287–293. Tokyo: Iwanami shoten, 2011.
———. "Ishikawa Sanshirō to hininron" (1921). In *Yamakawa Kikue shū*, vol. 2, *Josei no hangyaku*, 241–247.
———. "Josei no hangyaku: seishin teki oyobi busshitsu teki hōmen yori mitaru sanji seigen mondai" (1921). In *Yamakawa Kikue shū*, vol. 2, *Josei no hangyaku*, 208–233.
———. "Sanji chōsetsu ron to shakai shugi" (1921). In *Yamakawa Kikue shū*, vol. 2, *Josei no hangyaku*, 267–286.
———. "Sanji seigen mondai" (1921). In *Yamakawa Kikue shū*, vol. 2, *Josei no hangyaku*, 234–236.
———. "Tasan shugi no noroi" (1920). In *Yamakawa Kikue shū*, vol. 2, *Josei no hangyaku*, 198–205.
Yamakawa Kikue seitan hyakunen o kinensuru kai. *Gendai feminizumu to Yamakawa Kikue: renzoku kōza "Yamakawa Kikue to gendai" no kiroku.* Tokyo: Yamato Shobō, 1990.
Yamamoto Senji. "Jinsei seibutsugaku shōin." In *Yamamoto Senji zenshū*, vol. 1, 47–140.
———. "Kensetsu teki sanji chōsetsu to wa donna mono ka: eikoku no sanji chōsetsu no kinjō (II)." *Sanji chōsetsu hyōron*, no. 2 (March 1925): 12–16.
———. "Sanga joshi Kazoku seigen hō hihan" (1922). In *Yamamoto Senji zenshū*, vol. 3, 25–98.
———. "Sanji chōsetsu hyōron kara sei to shakai e (I)." *Sei to shakai*, no. 9 (1925): 2–15.
———. "Sanji chōsetsu, ketsuron, sono igō" (1926). In *Yamamoto Senji zenshū*, vol. 3, 591–601.
———. "Sanji chōsetsu wa tenri ni somuku ka." *Sei to shakai*, no. 13 (March 1926): 18–23.
———. "Seiteki inpeishugi no tameni okiru heigai no ichirei" (1922). In *Yamamoto Senji zenshū*, vol. 3, 99–113.
Yanaihara Tadao. *Jinkō mondai*. Tokyo: Iwanami shoten, 1928.
Yokoyama Takashi. *Nihon ga yūseishakai ni narumade: kagaku keimō, medhia, seishoku no seiji*. Tokyo: Keiso shobo, 2015.
Yosano Akiko. "Josei no tettei shita dokuritsu" (1918). In *Shiryō bosei hogo ronsō*, edited by Nobuko Kōuchi, 85–86. Tokyo: Domesu shuppan, 1984.

KOREAN

An T'ae-yun. *Singmin chŏngch'i wa mosŏng*. P'aju: Han'guk haksul chŏngbo, 2006.

Chŏng Ilyŏng. "Ilche sikminchiki chosŏn kanisaengmyŏngpohŏm ŭl t'onghae pon 'kongkong' ŭi kimansŏng." *Yŏksahakyŏn'gu*, no. 75 (2019): 179–214.

Im Sŏngmo. "Manchu nongŏpimin chŏngch'aek ŭl tullŏssan kwantongkun, chosŏn ch'ongtokpu ŭi taelip kwa kŭ kwikyŏl." *Ilbonyŏksayŏn'gu*, no. 29 (2009): 133–162.

Pak Yangsin. "Sikmin chŏngch'aekhak ŭi sinchip'yŏng kwa manchu munche insik—Yanaihara Tadao lŭl chungsimŭlo." *Manjuyŏn'gu*, no. 21 (2016): 157–188.

INDEX

ABCL, see American Birth Control League
Abe Ayao, 23
Abe Isoo, 16, 17, 27, 28–30, 31, 58, 175n60, 178n92
Abe Shinzo, 163
Abortions, 159, 161–62, 186n87
Absolute surplus population, 38, 64
Ackerman, Edward, 160
Agamben, Giorgio, 125, 197n68
Agrarian imperialism, 89–90, 95–99
Agrarianism (nōhonshugi), 95–96
Agricultural depression, 92
Agricultural economics, 83, 86. See also Nasu Shiroshi
Akamatsu Akiko, 58
Akamatsu Tsuneko, 58
Allied Translator and Interpreter Section (ATIS) report, 154–55, 155 (fig.)
Aly, Götz, 107, 193n10
American Birth Control League (ABCL), 26, 181n19. See also Birth Control Review
An T'ae-yun, 149
Aoyama Chise, 60–61
Asia-Pacific War, see Wartime period

Bashford, Alison, 7–8, 17, 74
Bebel, August, 18, 63–64
Belgium, 83, 89
Biopolitical state: gender and, 12, 134–35, 136–37, 148, 149, 157; implications, 132; race and, 116, 134; in wartime Japan, 5, 11, 104–5, 106, 115, 125–26, 132, 134–35, 148
Biopolitics: in everyday life, 130; Foucault on, 9–10, 74; governmentality and, 10–12; imperialism and, 88; in postwar period, 158–59, 162; voluntary motherhood and, 57–58; wartime population policies and, 5, 125–26, 130, 132, 134
Biopower, 10, 57, 105
Birth control: clinics, 53, 58, 59, 186n87; contraceptives, 44, 48, 58, 82; eugenics arguments, 30–31, 34–35, 39–40, 53, 68–69, 79, 178n96; postwar family planning campaign, 159, 160–61, 163; scholars' views, 81–82; state policies, 69–70, 79, 81–82, 160; sterilization policies, 31, 32, 120–23, 161–62, 175n60. See also Birth strike; Neo-Malthusianism, birth control advocacy and
Birth Control League, see American Birth Control League; Japan Birth Control League
Birth control movement: comparison to think tank scholars, 72–73, 75; eugenics arguments, 2, 39–40, 53, 68–69, 178n96; Japanese supporters, 2, 16–17, 28, 40, 48–49, 54–59; leftists in, 20, 33–34, 35–40, 41–44, 65–68; legacy, 44; Pro-BC, 41–42, 43 (fig.), 180n110; Seigenkai, 35–40, 41; state repression, 44, 69–70;

225

Birth control movement (*cont.*)
transnational, 54; views of population problem, 73, 75; in Western countries, 26, 39–40, 49, 54, 181n19, 182n24. *See also* Chōsetsukai; Feminists, birth control activism and; Sanger, Margaret; Voluntary motherhood

Birth Control Review (ABCL), 39, 49–50, 51 (fig.), 54, 181n19

Birth Control Review (*Sanji chōsetsu hyōron*), *see* Hyōron

Birth rates: efforts to increase, 1–2, 118, 126, 163; in interwar period, 76, 80. *See also* Fertility rates; Pronatalist policies

Birth strike (*shussan sutoraiki*), 60, 65, 69

Bismarck, Otto von, 106–7

Bodies: of colonial others, 115–16; desirable traits, 126–27; inferior, 121–23, 162; national security role, 110; physical health and strength, 108, 110–11, 112, 130, 142–43, 195n36; scientific management, 105, 111, 116–17; state control and surveillance, 7, 134–35, 141–45, 148, 155–56, 157. *See also* Eugenics; Women's bodies

Book of Documents (*Shūjīng*), 113

Bosei hogo renmei, *see* League for Motherhood Protection

Boshi hogo-hō, *see* Mother-Child Protection Law

Brazil, Japanese immigrants, 94, 189n40

Briggs, Asa, 193n9

Britain: birth control supporters, 40, 178n96; Malthusian League, 17, 171n5, 178n96; welfare policies, 106, 193n9

Bureau of Health and Welfare (Kōseikyoku), Government-General of Korea, 148

Campaign for Healthy People (Kenmin undō), 112, 130, 142–43, 195n36

Capitalism: class disparities, 29–30, 36, 60; feminist critiques, 47, 60, 61, 62–63, 64; leftist critiques, 17–18, 19, 36–38, 75, 76, 78, 175n54; patriarchy and, 52; surplus laboring population, 30, 38, 64, 76

CASW, *see* Central Association for Social Work

Censorship laws, 33, 176n70

Censuses, 3, 20–22, 48, 85, 118

Central Association for Social Work (Chūō shakai jigyō kyōkai; CASW), 108, 111–12

Children: childcare, 148; families with large numbers of, 138–41, 140 (fig.), 141 (fig.), 142 (fig.); healthy, 138–41, 145, 147, 148; welfare programs for, 112, 137. *See also* Birth rates; Family; Motherhood; Reproduction

Children's Bureau (Jidō-kyoku), 112

Chodorow, Nancy, 45

Chōsetsukai (Nihon sanji chōsetsu kenkyūkai; Japanese Society for the Study of Birth Control), 27–31, 33, 56–57, 174nn45–46

Chūō shakai jigyō kyōkai, *see* Central Association for Social Work

Citizenship, gendered, 136, 139–40

Class disparities: in capitalism, 29–30, 36, 60; intersectionality, 68, 150, 151–52, 157; in knowledge distribution, 35. *See also* Poverty

Colonialism, *see* Imperialism; Japanese empire

Colonial studies (*shokumingaku*), 83, 88, 89

Comfort stations (*ianjo*), 150–51, 152–56, 201n47, 201n48

Comfort women (*ianfu*): ages, 151; differences from Japanese mothers, 152, 156–57; Japanese, 151–52, 202n51; medical care, 152; medical examinations, 154–55, 156, 157; motherhood denied, 136, 152–53; number of, 150–51, 201n47; places of origin, 151; pregnancies, 153–54; purpose of system, 152–53, 157; recruitment, 151–52; testimonies, 153, 155; treatment of, 152–55; Women's Tribunal, 153–54, 155, 202n56

Communists, 41, 61. *See also* Leftists; Socialists
Contraceptives, 44, 48, 58, 82. *See also* Birth control
Crenshaw, Kimberlé Williams, 150
Critical race theory, *see* Intersectionality
Curtis, Bruce, 7

Dai nihon yūsei kai, *see* Greater Japan Eugenics Society
Dai nippon fujinkai, *see* Greater Japan Women's Association
Dai tōa kyōeiken, *see* Greater East Asia Co-Prosperity Sphere
Darwin, Charles, 33
Dean, Mitchell, 10
Death rates, *see* Mortality rates
Deleuze, Gilles, 51–52
Democracy: in postwar period, 162; Taishō, 41, 92, 104, 176n70; universal male suffrage, 41, 179nn100–101; women's suffrage, 53
Demography, 186n1
Dennett, Mary Ware, 182n24
Discipline, 28, 29, 30
Drysdale, Charles Vickery, 17

Economists, *see* Agricultural economics; Scholars
Elections, *see* Democracy
Ellis, Havelock, 40
Emigration, *see* Migration
Ethnic nation (*minzoku*), 52, 77, 78, 98, 108, 187n12. *See also* Race hygiene
Ethnonationalism, 3, 63, 76, 187n12
Eugenic feminism, 53, 57, 59–60, 68–69, 136
Eugenicists: birth control advocacy, 30–31, 34–35, 79; Japanese, 2, 3, 23–25, 79, 120–21; views of modernity, 4, 24; in Western countries, 16–17, 40, 120. *See also* Eugenics
Eugenic marriage (*yūsei kekkon*), 32, 79, 127–30
Eugenic Marriage Consultation Office (Yūsei kekkon sōdansho), 127 (fig.), 127–30, 128 (fig.)
Eugenic Marriage Popularization Society (Yūsei kekkon fukyūkai), 128, 136
Eugenic motherhood, 53, 55–58, 59–60, 68–69, 136
Eugenic Protection Law (Yūsei hogo hō), 159, 161–62
Eugenics: birth control movement and, 39–40, 53, 68–69, 178n96; defined, 22–23; definition of unfit, 31; fascism and, 32; maternal feminism and, 32; National Eugenic Law, 6, 23, 31, 82, 122–23, 127, 161, 162; negative, 23–24, 30–31, 121, 161–62; political outlooks associated with, 39; population quality and, 3, 6, 23, 24–25, 126–27; positive, 23–24, 29, 39–40, 126–27; in postwar period, 161–62, 163; research, 116–17, 120; scholarship on, 6; sterilization policies, 31, 32, 120–23, 161–62, 175n60; voluntary motherhood idea and, 50. *See also* Population quality
Europe: birth control movement, 40; censuses, 20–21; colonialism, 89; emigration, 89; imperialism, 21, 89; Neo-Malthusianism, 16–17, 171n5; tensions of modernity, 19; welfare policies, 106–7. *See also* Britain; Germany
Euthenics, 176–77n73
Evolution, 34–35

Family: Foucault on, 119; large numbers of children encouraged, 138–41, 140 (fig.), 141 (fig.), 142 (fig.); as model and instrument, 119–20; norms, 2, 119–20, 138, 163; parental morality, 28–29; patriarchal, 47, 52, 60, 62–63. *See also* Fertile womb battalion; Reproduction; Women's roles
Family planning campaign (postwar), 159, 160–61, 163. *See also* Birth control

Family Planning Federation of Japan (Nihon kazoku keikaku renmei), 161
Family-state (*kazoku kokka*) ideology, 134, 156
Family system, 45–46, 134
Farmers, emigration of, 86–87, 95, 98–99. *See also* Agrarian imperialism
Fascism, 5, 32, 104–5. *See also* Total war system; Wartime period
February 26 Incident (1936), 99, 109, 111, 194n19
Feminism: eugenic, 53, 57, 59–60, 68–69, 136; first-wave, 137; maternal (matricentric), 32, 46–47, 53, 57, 61, 135–36, 137, 180n6; socialist, 47, 60, 61–62, 65–68. *See also* Voluntary motherhood
Feminists: birth control activism and, 2, 27, 48–49, 53, 69, 161; co-opted by state in wartime, 32, 135; debates on motherhood, 46–47, 52; heterogenous approaches, 52–53, 68–69; identity categories, 52; in interwar period, 45–49, 137; in postwar period, 47, 161. *See also* Hiratsuka Raichō; Ishimoto Shizue; Voluntary motherhood; Yamakawa Kikue
Fertile womb battalion (*kodakara butai*), 2, 138–41, 198n10, 199n14
Fertility: infertility treatments, 1–2; patriotic, 138–41, 145; statistical research, 118–19. *See also* Birth control; Motherhood; Pronatalist policies; Reproduction; Sterilization policies
Fertility rates: demographic challenges related to, 1, 2; in interwar period, 2, 55; in postwar period, 1; recent, 163; in wartime, 119. *See also* Birth rates
Forced labor mobilization, 117, 132, 195n36
Foucault, Michel: on biological-type relationships, 57; on biopolitics, 9–10, 74; on colonialism, 12; on family, 119; on governmentality, 9, 10–11, 73, 81; on problematization, 1, 4; on science of the state, 21; on technologies of the self, 29

Fujimura Yoshirō, 78
Fujin dōmei, *see* Women's Birth Control League of Japan
Fujino Yutaka, 195n36
Fujitani, Takashi, 115
Fukuda Tokuzō, 77, 78, 79

Galton, Francis, 22–23, 25
Gender: biopolitical state and, 12, 134–35, 136–37, 148, 149; citizenship and, 136, 139–40; debates on differences, 45–47; equality, 46, 47; intersectionality, 68, 150, 151, 157; masculinity, 69; patriarchy, 47, 60, 62–63; reification of binary, 12; scholarship on, 6; segregation, 134, 136; wartime population policies and, 136. *See also* Feminism; Women
Gender roles, *see* Women's roles
General Headquarters of Allied Powers (GHQ), 160
Germany: censuses, 20–21; Nazi regime, 107, 122, 138, 193n3, 193n10; race hygiene, 120; Weimar period, 103, 193n3; welfare policies, 106–7, 193n10
GHQ, *see* General Headquarters
Gluck, Carol, 169n18
Gordon, Linda, 49
Governmentality: biopolitics and, 10–12; defined, 10, 73; Foucault on, 9, 10–11, 73, 81; imperialism and, 74, 85, 98, 100; in Japan, 73, 74, 100; social forces initiating, 32–33
Great Depression, 92, 95, 111
Greater East Asia Co-Prosperity Sphere (Dai tōa kyōeiken), 123, 124, 125–26, 130
Greater Japan Eugenics Society (Dai nihon yūsei kai), 23
Greater Japan Women's Association (Dai nippon fujinkai; *Nippu*), 145, 147–48, 200n36
Greenhalgh, Susan, 170n29, 186n4
Guattari, Félix, 51–52

Hamada Kunimatsu, 194n19
Hamaguchi Osachi: attack on, 92; cabinet, 84, 92

Handbook for the Expectant Mother (Ninsanpu techō), 143–45, 144 (fig.), 148, 156
Hanihara Masanao, 174n42
Harmful Contraceptive Devices Control Regulation (Yūgai hininyō kigu torishimari kisoku), 44, 82
Hashimoto Denzaemon, 95, 96
Healthcare: examinations of comfort women, 154–55, 156, 157; infertility treatments, 1–2; for pregnant women and mothers, 119, 143–48; shortage of medical professionals, 145, 199–200n25. *See also* Public health
Health insurance, national, 1, 114–15
Healthy People Bureau (Kenminkyoku), 106, 132
Heiminsha (Commoners' Society), 61
Hiratsuka Raichō, 32, 46–47, 57, 58, 136, 180n4
Hirohito, Emperor, 158
Hirota Kōki, cabinet, 97, 194n19
Home Ministry (Naimu-shō), 33, 82, 93, 174n42, 176n70
Household registration system (*koseki*), 20
Human resources (*jintekii shigen*), wartime mobilization, 100–101, 102–3, 105, 124–25, 162–63
Hygiene: military, 108–9; policy recommendations, 79–81; research, 7. *See also* Public health; Race hygiene
Hyōron (*Birth Control Review*; *Sanji chōsetsu hyōron*), 39–40, 41, 178n92

Ichikawa Fusae, 136, 137
Ichikawa Genzō, 23
Ikoma Takatsune, 95
Imperialism: agrarian, 89–90, 95–99; biopolitics and, 88; economic exploitation of colonies, 87–88, 89–90, 91, 94–95; European, 21, 89; governmentality and, 74, 85, 98, 100; Nitobe on, 88, 91; settler colonies, 87–88, 89, 91. *See also* Japanese empire

Inequality, 46, 47, 60. *See also* Class disparities
Infertility treatments, 1–2
Inoue Masaji, 78, 93, 94–95
Institute of Pacific Relations (IPR), 84, 89, 91
Institute of Population Problems (Jinkō mondai kenkyūsho; IPP), 99, 113, 116–19, 124, 159–60, 192n80
Intellectuals, *see* Scholars
International Planned Parenthood Federation (IPPF), 161
International Union for the Scientific Investigation of Population Problems (IUSIPP), 82–83, 84, 93, 188n29
Intersectionality, 68, 149–50, 151, 157
Interwar period: birth and fertility rates, 2, 55, 76, 80; censorship laws, 33, 176n70; censuses, 21–22; economy, 19; feminists, 45–49, 137; food crises, 19, 22; mortality rates, 80; political turmoil of 1930s, 92–93; population growth, 2, 28, 85; population policies, 7, 72, 78–82; welfare programs, 108–12. *See also* Population discourse in interwar period; Taishō period
Inukai Tsuyoshi, 92
IPP, *see* Institute of Population Problems
IPPF, *see* International Planned Parenthood Federation
IPR, *see* Institute of Pacific Relations
Ishida Sentarō, 149
Ishiguro Tada'atsu, 95, 96
Ishikawa Sanshirō, 66–67
Ishimoto (Katō) Shizue: arrest, 70, 198n3; birth control advocacy, 48–49, 50–51, 52, 53, 54–59, 68–69; on eugenic motherhood, 53, 55–58, 59–60, 68–69; family planning campaign and, 161; founding of Chōsetsukai, 27; life of, 48, 53–54, 58, 183n47; Sanger and, 54; "Shin-marusasu shugi" (Neo-Malthusianism), 50–51, 54; on voluntary motherhood, 50–51, 52, 62, 68, 135. *See also* Chōsetsukai

Ishimoto Keikichi, Baron, 16–17, 22, 27, 53–54, 58, 183n47
IUSIPP, *see* International Union for the Scientific Investigation of Population Problems

Jameson, Fredric, 26
Japan Birth Control League (Nihon sanji chōsetsu renmei), 58
Japanese Association of Race Hygiene (Nihon minzoku eisei kyōkai), 23, 120, 121, 128
Japanese Communist Party, 61
Japanese empire: birth control movement in colonies, 39; censuses, 21–22; economic development, 87, 88, 89–90, 190n55; emigration to colonies, 86–88, 89, 90, 93–99, 192n76; end of, 158; expansionism, 92; migration barriers, 189n45; military conscription, 148–49; natural resources, 91, 94–95; Pan-Asianism, 92, 116; population governance, 12, 85; pronatalist policy, 149; racial ideologies, 115–16; role in addressing population problem, 86–89; wartime mobilization, 123–24; welfare and public health programs, 115–16, 195n36. *See also* Korea; Manchukuo; Taiwan
Japanese Society for the Study of Birth Control, *see* Chōsetsukai
Japanese (Yamato) race, 3, 99, 108, 116, 192n80. *See also* Ethnic nation; Race hygiene
Japan Federation of Labor, *see* Sōdōmei
Jasanoff, Sheila, 186n3
Jidō-kyoku, *see* Children's Bureau
Jinkō, *see* Population
Jinkō-kyoku, *see* Population Bureau
Jinkō mondai kenkyūkai, *see* Population Problem Research Society
Jinkō mondai kenkyūsho, *see* Institute of Population Problems
Jinkō mondai shingikai, *see* Population Problem Inquiry Council
Jinkō mondai zenkoku kyōgikai, *see*

National Council for Population Problems
Jinkō shokuryō mondai chōsakai, *see* Population and Food Problems Investigation Committee
Jünger, Ernst, 102, 103, 193n3

Kaigai kōgyō kabushiki gaisha, *see* Overseas Enterprise Co., Ltd.
Kaizō-sha, 26, 34
Kaji Tokijirō, 17, 27, 58, 178n92
Kaneko Shigeri, 58, 136, 137
Kanemitsu Tsuneo, 124
Kasza, Gregory J., 107
Katō Kanji, 95–96
Katō Kanjū, 48, 183n47
Katō Shizue, *see* Ishimoto Shizue
Kawakami Hajime, 75, 76, 175n54
Kawasaki Natsu, 58
Kelly, M. G. E., 186–87n5
Kenmin-kyoku, *see* Healthy People Bureau
Kenmin undō, *see* Campaign for Healthy People
Key, Ellen, 32, 46, 180n4
Kikaku-chō, *see* Planning Agency
Kim Bok-Dong, 153
Kinoshita Seichū, 145
Kiyoura Keigo, 112
Kobayashi Takiji, 42
Koike Shirō, 39
Koizumi Chikahiko, 108, 109
Kokudo keikaku settei yōkō, *see* National Land Planning
Kokumin kenkō hoken hō, *see* National Health Insurance Law
Kokumin yūsei hō, *see* National Eugenic Law
Kokuritsu kōshū eiseiin, *see* National Institute of Public Health
Konoe Fumimaro: cabinet, 109–11, 112, 124; total war policy, 102
Kōra Tomiko, 136
Korea: birth control movement, 39; Campaign for Healthy People, 195n36; Government-General, 86, 115, 148, 189n45; health insurance, 115; Japanese settlers, 86, 91, 189n45, 191n60; labor conscription,

195n36; military conscription, 148–49; pronatalist policy, 149
Koschmann, J. Victor, 8, 104, 169n17
Kōsei, use of term, 113
Kōsei rōdō-shō, see Ministry of Health, Labor, and Welfare of Japan
Kōsei-shō, see Ministry of Health and Welfare
Koya Yoshio, 160, 161, 192n80
Kropotkin, Peter, 63
Kurahara Korehito, 179n107
Kutsumi Fusako, 36, 178n91
Kwantung Army, 96, 97

Labor: as commodity, 29–30; forced, 117, 132, 195n36; surplus laboring population, 30, 38, 64; women in workforce, 46, 61, 66. See also Working class
Labor activists, 19–20, 27, 35–36, 40–41, 61, 187n7
Land planning, see National Land Planning
Latin America, migration to, 94, 189n40
League for Motherhood Protection (Bosei hogo renmei), 137
League of Nations, 82–83, 84, 92, 191n58
Leftists: birth control advocacy, 20, 33–34, 35–40, 41–44, 65–68; critiques of capitalism, 17–18, 19, 36–38, 75, 76, 78, 175n54; critiques of Malthusian theory and Neo-Malthusianism, 17–20, 33, 36–38, 63–65, 76, 185n79; divisions over birth control, 38, 63, 178n91; eugenics views, 39–40; factionalism, 40–41; gender issues and, 65–67, 185n79; goals, 26; political parties, 41; scholars, 76; state repression, 40, 41, 42. See also Socialists
Lenin, Vladimir, 18

MacArthur, Douglas, 154
Majima Kan, 58, 161, 178n92
Malthus, Thomas Robert, 17–18
Malthusian League, 17, 171n5, 178n96

Malthusian theory of population: application in Japan, 22, 95, 98, 159; leftist critiques, 17–18, 33, 36–38, 63, 171n8. See also Neo-Malthusianism
Manchukuo: founding, 85, 90, 91, 92, 100, 179–80n108; migration policies, 74, 90, 91, 94–99, 111; natural resources, 91; peasant migration, 96, 97–98
Manchuria: birth control movement, 39; as lifeline of Japan, 91, 95, 191n58
Manchurian Incident, 42, 85, 90, 179–80n108
Manila, comfort women, 154–55
Marco Polo Bridge Incident, 106, 193n8
Marriage: ages of women, 119; eugenic, 32, 79, 127–30; formation of families, 119–20; maxims, 128, 129 (fig.); norms, 2. See also Family; Women's roles
Maruyama, Masao, 8
Marx, Karl, 16, 17–18, 38, 63, 64, 78, 171n8, 185n71
Marxists, see Leftists
Masculinity, 69
Maternal (matricentric) feminism, 32, 46–47, 53, 57, 61, 135–36, 137, 180n6. See also Motherhood
Matsuda Tokiko, 180n110
Matsumura Shōnen, 30–31
Matsuoka Yōsuke, 191n58
Mbembe, Achille, 105
Medical care, see Healthcare; Health insurance
Meiji period: family-state ideology, 134, 156; family system, 45–46, 134; household registration system, 20; population discourse, 3; population growth, 85; population statistics gathered, 3, 20–22; women's domestic roles, 45–46
MHW, see Ministry of Health and Welfare
Migration: barriers, 86, 189n45; destinations, 86; of farmers and peasants, 86–87, 95, 96, 97–99;

Migration (*cont.*)
  to Japanese colonies, 86–88, 89, 90, 93–99, 192n76; to Latin America, 94, 189n40; to Manchukuo, 74, 90, 91, 94–99, 111; to relieve population pressures, 86–87, 89, 93–99, 192n76
Military: conscription, 108–9, 148–49, 200n38; power, 92, 99, 194n19. *See also* Ministry of Army
Military hygiene (*gunjin eisei*), 108–9
Military sexual slaves, *see* Comfort women
Miller, Ruth A., 139–40
Minami Ryōzaburō, 76
Ministry of Army (Rikugun-shō), 97, 108–10, 152, 202n51
Ministry of Colonial Affairs (Takumu-shō), 95, 96
Ministry of Health, Labor, and Welfare of Japan (Kōsei rōdō-shō), 1–2
Ministry of Health and Welfare (Kōsei-shō; MHW): Campaign for Healthy People, 112, 130, 142–43, 195n36; establishment, 74, 104, 105, 106, 107–13, 114; Eugenic Marriage Consultation Office, 127 (fig.), 127–30, 128 (fig.); Eugenics Bureau, 120; family planning campaign, 160–61, 163; functions, 106, 114; goals, 116, 126, 130; healthcare assistance, 199–200n25; ministers, 108, 124; name, 113; Population Bureau, 126–27, 130, 132, 145; population policies, 100; in postwar period, 159–60; promotion of motherhood, 138–41; structure, 114, 126, 132; in wartime period, 112–13; welfare programs, 107. *See also* Healthy People Bureau; Institute of Population Problems; Race Hygiene Research Society; Wartime population policies; Welfare programs
Ministry of Home Affairs (Naimu-shō), 3, 21, 23, 109, 114, 202n51
Ministry of Social Affairs (Shakai-shō) proposal, 79, 111, 112
Minzoku, *see* Ethnic nation; Race hygiene
Minzoku eisei kenkyūkai, *see* Race Hygiene Research Society
Mitamura Shirō, 35, 36
Mitsui Mining Company, 54
Mitsukoshi department store, Eugenic Marriage Consultation Office, 127 (fig.), 128 (fig.)
Miyake, Yoshiko, 134
Modernity: defined, 19; eugenicists' views, 24; family system and, 45–46; fascism as deviation from, 104–5; gendered, 69; Japanese, 9; motherhood and, 69; nationalism and, 8–9; population discourse and, 2–3, 4–5, 7, 8, 9, 162; tensions, 19–20; Western, 8–9, 19
Molony, Barbara, 46
Mongolia, 87, 91, 94–95, 96
Mortality rates, 79, 80, 81, 118, 126
Mother-Child Protection Law (Boshi hogo-hō), 137
Motherhood (*bosei*): burdens, 66; denied to comfort women, 136, 152–53; discursive construction of, 12; eugenic, 53, 55–58, 59–60, 68–69, 136; feminist debates, 46–47, 52; healthcare, 143–48; in modern context, 69; nationalist, 136, 145–48; natural, 66, 67; as public duty, 32, 142–43, 145; state protections, 70, 81, 134, 137–38, 148, 156; wartime promotion, 134–35, 137–48, 156, 162–63; welfare programs, 134, 137. *See also* Maternal feminism; Pregnancies; Pronatalist policies; Voluntary motherhood
Motherhood protection debate (*bosei hogo ronsō*), 46–47, 60, 61
Muraoka Hanako, 58
Musansha sanji seigen dōmei (Proletariat Birth Control League), *see* Pro-BC

Nadkarni, Asha, 53
Nagai Hisomu, 3, 23, 78, 79, 81–82, 120–21, 188n19
Nagai Tōru, 71, 75, 77–79, 85, 93, 94, 160–61

Naimu-shō, *see* Ministry of Home Affairs
Naitō Morizō, 21
Nasu Shiroshi, 75, 78, 85, 86, 93, 94, 95, 96
National Commendation for Families with Many Healthy Children (Yūryō tashi katei hyōshō), 138–41
National Council for Population Problems (Jinkō mondai zenkoku kyōgikai), 124
National Eugenic Law (Kokumin yūsei hō), 6, 23, 31, 82, 122–23, 127, 161, 162
National Health Insurance Law (Kokumin kenkō hoken hō), 114–15
National Institute of Public Health (Kokuritsu kōshū eiseiin), 160
Nationalism: agrarianism and, 95–96; birth control advocacy and, 53; ethno-, 3, 63, 76, 187n12; eugenic feminism and, 59–60; imperial, 115, 130; maternal feminism and, 32; modernity and, 8–9; in wartime period, 8
Nationalist motherhood, 136, 145–48
National Land Planning (Kokudo keikaku settei yōkō), 123–24, 197n62
National Mobilization Law (Kokka sōdōin hō), 102–3, 117
Natural selection, 34–35
Necropower, 105, 148
Neo-Malthusianism: global rise, 16–17; goals, 17, 26, 35; in interwar period, 4, 16–17, 22, 25–26, 75; leftist critiques, 17–20, 36–38, 63–65, 76, 185n79; scholarly critiques, 76, 77–78; views of population problem, 5, 55, 73; in Western countries, 16–17, 171n5
Neo-Malthusianism, birth control advocacy and: arguments, 5, 29–31, 32, 35; international conferences, 16–17; Ishimoto on, 54–55, 57; in Japan, 26–31, 43–44, 187n7; as solution to poverty, 18, 20
Nihon bosei hogokai, *see* Society for the Protection of Mothers

Nihon bungaku hokokukai, *see* Patriotic Association for Japanese Literature
Nihon kazoku keikaku renmei, *see* Family Planning Federation of Japan
Nihon minzoku eisei kyōkai, *see* Japanese Association of Race Hygiene
Nihon rōdō kumiai sōdōmei, *see* Sōdōmei
Nihon sanji chōsetsu fujin dōmei, *see* Women's Birth Control League of Japan
Nihon sanji chōsetsu kenkyūkai, *see* Chōsetsukai
Nihon sanji chōsetsu renmei, *see* Japan Birth Control League
Niizuma Ito(ko), 58
Nippu, *see* Greater Japan Women's Association
Nitobe Inazō, 75, 77, 78, 83–84, 88–91, 95, 190n55
Noda Kimiko, *Sanji seigen kenkyū* (The study of birth control), 36–37, 37 (fig.), 38

Ogawa Ryūshiro, 58
Ogino Miho, 199n23
Ōhara Institute for Social Research (Ōhara shakai mondai kenkyūsho), 24–25, 48
Oka Asajirō, 23
Okazaki Ayanori, 118
O'Reilly, Andrea, 180n6
Osaka Asahi Shinbun, 36, 94, 177n82
Osaka Mainichi Shinbun, 36, 177n84
Ōshima Yoshiharu, 54
Ōta Tenrei, 161
Ōuchi Hyōe, 76
Overpopulation: feminist views, 55–57, 64–65, 68; in population discourse, 22, 27–28, 55, 192n77; in postwar period, 159; surplus laboring population, 30, 38, 64, 76. *See also* Birth control; Malthusian theory of population; Neo-Malthusianism; Population control; Population growth; "Population problem"; Population quantity

Overseas Enterprise Co., Ltd. (Kaigai kōgyō kabushiki gaisha), 94, 189n40
Pan-Asianism, 92, 116
Parental morality, 28–29, 36. *See also* Children; Family; Motherhood; Reproduction
Patriarchal family, 47, 52, 60, 62–63
Patriotic Association for Japanese Literature (Nihon bungaku hokokukai), 139, 199n16
Paul, Diane B., 39
Pearl, Raymond, 83
PFIC, *see* Population and Food Problems Investigation Committee
Planning Agency (Kikaku-chō), 108, 110, 111, 112, 114, 132
Ploetz, Alfred, 120
Population (*jinkō*): biopolitics and, 10; defining, 76, 82; introduction of concept, 3, 20–22; as target of government policy, 78, 82; in wartime discourse, 105. *See also* "Population problem"; Population quantity
Population and Food Problems Investigation Committee (Jinkō shokuryō mondai chōsakai; PFIC): compared to PPRS, 93; Department of Population, 76–77, 78–79, 82, 84; establishment, 75, 76; goals, 93; reports by special committee, 78–82, 90; scholars, 76–82, 84–85, 99; scholarship on, 7; structure, 76–77; study of colonies, 86–88
Population Bureau (Jinkō-kyoku), 126–27, 130, 132, 145
Population control policies, 4, 5, 6–7, 79, 80–81, 159, 160–61. *See also* Birth control; Migration; Neo-Malthusianism; Population governance; Wartime population policies
Population discourse: defined, 3; historical continuity, 6–7, 9; historical legacy, 159, 161, 163; in Meiji period, 3; modernity and, 2–3, 4–5, 7, 8, 9, 162; politics and, 7; in postwar period, 159–63; scholarship on, 6–7; scope, 7–8; transnational patterns, 3; in wartime period, 5, 9, 99, 103, 105, 162, 192n80. *See also* "Population problem"
Population discourse in interwar period: debates, 2, 19–20, 33, 36–39, 43–44, 174n45; Japanese government involvement, 32–33; multiplicity, 4, 20; "population problem," 2, 4, 19–20, 22, 24, 55–56, 75–76; relationship to wartime period, 5, 103–5, 107, 126; socioeconomic issues, 3–4, 27, 28, 75, 78, 103, 111, 162; utopian remedies, 25–26, 33, 44. *See also* Birth control movement; Eugenics; Feminism; Neo-Malthusianism
Population governance, 73, 74, 79–82, 85, 99, 100. *See also* Migration; Population science
Population growth: benefits, 63–64; in interwar period, 2, 28, 85; neo-Malthusian view, 26–27, 28, 63, 64; in postwar period, 159; quality improvements and, 25. *See also* Overpopulation; Population quantity; Pronatalist policies
Population Guidelines (Jinkō seisaku kakuritsu yōkō), 113–14, 124–25, 126
"Population problem" (*jinkō mondai*): feminist view, 55–56; in interwar period, 2, 4, 19–20, 22, 24, 48, 55, 75–76; in postwar period, 159, 163; problematization, 4, 7, 9, 19–20, 22, 25, 73, 80, 163; role of state intervention, 2, 4, 9, 30–31, 73; scholars' views, 73, 75–76, 77–78, 82, 86, 98–99, 100; utopian remedies, 25–26, 33, 44. *See also* Birth control; Neo-Malthusianism; Overpopulation; Population discourse; Population quantity
Population Problem Inquiry Council (Jinkō mondai shingikai), 132, 159–60
Population Problem Research Society (Jinkō mondai kenkyūkai; PPRS): activities, 93, 99; conference (1940),

124; emigration policy proposals, 94–95, 97–99, 192n76; establishment, 75, 84–85, 92–93; goals, 98; in postwar period, 159–60; research, 94; scholars, 85, 93, 99, 100; views of population, 98–99, 100

Population quality (*jinkō no shitsu*): eugenics goals, 3, 6, 23, 24–25, 79, 126–27; relationship to quantity, 3, 4, 126–27; wartime policies, 5, 113–14. *See also* Eugenic motherhood; Eugenics

Population quantity (*jinkō no ryō*): absolute surplus, 38, 64; density, 85–86; quantification, 3, 22; recent decline, 1, 163; relationship to quality, 3, 4, 126–27; relative surplus, 18, 38, 64, 185n71; statistics gathering, 3, 20–22, 48, 80, 85, 118–19. *See also* Censuses; Migration; Overpopulation; Population control; Population growth

Population science: development, 72–73, 186n1; international cooperation, 82–83, 84; policy recommendations, 5, 73, 79–82, 85–86, 90, 100; in postwar period, 159–60; scope, 186n1; in wartime period, 117–19. *See also* International Union for the Scientific Investigation of Population Problems; Population governance; Scholars

Postwar period: biopolitics, 158–59, 162; break with wartime regime, 8–9; democracy, 162; eugenics, 161–62, 163; family planning campaign, 159, 160–61, 163; feminism, 47; fertility rates, 1; modernity and, 8–9; occupation forces, 160; population growth, 159; population policies, 132, 168–69n11; "population problem," 159, 163; population science, 159–60; sterilization policies, 161–62; welfare policies, 107, 132, 163

Poverty: debate on causes, 17–19, 29, 36–38, 63, 65, 174n45; rural, 97, 111. *See also* Class disparities; Welfare programs

Power: bio-, 10, 57, 105; disciplinary, 10; Foucault on, 9–11; necro-, 105, 148. *See also* Governmentality

PPRS, *see* Population Problem Research Society

Pregnancies: abortions, 159, 161–62, 186n87; of comfort women, 153–54; healthcare, 119, 143–48. *See also* Motherhood

Prewar period, 2. *See also* Meiji period

Pro-BC (Musansha sanji seigen dōmei; Proletariat Birth Control League), 41–42, 43 (fig.), 180n110

Procreation, *see* Reproduction

Proletarian revolution, 18, 20

Proletariat Birth Control League (Musansha sanji seigen dōmei), *see* Pro-BC

Pronatalist policies: advocates, 31, 36; fertile womb battalion, 2, 138–41, 198n10, 199n14; "give birth and multiply" slogan, 119, 159; scholarship on, 7; in wartime period, 2, 70, 99, 103, 118, 119–20, 138–48, 149

Public health: in colonies, 115–16, 195n36; eugenics and, 23, 31, 40; government programs, 73, 106, 107, 108, 109, 110–11, 114; for mothers and children, 147; policy recommendations, 79–81; population discourse and, 3, 6; sexually transmitted disease prevention, 29, 152–53, 154–55, 157

Qiu, Peipei, 201n47

Race: biopolitical state and, 116, 134; colonial others, 116; intersectionality, 150, 151–52, 157; Japanese (Yamato), 3, 99, 108, 116, 192n80; polite racism, 115; schema, 116; welfare policies and, 115–16

Race hygiene (*minzoku eisei*), 120–23, 128, 132

Race Hygiene Research Society (Minzoku eisei kenkyūkai; RHRS), 113, 116–17, 120, 121–22, 128

Radio Calisthenics (Rajio taisō), 130, 131 (fig.)
Red Wave Society (Sekirankai), 61
Relative surplus population, 18, 38, 64, 185n71
Report on Productivity Growth (Seisanryoku zōshin ni kansuru tōshin-an), 90
Reproduction: eugenic marriage and, 127–30; family as normative unit, 119–20; sterilization policies, 31, 32, 120–23, 161–62, 175n60; as woman's role, 2, 57, 59–60, 134–36, 139–40, 156. *See also* Birth control; Fertility; Motherhood; Pregnancies; Pronatalist policies; Voluntary motherhood
Reproductive labor, 49, 66–67, 135
Research organizations, *see* Institute of Population Problems; Population and Food Problems Investigation Committee; Population Problem Research Society; Scholars
RHRS, *see* Race Hygiene Research Society
Rice Riots, 19
Richards, Ellen S., 176–77n73
Rikugun-shō, *see* Ministry of Army
Robertson, Jennifer, 198n10
Rockefeller Foundation, 160

Saitō Itsuki, 23, 24
Saitō Makoto, 92, 93
Sakai, Naoki, 170n19
Sakai Magara, 137
Sakai Toshihiko, 65, 185n79
Sanger, Margaret: eugenics views, 50, 62; "Family Limitation," 33, 34; influence in Japan, 39, 49–50, 51, 52, 62, 68; Ishimoto Shizue and, 54; IUSIPP founding and, 82–83; lectures in Japan, 26–27, 34, 174n42; neo-Malthusian views, 27, 55, 62, 64–65; on voluntary motherhood, 49–50, 62, 68, 182n24; *Woman and New Race*, 45, 50. *See also* Birth Control Review
Sanji chōsetsu hyōron (*Birth Control Review*), *see* Hyōron

Sanji seigen kenkyū (The study of birth control), 36–37, 37 (fig.), 38
Sanji seigen kenkyūkai, *see* Seigenkai
Schaffer, Simon, 71
Scholars: influence on population policies, 72–73, 74, 75, 100; Marxist, 76; at PFIC, 76–82, 84–85, 99; relations with government, 72; views of birth control, 81–82; views of population problem, 73, 75–76, 77–78, 82, 86, 98–99, 100. *See also* Population science
Schreiner, Olive, 46, 180n4
Scientific knowledge, 74, 82–83, 84. *See also* Population science; Scholars
Second Sino-Japanese War, *see* Wartime period
Seigenkai (Sanji seigen kenkyūkai), 35–40, 41
Seisanryoku zōshin ni kansuru tōshin-an, *see* Report on Productivity Growth
Sekirankai, *see* Red Wave Society
Settler colonialism, 87–88, 89, 91. *See also* Imperialism; Japanese empire; Korea; Manchukuo; Taiwan
Sex education, 29, 34, 177n81
Shibahara Urako, 58, 70, 186n87
Shigemitsu Mamoru, 158
Shimojō Yasumaro, 124
Shimomura Hiroshi, 78, 94
Shino family, 141 (fig.)
Shiroto family, 139, 140 (fig.)
Shiroto Kimi, 139, 140
Shōwa Depression, 92, 95, 111
Smedley, Agnes, 54
Social Darwinism, 24, 88, 188n19
Socialist feminism, 47, 60, 61–62, 65–68
Socialists: American, 54; birth control debates, 66–68; Diet members, 161; eugenics and, 39; feminists, 47, 60, 61–62, 65–66; indifference to birth control movement, 65; Sekirankai (Red Wave Society), 61. *See also* Leftists; Marx, Karl; Yamakawa Kikue
Social reformers, 27, 75, 187n7. *See also* Birth control movement;

Central Association for Social Work; Ishimoto Keikichi, Baron; Ishimoto Shizue; Labor activists; Leftists
Social science, see Population science; Scholars
Society for the Protection of Mothers (Nihon bosei hogokai), 145–47
Sōdōmei (Nihon rōdō kumiai sōdōmei; Japan Federation of Labor), 35, 178n91
Sō Mitsuhiko, 95, 96
State of exception, 125–26, 197n68
Statistics, 3, 20–22, 118–19. See also Censuses; Population quantity
Sterilization policies, 31, 32, 120–23, 161–62, 175n60
Stoler, Ann Laura, 21
Stopes, Marie, 40, 178n96
Sugi Kōji, 20–21
Surplus laboring population, 30, 38, 64, 76
Suzuki Bunji, 27, 178n92, 187n7

Tachi Minoru, 160, 192n80
Taishō Democracy, 41, 92, 104, 176n70
Taishō period: censorship laws, 33, 176n70; feminism, 137; universal male suffrage, 41, 179nn100–101. See also Interwar period
Taiwan: birth control movement, 39; censuses, 21; economic development, 89–90, 190n55; Government-General, 89, 115; insurance industry, 115; Japanese settlers, 86–87, 91, 191n60; labor conscription, 195n36; military conscription, 148, 200n38; National Physical Fitness Law, 195n36
Takamure Itsue, 32
Takano Iwasaburō, 24–25
Takata Yasuma, 75–76, 187n12
Takeuchi Shigeyo, 136
Takeuchi, Yoshimi, 19
Takeuchi-Demirici, Aiko, 54
Takumu-shō, see Ministry of Colonial Affairs
Tanaka Giichi, 76
Tatsuno Kyūshi, 139

Ten Maxims for Marriage (Kekkon jyūkkun), 128, 129 (fig.)
Terauchi Hisaichi, 108–9, 194n19
Thompson, Warren, 160
Titmuss, Richard Morris, 106
Tokyo Asahi Shinbun, 117
Tokyo Imperial University, 24, 33, 54, 86, 88, 90
Total war (*sōryokusen*), 102
Total war system (*sōryokusen taisei*): human resources mobilization, 100–101, 102–3, 105, 124–25, 162–63; population policies, 2, 5, 74, 100–101, 104; postwar break with, 8–9; as state of exception, 125–26. See also Wartime period
Translation, meaning of, 51–52
Tsuda Umeko, 61
Tsunoda family, 142 (fig.)
Tsurumi Yūsuke, 53

Ueda Teijirō, 76, 78, 85, 86, 93, 94
Ueno Chizuko, 133, 136
Ujihara Sukezō, 23–24
United States: birth control movement, 26, 54, 181n19; demographic research, 186n1; immigration, 86, 89; occupation of Japan, 160; "population crisis," 169n14; sterilization policies, 31; voluntary motherhood supporters, 49–50. See also Sanger, Margaret
Unno Yukinori, 3, 23, 178n92
Utopias, 26

Voluntary motherhood: eugenics goals, 50, 62, 135; Ishimoto on, 52, 62, 68, 135; Japanese supporters, 44, 49, 50–51, 56–58, 67–69, 135; Sanger's support, 49–50, 62, 68, 182n24; transpacific translations, 49–52; wartime population policies and, 135; Western supporters, 49–50, 182n24; Yamakawa Kikue on, 50, 52, 62–63, 67–68, 69

Wakatsuki Reijirō, 92
Wartime period: casualties, 158; final battles, 158; historiography, 8, 104–5;

Wartime period (*cont.*)
National Mobilization Law, 102–3; population discourse, 5, 9, 99, 103, 105, 162, 192n80; population science, 117–19; scholarship on, 8; welfare programs, 112–13, 114–15, 134. *See also* Biopolitical state; Comfort women; Fascism; Total war system

Wartime population policies: biopolitics and, 5, 125–26, 130, 132, 134; development, 5, 106, 113–14; eugenic, 120–23, 126–27; gender and, 136; "healthy soldiers and healthy people" (*kenpei kenmin*) slogan, 5, 100, 101, 104; human resources focus, 100–101, 102–3, 105, 124–25, 162–63; National Land Planning, 123–24, 197n62; obstacles, 132; population control, 5, 7; population distribution planning, 124; Population Guidelines, 113–14, 126; population quality, 5, 113–14; promotion of motherhood, 134–35, 137–48, 156, 162–63; pronatalist, 2, 70, 99, 103, 118, 119–20, 138–48, 149; quantity and quality, 113–14; research, 116–19; scholarship on, 7; statistics gathering, 118–19; sterilization, 121–23; total mobilization goal, 102–3, 117, 123–24; voluntary motherhood and, 135. *See also* Ministry of Health and Welfare

Welfare Calisthenics of Great Japan (Dai nihon kōsei taisō), 130

Welfare programs: development in Japan, 107–12, 114; goals, 110–11; in Japanese colonies, 115–16, 195n36; links to warfare, 106–7, 193n9; for mothers and children, 112, 134, 137; in postwar period, 107, 132, 163; in wartime period, 112–13, 114–15, 134. *See also* Ministry of Health and Welfare

Western countries: birth control movement, 39–40, 49, 54, 182n24; eugenicists, 16–17, 40, 120; modernity, 8–9, 19; neo-Malthusianism, 16–17, 171n5; voluntary motherhood supporters, 182n24. *See also* Europe; United States

Wilson, Sandra, 147

Winckler, Edwin A., 170n29

Wombs, *see* Pregnancies; Reproduction; Women's bodies

Women: economic empowerment, 46, 163; emancipation, 60; employment, 46, 61, 66; ideal virtues, 134, 147; identity categories, 52; patriotic activities, 147; political rights, 47, 52, 67–68, 182n26; reproductive labor, 49, 66–67, 135; reproductive rights, 161; suffrage, 53; working class, 54, 60, 61, 66. *See also* Comfort women; Feminists; Gender; Motherhood

Women's Birth Control League of Japan (Nihon sanji chōsetsu fujin dōmei), 58–59

Women's bodies: biopolitical state and, 12, 134–35, 136–37, 148, 149, 157; comfort women, 150–57; health improvements, 81; of mothers, 12, 59–60, 135, 141–45; state control and surveillance, 6, 155–56, 157. *See also* Pregnancies; Reproduction

Women's International Tribunal on Japanese Military Sexual Slavery, 153–54, 155, 202n56

Women's movement, *see* Feminism

Women's roles: domestic, 45–46, 47, 134; reproduction, 2, 57, 59–60, 134–36, 139–40, 156

Working class: birth control advocacy for, 20, 30, 35–36, 38–40, 41–43, 52; coal miners, 54; consequences of population growth, 29–30; exploitation, 38; sterilization policies, 31; surplus laboring population, 76; women, 54, 60, 61, 66. *See also* Class disparities; Labor

World Population Conference, 82–83

World War II, impact on welfare policies, 106, 193n9. *See also* Wartime period

Yamada Waka, 46, 47, 136, 137
Yamakawa Hitoshi, 61
Yamakawa Kikue: activism, 61–62; birth control advocacy, 48–49, 52, 60, 62–63, 65–68, 69; on birth strike, 60, 65, 69; critique of neo-Malthusianism, 63–65, 174n45; founding of Chōsetsukai, 27; gender and class critique, 60, 61, 62–63, 66–68; life of, 60–61; on matricentric feminism, 47; role in feminist movement, 46, 60; on voluntary motherhood, 50, 52, 62–63, 67–68, 69; wartime activities, 70; on women's roles, 67
Yamamoto Kotoko, 180n110
Yamamoto Senji: *Hyōron* and, 39–40, 178n92; political activism, 41; Sanger's visit to Japan and, 27, 34; as scientist, 33–34; support of birth control, 36, 41, 177n81, 177n84, 177–78n90; sympathy to women's issues, 65; translation of Sanger's "Family Limitation," 33, 34–35
Yamamoto Sugiko, 59
Yamamuro Tamiko, 58–59
Yamanouchi Shigeo, 23
Yamato race, *see* Ethnic nation; Japanese race
Yamazaki Yoshio, 95
Yanagisawa Yasutoshi, 93
Yanaihara Tadao, 76, 84, 90
Yasui Hiroshi, 127–28, 128 (fig.)
Yosano Akiko, 46–47
Yoshida Hideo, 76
Yoshimi, Yoshiaki, 152
Young, Louise, 97–98
Young, Robert, 87
Yūryō tashi katei hyōshō, *see* National Commendation for Families with Many Healthy Children
Yūsei hogo hō, *see* Eugenic Protection Law
Yūsei kekkon fukyūkai, *see* Eugenic Marriage Popularization Society
Yūsei kekkon sōdansho, *see* Eugenic Marriage Consultation Office

The authorized representative in the EU for product safety and compliance is:
Mare Nostrum Group
B.V Doelen 72
4831 GR Breda
The Netherlands

www.ingramcontent.com/pod-product-compliance
Lightning Source LLC
Chambersburg PA
CBHW031806220426
43662CB00007B/548